# China Labor Relations Research

## 2021

Edited by Fu Deyin

中国财经出版传媒集团

经济科学出版社
Economic Science Press

**图书在版编目（CIP）数据**

中国劳动关系研究. 2021=Research on Labor
Relations in China 2021：英文 / 傅德印主编. --
北京：经济科学出版社，2022.8
ISBN 978-7-5218-3789-6

Ⅰ. ①中…　Ⅱ. ①傅…　Ⅲ. ①劳动关系 – 研
究报告 – 中国 –2021– 英文　Ⅳ. ①F249.26

中国版本图书馆CIP数据核字（2022）第113164号

责任编辑：吴　敏
责任校对：徐　昕
责任印制：张佳裕

中国劳动关系研究2021　傅德印　主编
China Labor Relations Research 2021　Edited by *Fu Deyin*
经济科学出版社出版、发行　新华书店经销
社址：北京市海淀区阜成路甲28号　邮编：100142
编辑工作室电话：010-88191375　发行部电话：010-88191522
网址：www.esp.com.cn
电子邮箱：esp@esp.com.cn
天猫网店：经济科学出版社旗舰店
网址：http://jjkxcbs.tmall.com
北京季蜂印刷有限公司印装
787 × 1092　16开　16.25印张　330000字
2022年8月第1版　2022年8月第1次印刷
ISBN 978-7-5218-3789-6　定价：65.00元
（图书出现印装问题，本社负责调换。电话：010-88191510）
（版权所有　侵权必究　打击盗版　举报热线：010-88191661
QQ：2242791300　营销中心电话：010-88191537
电子邮箱：dbts@esp.com.cn ）

# Preface

*Fu Deyin*

Labor relation is a crucial part of production relations, and is the most important and basic economic relations in modern society. General Secretary Xi Jinping pointed out that building a harmonious labor relationship with Chinese characteristics was an essential part of keeping the path of socialism with Chinese characteristics, implementing the theory of socialism with Chinese characteristics, and improving the system of socialism with Chinese characteristics. Since the reform and opening up in the new era, China has explored the labor relations governance, and has accumulated valuable experience in functions of government, the establishment of governance mechanisms, and the realization of labor rights and interests, making important contributions to the improvement of the market economy system and the promotion of rapid economic development.

Since the reform and opening up, with China's transition to a market economy, the subject of labor relations gradually has transitioned from government administrative management to market-oriented adjustment, fully mobilizing the enthusiasm of labors, continuously releasing labor mobility, and guaranteeing labors' rights and interests in the realization of economic development and social progress. In the new century, with the continuous deepening of economic system reforms and the completion of the market-based development of labor relations, it has become clearer that the main goal of labor relations governance is to achieve full employment and to protect the legitimate rights and interests of workers in accordance with the law. Since the new era, China has taken new steps in the exploration of harmonious labor relations. In 2015, the Central Committee of the Communist Party of China (CPC) and the State Council issued *Opinions on Building Harmonious Labor Relations*, which clearly stated to explore the way to harmonious labor relationship with Chinese characteristics without copying the model of industrialized market economy. The report of the 19th National Congress of the Communist Party of China pointed out the necessity to improve the negotiation and coordination mechanism involving the government, trade unions, and enterprises to build harmonious labor relations. The Fourth Plenary Session of the 19th Central Committee proposed to improve the coordination mechanism to build harmonious labor relations, and promote decent work and all-round development of the majority of workers. Under the leadership of the CPC, the working class has a special status in the China's political and economic system, thus building a harmonious labor relationship is not only an objective need for China's economic and social development, but also an important achievement in adhering to the path of socialism with Chinese characteristics, which fully demonstrates the advantages of the socialist system, and further strengthens confidence in the path, theory, system,  and culture of socialism with Chinese characteristics.

**Building harmonious labor relations is an inevitable need for China's economic and social development**. As people's living standards have improved significantly, and their aspiration for a better life has become stronger, the main social contradiction in China has been transformed into a contradiction between the people's ever-growing need for a better life and unbalanced and inadequate development. In the new era, the people's needs are more diversified, multi-layered, multi-faceted, and becoming more extensive, represented by not only higher requirements on material and cultural life, but also increasing demand on democracy, the rule of law, fairness, justice, security, and the environment. Labor relations, as it intuitively reflects the wage income, working environment, labor security, and economic and social status of labors, is closely related to the requirements of the people. The contradiction between people's ever-growing need for a better life and unbalanced and inadequate development is still the contradiction between subjective needs and objective development, and in essence, the complex contradictions between productivity and production relation, and between economic foundation and the superstructure. To address the contradiction, we must further unleash and develop social forces of production, vigorously improving the quality and level of development; and endeavor to adjust production relations and improve the superstructure. In this sense, building a harmonious labor relationship is a people-centered development philosophy, which allows the fruits of the reform to benefit all the people and truly realize the common prosperity for all.

**Building harmonious labor relations is an important manifestation of improving national governance capabilities**. The key to comprehensively deepening reforms and addressing the current contradictions and challenges faced lies in the modernization of the governance system and governance capabilities. *Opinions on Building Harmonious Labor Relations* issued by the Central Committee of the Communist Party of China and the State Council clearly stated that China is in a period of economic and social transformation, with the subjects and demands of labor relations becoming more diversified, contradictions in labor relations have become more prominent, and the task of building a harmonious labor relationship is arduous. Efforts to build harmonious labor relations with Chinese characteristics and modernize labor relations governance systems and governance capabilities are of great and far-reaching economic, political and social significance. Building harmonious labor relations is the main goal of China's labor relations governance, which fully reflects the real needs of the modernization of the national governance system and social governance capabilities. Through the standardization, scientific development and procedure sophistication of the governance system, social entities can actively and effectively participate in the process of labor relations governance, achieving a benign interaction and win-win results among the government, labors, and capital.

**Building harmonious labor relations is the main content of China's contemporary worker's movement**. As the representative and defender of the legitimate rights and interests of workers in the labor relationship, the trade union bears a crucial responsibility in promoting and building harmonious labor relations, and serves as an important channel and force for standardizing the expressions of demands of workers, safeguarding their rights and interests, and building a harmonious labor relationship. General Secretary Xi Jinping has repeatedly stressed that trade unions must play a good role in coordinating labor relations, meaning not only speak and act for workers and safeguard their interests, but also strengthen the guidance of workers from the perspective of maintaining social stability and promote the development of harmonious labor relations. Worker's movement is important for the CPC, while the task of trade union is a regular and basic work of the governance of China. The economic prosperity and social progress of contemporary China is the result of the joint efforts of millions of workers, and a solid foundation for the continued development of worker's movement in China. As the representatives of hundreds of millions of workers, the Chinese trade union shall not only actively participate in legislation and policy formulation to protect the interests of workers, but also understand and execute the policies to safeguard the interests of workers and to ensure social harmony.

China University of Labor Relations (CULR) is the only subordinate higher education institution of All-China Federation of Trade Unions. Now, CULR has formed a cluster of labor relations subjects with the characteristics of "Trade Union +" and "Labor +" to conduct in-depth study of prominent problems in the field of labor relations, analyze specific issues in detail, and make targeted efforts on specific topics. "Telling China stories well, telling stories of China's labor relations and trade unions well" is an important responsibility of CULR. Since 2015, faculties and researchers of CULR have completed a number of research papers on the theory and practice of building harmonious labor relations with Chinese characteristics. As the international research literatures cannot reflect the current labor relations in China, we selected papers of Chinese scholars, and translated into English, hoping to further stimulate discussion and communications on the new model of China's harmonious labor relations.

This collection includes achievements of Chinese scholars on harmonious labor relations with Chinese characteristics in recent years at multiple levels and from multiple aspects, including discussions of the external environment of harmonious labor relations with Chinese characteristics, and in-depth studies of the subjects of labor relations. For example, Ji Shao presented a full perspective of the rural labor mobility and labor market system since the reform and opening up, Yang Dongmei summarized the historical evolution and experience of model workers in the past 70 years in China, Wu Jianping reviewed the trends and characteristics of changes in the mechanisms of China's trade union since the reform and opening up, and Ji Wenwen and Xiao Zhu discussed the employment status, identity confirmation and rights protection of workers with emerging form of employment in the context of the digital economy. Some scholars discussed related systems of labor relations. For example, Guo Peng explored the historical changes and reforms of China's basic pension system "combining social pooling and personal accounts", Li Ke *et al.* reviewed the historical evolution of labor education in China, and Ye Ying studied cases of building a cross-cultural and harmonious labor relationship management system in overseas Chinese-funded enterprises. In terms of the theoretical research on labor relations in China, Liu Xiangbing *et al.* believe that the theory of labor relations in China is rooted in the country's historical and practical experience, as well as national and social conditions, and has formed a theory system on labor relations with Chinese characteristics, that is, labor relations are derived from economic relations, and also involve political relations, with the fundamental interests of both parties in labor relations being consistent. Therefore, the contradiction in the field of labor relations is the contradiction among specific interests based on the consistence of the fundamental interests, which forms the theoretical basis of the state-led governance system of labor relations in China. With regard to the coordination mechanism of China's labor relations, Wen Xiaoyi believes that due to changes of supply and demand in the labor market, the strengthened positions of workers in negotiation, and the self-adjustment of roles of local governments and employers, China's collective negotiation system has been more diverse compared to the previous state-led model, as it has been driven by more diversified subjects. Jiang Ying *et al.* believe that China's labor-dispute arbitration system is not only the result of historical development, but also supported by international comparative experience. It is a quasi-judicial compulsory dispute resolution mechanism, which strengthens the role of the non-litigation dispute resolution mechanism in resolving litigation and litigation procedures.

Contemporary China is experiencing extensive and profound social changes. Researches and discussions on the development process and practical experience of China's harmonious labor relations not only help to understand the operation and structure of contemporary China's social governance, but also have a great reference value to the coordination of labor relations of global industrialized market economies. Modern scientific and technological revolution, as well as the industrial revolution, especially the digital economy, will have a profound impact on the economy and society of all countries in the world. The new journey of economic and social development has begun, and building harmonious labor relations and the scientific management of labor relations will deepen, while academic researches on China's labor relations will still be the focus of our attention. Therefore, we plan to publish one edition of *Research on Labor Relations in China* every year starting from this collection to present the latest research achievements of our faculties and researchers to foreign readers, hoping to get more attention and feedback, and to jointly contribute to build harmonious labor relations in China.

Finally, it should be pointed out that the International Exchange and Cooperation Office of our University has made great efforts in preparing and selecting articles, editing and publishing of this book. The editors of Economic Science Press have provided useful editorial advice on this book, and also made many contributions in language translation. Therefore, as this book is about to be published, I would like to express my gratitude to all of you.

# Contents

# Labor History

- Achievements and Experience of the Cause of Model Workers in the Past 70 Years Since the Founding of the People's Republic of China

# Achievements and Experience of the Cause of Model Workers in the Past 70 Years Since the Founding of the People's Republic of China[*]

*Yang Dongmei*[**]

**Abstract:** There are mainly two periods for the development of the cause of model workers since the founding of the People's Republic of China: first, the period of socialist development; second, the period since the reform and opening up. During the past 70 years, model workers have made significant achievements in promoting political and economic development, leading advanced culture, and building the model workers system. And there are four lessons learned for the development of the cause of model workers in China: the leadership of the CPC should be strengthened; the undertakings of model workers should serve the big picture of the CPC and the whole country; the methods and means of model works should be innovated to meet the changing demand over time; theoretical studies should be enhanced to further understand the principles of the cause of model workers.

**Keywords:** 70 years since the founding of the People's Republic of China; model workers; advanced worker; model workers selection system

Since the founding of the People's Republic of China, under the leadership of the Communist Party of China (CPC), model workers have been selfless with their ordinary work, making important contributions to the country's economic and social development, as well as the reform and opening up. Statistics show that, from 1949 to 2015, the Central Committee of the Communist Party of China and the State Council have held 15 national commendation conferences for model workers, honoring a total of 10,667 advanced collectives and 31,515 model workers and advanced workers, among

[*] This paper was published in *Hubei Social Sciences*, Issue 8, 2019.

[**] Yang Dongmei, professor, Dean of the School of Labor Union, China University of Labor Relations. She specializes in the trade union theory and work, working class, labor relations, etc.

which 23 model workers were honored in 7 conferences after 1979 (Li, 2018), and there were more model workers honored at conferences of lower levels. The year 2019 marked the 70th anniversary of the founding of the People's Republic of China. It is of great practical significance to analyze the glorious history and outstanding achievements of model workers over the past 70 years and to study and summarize the rich experience, so as to continue to improve the work related to model workers in the new era.

## I. 70 Years of Development of the Cause of Model Workers Since the Founding of the People's Republic of China

The cause of model workers in the past 70 years since the founding of the People's Republic of China is closely related with the historical background, the level of economic and social development, the political and cultural orientation and the undertakings of trade unions of different periods. Based on the historical development of the cause of model workers, it can be divided into two periods, one is the period of socialist development, and the other is the period since the reform and opening up. The former is the period of formation of the cause of model workers, while the latter is the period of institutionalization and standardization.

### 1. The Period of Socialist Development (1949-1966)

During this period, four conferences were held to honor model workers: National Conference of Representatives of Model Workers, farmers and Soldiers (1950), National Conference of Representatives of Advanced Workers (1956), National Conference of Representatives of Advanced Collectives and Advanced Workers of Industry, Transportation, Capital Construction, Finance and Trade in Socialist development (1959), and National Conference of Representatives of Advanced Units and Advanced Workers of Education and Culture, Health, Sports and Journalism in Socialist development (1960).

*1.1 The National Conference of Representatives of Model Workers, farmers and Soldiers*

After the founding of the People's Republic of China, the working class, as masters and builders of the new country, actively participated in various economic and social reforms and production activities, and played a significant role in the restoration of production and political movements. In order to honor the individuals who made significant contributions to the restoration of production, from September 25th to October 2nd 1950, the State Council held the National Conference of Representatives of Model Workers, farmers and Soldiers in Beijing, and 464 people were honored with National Model Workers. These model workers were mainly from industrial, agricultural sector and the military. In the preparatory meeting for this conference, the State Council stipulated that the representatives of model workers were to be selected on the basis of the model worker movement organized and carried out by the trade unions.

### 1.2 The National Conference of Representatives of Advanced Workers

According to the requirements of the general guideline of the CPC during the transitional period, the First Five-year Plan (1953-1957) was implemented for the development of economy, and a great number of workers have actively participated in the socialist development. From 1953 to 1956, the Central Committee of the Communist Party of China and All-China Federation of Trade Unions successively carried out labor competition campaigns such as the campaign for increasing production and saving, and the campaign for advanced workers, which stimulated the enthusiasm and creativity of workers; as a result, there were more advanced collectives and individuals from different sectors. In order to sum up the experience and honor the advanced workers, National Conference of Representatives of Advanced Workers was held in Beijing from April 30th to May 10th 1956, in which 853 were honored with National Advanced Collective and 4,703 were honored with National Advanced Worker (People's Daily, 2005). Most of the individuals and collectives honored were from the industrial sector. The criteria for the selection of model workers included "meeting the targets of the First Five-year Plan ahead of schedule", "meeting the targets of superior quality", "achievements in learning and promoting experience or in using advanced technology in trial production", etc (People's Daily, 1956).

### 1.3 Two national conferences held to honor model workers in 1959 and 1960

In 1957, when China entered the period of socialist development, the main task of the working class was to adhere to the guideline of diligence and thrift, initiate a new upsurge of production for the Second Five-year Plan, and meet or even overfulfill the targets of the new national plan. All-China Federation of Trade Unions has actively mobilized workers to engage in production, and promoted the development of the campaign of increasing production and saving in various ways. In 1959, All-China Federation of Trade Unions urged workers all over the country to "initiate a new upsurge of the increasing production and saving campaign to sustain a continuous leap of the national economy in 1959". Workers from different sectors took actions accordingly and new peaks were reached. Statistics show that, there were more than 300 thousand advanced collectives and 3 million advanced workers nationwide in 1959; workers have put forward about 81.48 million rational proposals, of which about 37.75 million were put into practice (Wang, He and Cao, 2005).

In order to honor advanced units and individuals from the industrial sector during the Great Leap Forward, the Central Committee of the Communist Party of China and the State Council held National Conference of Representatives of Advanced

Collectives and Advanced Workers of Industry, Transportation, Capital Construction, Finance and Trade in Socialist development (National Conference of Outstanding Workers for short) from October 25th to November 8th 1959, in which 2,565 national advanced units and 3,267 national advanced individuals were honored. From June 1st to 11th 1960, the Central Committee of the Communist Party of China and the State Council held National Conference of Representatives of Advanced Units and Advanced Workers of Education and Culture, Health, Sports and Journalism in Socialist development (Conference of Outstanding Workers in Cultural and Educational Fields for short), in which 3,092 advanced units and 3,267 advanced workers were honored (People's Daily, 2005).

The scope of selecting model workers in 1959 and 1960 was further expanded to include not only the sectors of industry, transportation, capital construction, finance and trade, but also education, culture, health, sports and journalism, while the number of model workers from rural areas was drastically reduced. In these two conferences, Wang Chonglun, Ni Zhifu, Zhang Binggui, Shi Chuanxiang, Wang Jinxi and Zhao Mengtao were selected as model workers. Their meritorious deeds are still widely known today and they have become role models for the whole country.

## 2. The Cause of Model Workers in the Period Since the Reform and Opening Up (1977-2019)

Due to the Cultural Revolution and other factors, nationwide selection activities of model workers were suspended for 17 years. As the Cultural Revolution ended, the Chinese society gradually went back on track. With the support of the CPC and the government, the selection of model workers was resumed, which marked the second upsurge of the model worker movement. From April 1977 to December 1979, the Central Committee of the Communist Party of China and the State Council held five consecutive national model worker conferences, and there weren't any selection of national model worker carried out from 1979 to 1988. From 1989 to the present, a total of six national conferences of commendations were held. They were all called "National Model Worker and Advanced Worker Commendation Conference", and the time was fixed – once every five years. The selection and commendation of model workers began to "enter a normalized and institutionalized stage" (Li, 2018).

*2.1 Five conferences held to honor model workers at the early stage of the reform and opening up*

These five conferences were held before and after the Third Plenary Session of the Eleventh Central Committee of the Communist Party of China, which served as a link between the past and the future. Three conferences – National Conference that advocated the industrial sector to learn from the experience of Daqing oilfield,

National Conference that advocated the finance and trade sector to learn from the experience of Daqing oilfield and Dazhai village, and National Science Conference – were held before the Third Plenary Session by the Central Committee of the Communist Party of China and the State Council; and model workers selected from 1960 to 1978 were honored. Two conferences – National Conference of Advanced Enterprises and Model Workers from the Sectors of Industry, Transportation and Capital Construction, and National Conference of Advanced Units and Model Workers from the Sectors of Agriculture, Finance and Trade, Education, Health and Scientific Research were held after the Third Plenary Session by the State Council; and model workers selected from 1978 to 1979 were honored. The theme of these two conferences began to shift to economic development and the reform and opening up. There were a total of 2,541 model workers and advanced workers from the sectors of industry, science and technology, finance and trade, transportation, capital construction, agriculture, education, health, and scientific research, and 4,157 advanced units were selected nationwide. These five selections were carried out in different sectors, which "indicated the urgent needs of the country for the development of specific fields at specific historical stages, and demonstrated distinctive features of that period" (Wang, 2018).

Since the reform and opening up, with economic development became the major task of the county, the criterion for selecting model workers has also changed. In 1979, the concept of "advancement" was defined for the first time as "Model workers and advanced collectives of all sectors must be outstanding representatives of the advanced productivity that demonstrates the direction of social development" (You, 1997). The criterion for assessment of model workers and advanced collectives was also clarified: "We need to see whether they have played a significant role in promoting the development of productivity, and whether they have made greater contributions to the socialist development" (China Co-op, 1986). Based on the selection criterion and conditions, it can be deducted that the main purpose of the selection of model workers in this period is to serve socialist modernization.

Among the national model workers honored at the five commendation conferences from 1977 to 1979, the group of intellectuals was particularly notable. Comrade Deng Xiaoping's assertion that "intellectuals have become part of the working class" expanded the scope of model workers, and greatly stimulated the enthusiasm of intellectuals and those engaged in mental work. The deeds of intellectuals and researchers represented by Chen Jingrun, Yuan Longping, Jiang Zhuying and Deng Jiaxian have inspired a generation to study science and technology, encouraged people of the whole country to reach new heights of science, and promoted the development of science in China.

*2.2 Six national conferences held to honor model workers since 1989*

In 1989, six national conferences were held to honor model workers, and a total of 17,535 model workers and advanced workers were commended, including a large number of knowledgeable, professional and well-rounded workers with characteristics of that period, such as Kong Fansen, Li Suli, Xu Hu, Li Bin, Xu Zhenchao, Deng Jianjun, Kong Xiangrui and Dou Tiesheng.

After 1989, with the development of socialist market economy, the scope of the selection of model workers has also changed. In the past, the honor was mostly granted to people in a certain sector. However, after 1989, not only the manual and mental workers from all sectors, but also those from new social organizations were included in the selection (Wang, 2018). For example, "workers, farmers, professionals, managers, ideological and political workers and other staff in the sectors of industry, agriculture, transportation, finance and trade, construction, education, scientific research, culture, health, sports, etc." were eligible for the selection in 1989[1]; the scope was clarified as "the reform and opening up, economic development, industrial and agricultural production and various social undertakings", and "professional and technical personnel, as well as managerial personnel" was further specified as "scientific and educational personnel, as well as corporate managerial personnel" in 2000; "the reform and opening up, economic development, industrial and agricultural production and various social undertakings" was changed to "the reform and opening up, economic development and the development of various social undertakings" in 2005, and at the same time, the term "other people" was clearly defined as "other people across every social stratum", and private entrepreneurs and urban migrant workers were also included in the selection (Economic and Technical Department of ACFTU, 2012).

Since the reform and opening up, whether significant contribution made to the reform and opening up and socialist modernization has become a major criterion for selecting model workers, which reflected its representativeness and the characteristics of the times. For example, in 1989, it was emphasized that the selected model workers should adhere to Four Cardinal Principles, support the reform and opening up, and make significant contributions to economic and intellectual civilization development. In 2010, achievements of promoting the transformation of economic development, optimizing economic structure, and improving the ability of independent innovation were highlighted in the selection. In 2015, the selection highlighted actively adapting to the new norm of economic development, improving the quality and efficiency of economic development, promoting economic transformation and

---

[1] Notice of the State Council on the Convening of the 1989 National Model Worker and Advanced Worker Commendation Conference[J]. Communique of the State Council of the People's Republic of China, 1989(12).

upgrading, facilitating new urbanization, implementing innovation-driven activities, strengthening risk prevention and control, and fostering stable and healthy economic development etc.

After 1989, the proportion of frontline workers in the selection of national model workers has been increasing. For example, it was stipulated that the proportion of workers should be no less than 30% in 1989; the proportion of frontline workers rose to 32% in 1995, and rose to 35% in 2000; in 2005, it was specified that enterprise workers should account for no less than 45% of the total number of recommended candidates, among which frontline workers and professional and technical personnel of enterprises should account for no less than 55% of the recommended corporate workers (Li, 2018). In 2015, among the selected model workers and advanced workers, frontline workers of enterprises accounted for 67.5% of the corporate candidates, 10.5% higher than the required ratio and 5.1% higher than the number of the previous selection; heads of enterprises accounted for 16.9% of the corporate candidates, 3.1% lower than the required ratio and 4.3% lower than the number of the previous selection; migrant workers accounted for 30.4% of farmers, 5.4% higher than the required proportion, and 17.7% higher than the number of the previous selection (Liu, 2015).

## II. Major Achievements of the Cause of Model Workers in the past 70 years Since the Founding of the People's Republic of China

In 2015, General Secretary Xi Jinping pointed out in his speech at the Conference to celebrate the International Labor Day that model workers and advanced individuals have shown people what it means to uphold the Chinese path, foster the Chinese spirit, and gather Chinese strength. With a strong awareness of their responsibility as masters of the country, they have set an example for all Chinese people to follow through their fine work, creations, and selfless devotion(Xi, 2015). In the past 70 years, great achievements were made in the cause of model workers in China, and model workers have contributed to consolidating the state power, promoting economic development, promoting advanced culture, and facilitating social progress. At the same time,  the cause of model workers in China has gradually matured despite twist and turns.

### 1. Participate in Political Development with a Sense of Ownership and Responsibility

The cause of model workers in China is developed under the leadership of the CPC, and is important for the Party and the country. On the one hand, the cause of model workers cannot be developed without the Party's leadership, which is the fundamental political guarantee for the healthy development; on the other hand, the leading and exemplary role of model workers can help to consolidate the class base and mass base of the Party. The Communist Party of China has always attached great importance to the important status and role of the working class and model workers. Over the past 70 years, model workers have participated in the political development of China with a sense of ownership and responsibility, and have always been firm supporters of the road to socialism with Chinese characteristics, playing an important role in accomplishing the political tasks of the Party and the country in various historical periods.

Over the past 70 years, a great number of model workers have been elected as Party delegates, deputies to People's Congress, the Chinese People's Political Consultative Conference(CPPCC) members and representatives of trade union congresses, or admitted into leading organs at all levels. They have played an equally active role in the management of state and social affairs. Since the 18th National Congress of the CPC, the political status of model workers has been further elevated, the channels of political participation have been expanded, and the proportion of model workers among Party delegates, deputies to People's Congress and CPPCC members at all levels has been increasing. Among 2,287 delegates to the 19th National Congress of CPC, there were 405 model workers from the provincial and ministerial level, accounting for 17.7%. Among 2,987 deputies to the 12th People's Congress, there were 593 model workers from the provincial and ministerial level, accounting for 19.9%; and 102 were front-line workers and farmers. Among 2,237 members of the 12th CPPCC, there were 113 model workers from the provincial or ministerial level, accounting for 5.1% (Li, 2018). At the 17th National Congress of Trade Unions, there were 977 advanced model workers honored by the institutions of the municipal level, accounting for 48.6%, including 127 national model workers and advanced workers (Wang, 2018). The increasing proportion of model workers among Party delegates, deputies to People's Congress and CPPCC members at all levels has created conditions for model workers to participate in politics and major social activities and play their important roles in the management of state and social affairs and democratic management at the grassroots level. In recent years, Xu Zhenchao, Guo Mingyi, Ju Xiaolin and other model workers from the frontline of production have served as part-time vice presidents of All-China Federation of Trade Unions; some model workers have worked as part-time vice presidents in Federation of Trade Unions of some provinces (autonomous regions and municipalities directly under the Central Government) and the national industrial unions. This is of great significance to maintaining and enhancing the political, advanced and mass nature of the work of trade union and trade union organizations, and strengthening the cultivation of trade union cadres.

## 2. Promote Economic Development by Creative Work

Over the past 70 years, in the periods of China's socialist development, the reform and opening up and the new era, with creative work, model workers have not only created huge economic benefits for enterprises and the country, but also played a leading role in social and economic development.

In the early years of the People's Republic of China, the CPC and the government, as well as trade unions at all levels, carried out various forms of model worker campaigns and model worker commending activities, such as technical innovation, advanced worker campaigns and rational proposal, in order to encourage all people to make concerted efforts and devote themselves to socialist production and development. Innovations, such as "Meng Tai Warehouse" of Meng Tai(worker of Ansteel), "Fine Yarn Working Method" of Hao Jianxiu(a textile worker), "Multifunctional Tire" of Wang Chonglun(a steelworker) and "Deep Pit Operation Method" of Ma Wanshui(the leader of the Ma Wanshui Group), improved production efficiency and contributed to the restoration of the national economy, the completion of the national economic plan, and the promotion of socialist industrialization.

Since the reform and opening up, in addition to frontline workers, there were more intellectuals, migrant workers and enterprise managers selected as model workers, and the economic contributions of model workers have also taken on new characteristics, for example, Yuan Longping, the national model worker and the "father of hybrid rice", has studied hybrid rice cultivation technology and successfully realized high and stable grain production in China. In the new century, advocated by All-China Federation of Trade Unions, the innovation studio was created by the grassroots role models and workers. It was developed as a carrier of economic and technological innovation, providing a new platform for model workers to conduct scientific research and technological innovation.

Since the 18th National Congress of CPC, under the leadership of the Party, government and trade unions, model workers have created one Chinese miracle after another with a strong sense of ownership, promoted the reform of industrial workforce and the transformation from "Made in China" to "Created in China", and helped to build a great modern socialist country. From 2012 to 2017, 460 million workers participated in professional skill competitions, with 3.295 million technical innovations, 941 thousand inventions, 58.166 million rational proposals and 899 thousand advanced operating methods; 120 million workers participated in professional skill competitions organized by trade unions, and 33.41 million workers participated in technical trainings organized by trade unions; 2.499 million people were selected as "gold medal workers", "chief technicians" and "chief employees"; 3.543 million mentor-apprentice pairs were formed among model workers (skilled personnel) (Worker's Daily, 2017), which contributed to the technological progress of enterprises and innovative development of industries.

### 3. Build the Spirit of Model Workers with Selfless Hard Work and Devotion

The spirit of model workers is formed in the practice of social production by workers and is a precious intellectual asset of the working class and the masses. The spirit of model workers, such as the spirit of Meng Tai, the spirit of Wang Jinxi, the spirit of "Two Bombs and One Satellite", the spirit of Shi Chuanxiang, and the spirit of Zhang Binggui, has converged to become a powerful source of strength. On April 28th 2005, Hu Jintao summarized the spirit of model workers in 24 Chinese characters for the first time. He said, generations of advanced model workers have fostered the great model worker spirit of "dedication to one's profession, pursuit of excellence, hard work, courageous innovation, indifference to fame and fortune, and readiness to sacrifices" with their own concrete actions (Economic and Technical Department of ACFTU, 2012).

The spirit of model workers embodies the professional ethics of "dedication to one's profession, pursuit of excellence", the hardworking, enterprising and innovative mindset of "hard work, courageous innovation", and the noble virtue of "indifference to fame and fortune, readiness to sacrifices". The spirit of model workers reflects the sense of ownership of the working class under the socialist system, embodies the socialist values, represents the spirit of the times, passes on the national tradition, and becomes an integral part of the Chinese ethos. It has played a vital role in promoting the concept that labor is honorable in the whole society, forming a social atmosphere of hardworking with passion and respecting labor, and stimulating the creativity of laborers.

Over the past 70 years, the spirit of model workers has been a powerful source of strength leading workers and the whole nation in periods of socialist development and the reform and opening up in China. In the 1960s, Wang Jinxi, a worker in Daqing Oilfield, as an outstanding representative of model workers, said that "I would rather give up 20 years of my life to complete the exploitation of the oil field". He was then deemed as the "Iron Man" of the oilfield. The "Iron Man Spirit" embodies the advanced nature of the working class in China, and still stimulates all Chinese people nowadays. In the new era, promotion of the spirit of model workers has become the main task of trade unions and an important lever of the cause of model workers. To better promote the spirit of model workers, it is necessary to give full play to the model workers' exemplary and guiding role, to lead the whole society with model workers' advanced concepts and noble character, to inspire workers to build a successful career, and to gather strong positive energy for the cause of socialism with Chinese characteristics.

## 4. Ensure the Sound Development of the Cause of Model Workers Through Institutional Development

In the past 70 years, in order to ensure the sound development of the cause of model workers, the government and relevant state organs have made provisions for the work related to model workers through legislation, and All-China Federation of Trade Unions and trade unions at all levels have also promulgated many normative documents for the selection, commendation, management and service of model workers. Systems for the education and training, regular health checkups, recuperation of model workers, and assistance for badly-off model workers have been established.

In 1982, it was stipulated in Article 42 of the Constitution of the People's Republic of China that "socialist labor competition is advocated, model workers and advanced workers will be awarded". In Article 6 of the Regulations on Rewards and Punishments for Enterprise Employees issued by the State Council on April 10th 1982, it was stipulated that "rewards for employees include record of merit, record of a great merit, promotion, issuance of commendatory order, and conferring honorary titles such as advanced laborer (worker) and model worker". In 1992, it was stipulated in Article 8 of the Trade Union Law of the People's Republic of China that, trade unions should organize workers to participate in socialist labor competitions, carry out activities of rational proposals, technical innovation and technical collaboration, improve labor productivity and economic efficiency, and develop social productivity. In 2001, it was stipulated in Article 32 of the Trade Union Law of the People's Republic of China that, commissioned by the government, trade unions and relevant state organs should work together in the selection, commendation, cultivation and management of model workers and advanced laborers (workers). Hence, the selection and commendation of model workers is fixed based on the basic laws of China and other relevant laws.

To optimize the work of trade unions, All-China Federation of Trade Unions has issued a series of rules and regulations, forming a more complete system of selection, commendation and management of model workers. On March 8th 1980, All-China Federation of Trade Unions issued a *Notice on the Trial Implementation of the Provisional Regulations on the Work of Model Workers*. The regulations were thereafter applied in selecting model workers, and other things related to model workers, such as management and benefits.

In addition, All-China Federation of Trade Unions and other institutions have also established systems for the regular health checkups and recuperation of model workers. In 1983, All-China Federation of Trade Unions, the Organization Department of the CPC Central Committee, Ministry of Labor and Personnel, and Ministry of Health formulated *Several Provisions on Protecting the Physical Health of Model Workers*. In 2000, All-China Federation of Trade Unions issued the *Notice on Organizing National Model Workers and Advanced Workers for Recuperation Activities*. And in 2005, All-China Federation of Trade Unions formulated *Administrative Measures on Organizing Model Workers' Activities in Recuperation Bases*.

In order to effectively address the difficulties in the life of some model workers and improve their living conditions, relevant institutions have formulated documents on increasing the pensions of model workers, forbidding the layoff of model workers, and providing them one-time rewards, so as to help model workers through funds and policies. These documents include *Interim Measures of the State Council on Workers' Retirement and Settlement* promulgated and implemented by the State Council in 1978, *Notice on Deepening the Reform of the Pension Insurance System for Enterprise Employees* issued by the State Council in 1995, *Notice on Further Solving the Problems of Social Security and Living Difficulties of Model Workers* jointly issued by Ministry of Human Resources and Social Security and other ministries in 2010, *Notice on Better Supporting the Badly-off Model Workers from the Provincial and Ministerial Level* issued by the General Office of the State Council in 2015, and *Regulations on the Treatment of Recipients of Meritorious Honors and Awards (for Trial Implementation)* and *Measures to Help Badly-off Recipients of Honors and Awards (for Trial Implementation)* issued by the General Office of the CPC Central Committee and the General Office of the State Council in 2018, etc.

## III. Lessons Learned from the Cause of Model Workers in the past 70 Years Since the Founding of the People's Republic of China

Over the past 70 years, the development of the cause of model workers has had its glories, and twists and turns, and rich experience has been accumulated. In the new era, it is necessary to effectively strengthen the leadership of the CPC in the management of model workers, strive to serve the big picture of the Party and the country, constantly enrich the methods and carriers of work related to model workers, and reach new heights for the cause of model workers.

### 1. Strengthen the Leadership of the Party to Ensure the Correct Direction of the Development of the Cause of Model Workers

The Party and the government have always cared about and attached great importance to the work related to model workers. Leaders of the Party have all given important instructions on the work related to model workers and attended the commendation conference of model workers. In September 1950, at the National Conference of Representatives of Model Workers, Farmers, Soldiers and War Heroes, Mao Zedong, on behalf of the Central Committee of the CPC, delivered a speech saying that the national war heroes and model workers "are exemplary figures of the country, the backbone of the advancement of causes of all areas, the reliable pillar of the government and the bridge between the government and the masses" (Mao, 1999). Since the 18th National Congress of CPC, General Secretary Xi Jinping has delivered several important speeches on the cause of model workers, stating that, it is of great importance that we promote the spirit of model workers and the spirit of labor throughout the society, publicize the deeds of model workers and other role models, and guide the general public to uphold the belief of hardworking, honest and creative work, so that the glory of labor and greatness of creativity can become the most powerful theme of our times, and the honor, sublimity, importance and beauty of labor can become a consensus (Xi, 2015). This has indicated the direction for the work related to model workers in the new era.

## 2. The Cause of Model Workers Must Serve the Big Picture of the Party and the Whole Country

The cause of model workers is a significant component of the cause of the Party and the country, and an important part of the work of trade unions. The success of the cause of model workers depends on whether it can serve the big picture of the Party and the whole country. Over the past 70 years, the goal of the cause of model workers has always been serving the big picture of the Party and the whole country. It is hoped that model workers can find their positions, play their roles and lead the masses of workers to work hard to complete the major tasks of the Party in different historical periods. In the new era, the cause of model workers should still serve the big picture of the Party and the country. Model workers should keep the goals of the 19th National Congress of CPC in mind and motivate workers to play a greater role in realizing the Chinese Dream of the great rejuvenation of the Chinese nation.

## 3. Continue to Innovate the Methods and Means of the Cause of Model Workers to Meet the Changing Demand over Time

The cause of model workers developed over the past 70 years. At different stages of history, the Party and the country as well as the trade unions found many methods and means with the characteristics of the times to meet the changing demand over time. In the early years of the PRC, national labor competitions such as the campaign to increase production and saving, and the advanced laborer campaign were the main means; in the period since the reform and opening up, the forms of labor competitions became more diversified, and a system of labor and professional  skill competition based on enterprise training and technical competitions, with national and industrial competitions as the main body and domestic competitions combining with international competitions, was gradually formed. Meanwhile, the innovation studio has become a new platform for model workers to showcase their talents, start their businesses and play their leading roles. In addition, in the selection of "pioneer of national workers", model workers also played exemplary role in mass economic and technological innovation activities such as technical innovation, technical collaboration, inventions, rational proposals, online training and "small inventions, small creations, small innovations, small designs and small proposals". At present, China is facing the major task of transforming the model of economic development and promoting industrial upgrading, and model workers should utilize innovative methods and means to promote the cultivation of industrial workforce.

### 4. Improve Theoretical Studies to further understand the principles of the Cause of Model Workers

With 70-year of development, Chinese trade unions have continued to innovate and become more mature. However, the theoretical researches of such a unique socio-historical phenomenon are not comprehensive enough. Most of the studies are the summary and compilation of the deeds of model workers, and the history of model workers is only touched upon in the introduction of the history of labor movement. In recent years, as more attention is paid to model workers, there are more studies on the history of model workers, the oral history of model workers, the culture and philosophy of model workers, and the spirit of model workers, which is a delightful phenomenon. In the future, researchers of model workers should expand the scope of study, reveal the principles of development of model worker cause in China in a multi-disciplinary, multi-angle and all-round way, explore the inner connection between the cause of model workers and political, economic, cultural, social and ecological development, and help people to better understand the cause of model workers, so that model workers can make greater contributions in the new era.

In the past 70 years, fine tradition formed during the revolutionary war time was inherited for the cause of model worker, and it has developed and changed along with the historical process of socialist development and reform and opening up, making great contributions, performing meritorious deeds and playing an irreplaceable role in political, economic and cultural development. At the same time, the work related to model workers has made substantial progress – a set of systems including selection, commendation, management and service of model workers were formed to better guarantee the sound development of the cause of model workers. At present, under the guidance of Xi Jinping Thought on Socialism with Chinese Characteristics for a New Era, the cause of model workers has new opportunities and gained more momentum of development. Therefore, an in-depth study and summary of the achievements and experiences of the development of the cause of model workers in the past 70 years and a deeper understanding of the principles of the development of the cause of model workers will help us to promote the innovative development of the cause of model workers in the new era, give full play to the leading and exemplary role of model workers, and unite and mobilize hundreds of millions of workers to together realize the Chinese Dream of the great rejuvenation of the Chinese nation.

## References

[1] Li Yufu. Introduction to the Labor-related and Economy-related Work of Trade Union[M]. Beijing: China Workers Publishing House, 2018.

[2] The Pulse of History: Brief Introduction to the Previous National Model Worker Conference[N]. People's Daily, 2005-4-29.

[3] All-China Federation of Trade Unions Issued a Notice to Hold a National Meeting of Representatives of Advanced Workers [N], People's Daily, 1956-2-21.

[4] Wang Yongxi, He Bufeng, and Cao Yanping. Brief History of Chinese Trade Unions[M]. China Workers Publishing House, 2005.

[5] Li Ke, Models and Guidance: The Evolution and Reflection of the Selection System of Model Workers[J], Teaching and Research, 2018(6).

[6] Wang Jiahao, The "Changed" and "Unchanged" of Model Workers in the 40 Years Since the Reform and Opening up[J]. Chinese Workers' Movement, 2018(12).

[7] You Zhenglin, Study of China's Model Worker Selection and Commendation System[J], Sociological Study, 1997(6).

[8] All-China Federation of Supply and Marketing Cooperatives, Selections from the History of All-China Federation of Supply and Marketing Cooperatives (Part 2 of Volume I). Beijing: China Financial and Economic Publishing House, 1986.

[9] Notice of the State Council on the Convening of the 1989 National Model Worker and Advanced Worker Commendation Conference[J]. Communique of the State Council of the People's Republic of China, 1989(12).

[10] Economic and Technical Department of All-China Federation of Trade Unions. New Workbook for Model Workers[M]. Beijing: China Workers Publishing House, 2012.

[11] Liu Weitao. The National Model Worker and Advanced Worker Conference Will Be Held in Beijing at the End of April[N]. People's Daily, 2015-4-27.

[12] Xi Jinping. Speech at the International Labor Day Celebration and National Model Worker and Advanced Worker Commendation Conference. People's Daily, 2015-4-29.

[13] Five Years of Hard Work: Build the Power of the Times to Hold Up the Chinese Dream – Record of the Trade Union's Work to Help Workers Improve Their Capabilities and Make Achievements Since the 18th National Congress of CPC[N], Workers' Daily, 2017-10-10.

[14] Selected Works of Mao Zedong (Volume 6)[M]. Beijing: People's Publishing House, 1999.

# Labor Market

- Rural Labor Transfer since Reform and Opening Up:
  Employment System, Policy Evolution and Innovation

# Rural Labor Transfer Since Reform and Opening Up: Employment System, Policy Evolution and Innovation[*]

*Ji Shao*[**]

**Abstract:** Since the reform and opening up, China has undergone a historical transformation from an agricultural country to an industrial one, developing rapidly into a major power in manufacturing, international trade and economy. Against the backdrop of economic and social transformation, China has the courage to conduct institutional innovation in exploring an employment system with Chinese characteristics for transferred rural labor in practices of deepening reform and opening up. Looking back on the magnificent process of transferring rural labor forces which has a far-reaching influence, the author believes that our most valuable experience would be conducting institutional innovation and cherishing respect towards people. This paper draws on a large volume of various sources, including major documents issued by the Central Committee of the Communist Party of China (CPC), the State Council and various ministries and commissions since the reform and opening up, authoritative reports by research institutions like the Development Research Center of the State Council, and iconic research achievements in the academia on rural labor mobility. On this basis, the paper reviews the employment system and policies in regard to China's rural labor transfer since the reform and opening up and summarizes the evolution process and future trends. Adhering to the principles of seeking truth from facts, objectivity and fairness, this paper tries to restore and present the magnificent historical course of China's rural labor transfer to readers.

**Keywords:** reform and opening up; institutional innovation; rural labor transfer; employment system

---

[*] This paper was originally published in *Economics and Management Research*, 2019, Issue. 1. Some of the data in the article was updated to 2020.

[**] Ji Shao, professor, doctoral supervisor, Dean of the School of Business Administration of China University of Labor Relations. She specializes in labor market theory and policy. Email: jshbj7483@sina.com.

Since the reform and opening up, tremendous changes have taken place in both China's rural and urban areas. From the demographic perspective, the proportion of China's urban population (urbanization rate) has rocketed from 17.9% in 1978 to 60.60%[1] by the end of 2020. This growth in urban resident population has been boosted by China's industrialization and urbanization process, to which China's rural labor transfer has made great contribution, changing China itself as well as benefiting the whole world. This fully demonstrates that the over 800 million farmers in China are the true heroes and masters of the nation, serving as strong power to push history forward. Since 1978, China has undergone a historical transformation from an agricultural country to an industrial one, developing rapidly into a major power in manufacturing, international trade and economy. Against the backdrop of economic and social transformation, China has the courage to conduct institutional innovation in exploring an employment system with Chinese characteristics for transferred rural labor in practices of deepening reform and opening up. Looking back on the magnificent process of transferring rural labor forces which has a far-reaching influence, the author believes that our most valuable experience would be conducting institutional innovation and cherishing respect towards people.

## I. An Employment System with Chinese Characteristics for Transferred Rural Labor Formed in Reform and Opening Up

### 1. Three Institutional Obstacles Restricted Rural Labor Transfer and Employment Before Reform and Opening Up

During the 28 years from the founding of the People's Republic of China to the reform and opening up, a dualistic system featuring urban-rural divide strictly restricted agricultural population from entering cities. The employment of China's transferred rural labor in these years can be divided into three stages, two of which witnessed severe setbacks.

The first stage is from 1950 to 1957, when the coexistence of multiple economic components in urban and rural areas allowed relatively free movement for rural population, who in turn contributed 60% of urban population growth. After 1955, a few restrictions emerged on rural labor transfer as the new dualistic household residential registration system (*hukou*[2] system) and people's commune system were established (Zhao, 2012).

The years between 1957 and 1963 marked the second stage, when rural labor transfer experienced drastic fluctuations. As the Great Leap Forward Movement was

---

[1] *National Population Development Plan (2016-2030).*

[2] *Hukou* means the household residential registration.

launched in 1958, the number of agricultural labor forces dropped from 192 to 151 million within just one year, transferring 40.82 million labor forces out of agriculture. The proportion of agricultural labor forces in social labor forces fell accordingly from 81.2% to 58.2%, a shrink of 23 percent points. Per capita grain dropped from 302 kg in 1957 to 108 kg in 1960, which set China's agriculture back to the level in the first few years of the People's Republic of China. This forced the state to coerce a number of labor forces back into agriculture from the secondary and tertiary industries, and more than 20 million people returned from urban to rural areas.

The third stage is from 1963 to 1977, when rural labor transfer was severely hindered by the *hukou* system which has imposed a dualistic household registration structure strictly separating urban and rural population. This system restricts rural population from moving into cities and flowing freely. In cities, jobs in non-agricultural sectors were under the unified planning and allocation of the state. From 1976 to 1977, 17.8 million urban youth went to rural areas in the Up to the Mountains and Down to the Countryside Movement, equal to 55% of newly created jobs in state-owned units from 1966 to 1977. In 1977, 15 million of them returned to cities, raising the urban unemployment rate to over 5% (Cui, 2017).

In summarizing rural labor employment before reform and opening up, we find that three institutional obstacles restrained rural labor transfer: the national strategy of prioritizing heavy industry, the *hukou* system and the dualistic system featuring urban-rural divide, and the collective management and laboring system of the people's commune. The three institutional obstacles hinder the free flow of labor forces and rational allocation of resources, thus undermining the efficiency of economic operations. In this context, institutional innovation became inevitable.

## 2. Rural Labor Forces Developed Their Wisdom and Ability to Conduct Institutional Innovation During Reform and Opening Up

General Secretary Xi Jinping pointed out in his keynote speech at the opening ceremony of Bo'ao Forum for Asia 2018 Annual Conference that the Chinese nation is a truth-seeking nation with an open mind, which is especially true since the reform and opening up. The people's efforts to open up their minds have advanced side by side with their endeavor of reform and opening up. Their search for new ideas and experiment of practices have been mutually reinforcing. The great strength of a guiding vision was fully demonstrated in rural labor transfer.

The reform and opening up introduced the household contract responsibility system to rural areas in China, which led to the emergence of township enterprises. This in turn gave farmers who lived near large and medium-sized cities and coastal areas opportunities to enter non-agricultural industries close to home, and initiated the trend of "rural labor transferring to local factories" of secondary and tertiary sectors which then swept the country. At its peak, there were more than 20 million township enterprises in China's rural areas, absorbing more than 120 million rural labourers for employment. These enterprises were reputed to account for half of the rural economy at the time (Du, 2018). As the reform of the economic system was deepened, a large number of joint ventures, foreign-invested companies, private enterprises and individual entrepreneurs appeared in cities, and many state-owned enterprises were revitalized through the reform as well. Moreover, as China opened itself to the world and foreign investment was introduced, many industries and businesses clustered in southeast coastal areas or areas that opened up early, creating huge local demand for labor. These changes in China's industrial layout, along with rural labor transfer that followed, caused most township enterprises scattering across China's rural areas to gradually lose their edge in the competition. Thus, the former mode of transferring rural labor to local township enterprises ran into trouble. In response to the rising tide of industrialization in coastal cities, farmers took a bold step of leaving their hometowns to pursue the various employment opportunities offered by industrialization and urbanization. This large-scale cross-regional migration of farmers for employment not only met the demand for labor from the rising wave of the industrialization in the cities, but also powerfully impacted the dualistic economic system featuring urban-rural divide that had been in place for many years, thus advancing China's economic reform to a deeper level.

Practice shows that China's rural labor mobility and employment did not go off without a hitch. The dualistic system featuring urban-rural divide system, which was not yet completely broken down, as well as the resulting policy system, concepts and social atmosphere, made the process of rural labor transfer full of hardships. However, the Chinese farmers are highly intelligent and innovative who dared to experiment and pioneer. With a good and relaxed policy environment, this pioneering and innovation capacity can be fully unleashed. The deepening of reform and opening up has been instrumental in continuously removing institutional barriers in the labour market and eliminating the shortcomings of various institutional mechanisms that hinder development, promoting the optimal allocation of labour resources and thus leading to the leapfrog development of China's economy.

At the beginning of reform and opening up, Fengyang County in Anhui Province was the first in China to adopt the household contract responsibility system, which liberated farmers and ensured their basic needs to be met. This can be called the first venture of Chinese farmers. The booming tide of migrant workers entering the city for work is the second venture of Chinese farmers. In recent years, migrant workers returned to their hometowns and started their own businesses with the knowledge, technology, business ideas, industrial operation experience and capital accumulated in the city, which can be seen as their third venture. All these were rational choices taken by Chinese farmers after integrating and weighing rural resources and their own. Essentially, these choices were the result of the interaction of institutional changes, economic transformation and cultural and psychological changes of the entire society in China's industrialization and urbanization process. Chinese farmers adapted to these changes and liberated themselves from the traditional natural economy. Transforming from relying on institutions for survival to utilizing institutions for development, they changed their role of passive participants into active players engaged in the market economy and resource competition. In fact, starting a business has become a major trend in China's economic and social development, and shifting from a survival-oriented to development-oriented approach has become a realistic choice for migrant workers to achieve social mobility. Migrant workers returning to their hometowns to start their own businesses have become an important force in promoting rural vitalization and achieving moderate prosperity for farmers. They have started thousands of private small and micro-sized enterprises (SMEs) and new types of agricultural businesses back in their hometowns and a number of entity operators and small entrepreneurs have grown up. Moreover, their market-oriented and localized businesses have contributed to the flourishing development of rural areas, led to the restructuring of the rural economy and drove institutional innovation in rural areas, being a key breakthrough in resolving many structural urban-rural contradictions in China's structural transformation. The connotation of "Chinese migrant workers" started to change, with a group of migrant workers with strong entrepreneurship emerging and growing. In this process, the government as well as the society must take major responsibility in creating a social atmosphere that encourages gaining wealth through hard work and law-abidance, creating a market environment valuing fair competition, and innovating the institutional system for labor mobility, employment and business start-ups.

## 3. Rural Labor Mobility and Employment Drove Reform and Innovation in the Labor Market System

The root causes of employment issues concerning Chinese migrant workers are as follows: (1) Since China has a large population and little land, there is a serious shortage of agricultural resources, with China's per capita arable land is only 1/4 of the world's average level and a long-standing surplus of rural labor. (2) The employment of transferred rural labor is hindered by restrictions such as China's large proportion of traditional agriculture and vast rural areas, underdeveloped urban industries and commerce, and the backward dualistic structure that provides scarce job opportunities (which is often seen in developing countries). (3) Planned economy, the national strategy of prioritizing heavy industry and a dualistic system featuring urban-rural divide, as well as the resulting policy system, concepts and social atmosphere excluded farmers from urban industrialization and reinforced the dualistic structure. (4) In the reform of implementing household contract responsibility system, farmers were granted with the right to manage their land, thus the right to dispose their labor force freely. (5) As the "three types of foreign-funded enterprises" (contractual joint ventures, cooperative ventures and solely foreign-funded enterprises) and private enterprises in coastal areas were autonomous to employ workers, they provide job opportunities for farmers to participate in industrialization. In summary, farmers gained an interest to lift themselves out of poverty because of the following drivers: the allocation of labor and land resources, the dualistic system featuring urban-rural divide, and economic and social contradictions impairing employment.

The substantial progress of industrialization is not only manifested in changes of industrial structure, but also in changes of employment structure, in labor transfer from agriculture to non-agricultural industries. As a developing country, China's development relies on industrialization and rural labor transfer. At the initial stage of industrialization when labor was still in surplus, the transfer and employment of massive surplus agricultural labor determines the degree of industrialization. Through implementing reform and opening up, the problem of ensuring the basic needs of farmers to be met that had long existed in China's rural areas was resolved. The main problem at present is the low income of farmers, and the key to solving it lies in their employment. Looking back on the course of reform and opening up, rural labor transfer gradually broke down the structure of urban-rural divide, creating a system in which industrialization, urbanization, and agricultural labor transfer naturally interact and integrate with each other through market economy. This is significant both in theory and practice in terms of solving the employment problem of surplus rural labor highly concerned in the rural areas, opening up new employment channels for rural labor, and promoting the building of a complete and competitive labor market.

Since the reform and opening up, rural labor mobility and employment reformed and innovated China's employment system in three aspects: (1) Reforming China's employment structure. Farmers obtained rights of finding jobs and managing their lands independently through the reform of implementing the household contract responsibility system. Surplus agricultural labor transferred into township enterprises, with self-employment and private enterprises as major destinations. Nowadays in China, some 30 million migrant construction workers play an active role in urban and rural projects. Agricultural product markets and small commodity markets with farmers as major buyers and sellers can be found in large, medium and small cities across China. Nearly 20 million rural labor forces work in low-end service industries in cities such as cleaning, security and babysitting. Some migrant workers have even entered the international labor market. A labor market with a large amount of transferred rural labor has become a reality of China's urban economy, fundamentally changing the traditional employment system. (2) Accelerating the shift from planned economy to market economy. Before the reform and opening up, more than 800 million farmers were bound by scanty arable land because of people's communes and the *hukou* system, stagnating in self-sufficient or semi-self-sufficient economies. The labor transfer to non-agricultural sectors severely lagged behind changes in the industrial structure. After the reform and opening up, township enterprises took the lead in introducing market mechanism into employment, and rural labor became a resource advantage for township enterprises and coastal foreign-funded enterprises, contributing greatly to attracting foreign investment, earning foreign exchange through exports, and boosting China's economic development. (3) Balancing resource allocation in urban and rural labor markets. Rural labor mobility and employment enabled farmers to come out of closed rural economies where they only care about meeting their basic needs. After entering the market economy in urban industries, their demands for social management system such as education, medical care, social security, housing, household residential registration (*hukou*) and participation in public affairs significantly pushed forward the unequal dualistic urban-rural system to evolve towards an integrated national treatment system. Through urban employment, they improved their competence, brought industrial civilization to rural areas and promoted agricultural modernization.

However, it must be noted that institutional barriers hindering rural labor transfer have not yet disappeared, and the policy system integrating farmers into cities is not yet complete. "Three price scissors, inequality of public resource allocation and public services, and one huge gap" brought by the dualistic system featuring urban-rural divide and related institutions still exist (Du, 2018)[1]. Therefore, it must be a complex and gradual process to establish a smooth and low-cost institutional

---

[1] "Three price scissors" refer to: First, price scissors between industrial and agricultural products. Second, price scissors between rural and urban land. Rural land cannot enter the primary market. Urban development zones and real estate land must be requisitioned by the government before entering the primary market, yet there is a huge gap between the expropriation price and the price at which the land is sold to developers (which is very high). This harms farmers' interests and makes farmers who lost their lands a new marginal group in society. Third, price scissors in wages between farmers and urban workers. "Inequality of public resource allocation and public service" means the distribution of resources such as education and health care is tilted towards cities. Rural laborers cannot enjoy the same treatment as urban employees in terms of employment, public services, and social security. "One huge gap" refers to the *hukou* system, or two different household registration systems in urban and rural areas. This makes it difficult for rural laborers to transform into urban residents.

mechanism and policy system on mobility and employment of migrant workers and transforming rural population into urban citizens.

## II. Evolution of Institutions and Policies on Rural Labor Mobility and Employment Since the Reform and Opening Up

### 1. Four Stages of Institutions and Policies on Rural Labor Mobility and Employment

Documents and reports by the Rural Economy Division under the Development Research Center of the State Council (DRC) and the Ministry of Human Resources and Social Security constitute the representative viewpoints on the main process that the state adjusted policies on rural labor mobility and employment since the reform and opening up and on policy orientation. Synthesizing their opinions, this article believes that China's institutions and policies for rural labor transfer and employment since 1978 can be divided into four stages (Jin and Shi, 2016).

**Stage 1:Passive response from 1978 to 1991.** After the Third Plenary Session of the 11th CPC Central Committee, the household contract responsibility system replaced the former "big pot" distribution system (under which everyone got the same "portion" irrespective of his work or contribution – translator's note). Faced with strong labor demand from township enterprises and coastal areas, China began to loosen its policy on rural population migrating to urban areas. In late 1980s, as the reform of economic system was deepened, major destinations of rural labor transfer shifted from township enterprises nearby to other provinces. During this period, the government mainly adopted measures to control farmers' mobility such as examination and approval, granting permits, collecting fees, fines, imposing restrictions on types of work, dismissal, and detention and  repatriation.

Major policies issued during this period are as follows: In January 1984, Central Document No. 1 of 1984 (*Circular of the CPC Central Committee on Rural Work During 1984*) initiated the reform of household residential registration in small towns, allowing migrant workers and other rural population who engaged in urban businesses and service industries to "take care of their own rations" and settle in those towns. In October 1984, the *Notice of the State Council on Farmers Settling Down in Cities* stipulated that public security organs grant permanent residence in towns to those who have the ability to run their own businesses, permanent address or a long-term job in township enterprises and count them as non-agricultural population. These policies provided opportunities for surplus rural labor to transfer into nearby towns. In July 1985, the Ministry of Public Security promulgated *Interim*

*Provisions on the Management of Temporary Resident Population in Cities*, internally setting the rate of "agricultural to non-agricultural population transfer" at 0.02% per year. In September 1985, the resident identity card system came into force. In October 1989, under domestic context, the household registration system was again tightened and the State Council issued the *Notice on Strictly Controlling Excessive Transfer of Agricultural Population to Non-Agricultural Industries*. In July 1990, the General Office of the State Council forwarded a *Report on Proposals Regarding Division of Labor in Managing "Agricultural to Non-Agricultural Population Transfer"*, originally published by the State Development Planning Commission along with other institutions. This report stipulated that policies on agriculture to non-agricultural population transfer be issued by the central government, and the transfer quota was greatly reduced.

The number of migrant workers was not large in this stage. Corresponding national policies mainly focused on managing their registered household and identity, which were loosened moderately at the start but tightened afterwards at the stage of passive response.

**Stage 2:Restricting while standardizing from 1992 to 2002.** A new wave of migrant workers surged after Deng Xiaoping's Southern Tour Speech in 1992. The central government affirmed the goal of developing market economy and supporting private economy, which facilitated free and orderly flow of surplus agricultural labor both between urban and rural areas and between regions. In the mid and late 1990s, however, with the reform of state-owned enterprises was intensified, urban employment was facing a severe situation aggravated by three factors: migrant workers seeking jobs in the city, the employment of new urban labor and the re-employment of laid-off workers as well as the unemployed, which slowed down the rural labor transfer. By the end of 1990s, the government began to pay more attention to migrant workers, a special group in China's structural transformation.

Major policy changes in this period are as follows: (1) The *hukou* system started to be loosened and gradually standardized. In June 1997, the State Council approved and circulated the *Pilot Reform Plan of the Ministry of Public Security for the Household Residential Registration System in Small Cities and Towns* and *Proposals on Improving the Household Residential Registration in Rural Areas*. In July 1998, the State Council approved and circulated the *Opinions of the Ministry of Public Security on Solving the Existing Conspicuous Problems in the Work of Residence Management*. In June 2000, the CPC Central Committee and the State Council issued *Several Opinions on Promoting Healthy Development of Small Cities and Towns*. In March 2001, the State Council approved and circulated *Proposals of the Ministry of Public Security on Reforming Household Residential Registration*

*System in Small Cities and Towns.* The core of these policies was to implement "blue stamp *hukou*" and change the standard of dividing agricultural and non-agricultural households from commodity grains to residence and occupation. A registration system was established based on three types of *hukou* (permanent residence, temporary residence and lodging residence), and documents gradually became the base for its management. By this point, the majority of small cities and towns have opened household registration to farmers. (2) Rural labor transfer and employment were restricted. In November 1994, the Ministry of Labor issued *Interim Provisions on Managing Cross-Provincial Mobility and Employment of Rural Labor* (repealed), requiring migrant workers to gain migrant employment permits before seeking jobs in other provinces. In October 1998, the General Office of the State Council issued *Proposals on Locally Settling Rural Labor Forces in Disaster-hit Areas and Organizing Orderly Movement of Migrant Workers*, stipulating that "people who blindly flow into cities should be persuaded to return to their hometowns", and that "behaviors such as illegal recruitment of rural labor, infringement of workers' legitimate rights and interests, and other acts that disrupt the labor market shall be investigated and severely punished." In January 2000, the Ministry of Labor and Social Security issued the *Notice on Publishing Proposals on Promoting Mobility and Employment of Surplus Rural Labor* (repealed). In March 2002, the General Office of the State Council issued the *Circular onImplementing Proposals of the CPC Central Committee and the State Council on Policy Issues Related to Doing Agricultural and Rural Work Well in 2002*, stating that it would work with the State Development Planning Commission, Ministry of Public Security, Ministry of Education, Ministry of Finance, Ministry of Labor and Social Security, Ministry of Health and other departments on "removing unreasonable restrictions and abolishing improper fees for migrant workers" and on "correcting the practice of returning migrant workers in an oversimplified and crude manner." (3) Explorations began on establishing management and service mechanism to support the "local enrollment" of migrant workers' children. In March 1998, the Ministry of Education and the Ministry of Public Security jointly released *Interim Regulations on Schooling for Migrant Children*. In May 2001, the State Council issued *The Decision on Reform and Development of Basic Education*, which paid attention to migrant workers' welfare and equal access to public services. In December 1998, the State Council issued *The Decision on Establishing the Basic Medical Insurance System for Urban Employees*. In December 2001, the Ministry of Labor and Social Security issued the *Notice on Improving Basic Pension Insurance for Urban Employees*, granting migrant workers access to social insurance for the first time.

**Stage 3: Proactively offering guidance from 2003 to 2005.** Since the 16th

CPC National Congress, in order to promote the integrated development of urban and rural areas and to increase farmers' income, the government decided to adopt an proactive approach to guide the employment of migrant workers through both quick-acting short-term measures and stable long-term policies. In December 2003, *Opinions of the Central Committee of the CPC and the State Council on Several Policies for Promoting the Increase of Farmers' Income* was released. This was considered as a programmatic document for solving employment issues of migrant workers, as 18 years passed since the central government addressed agricultural and rural issues in a No. 1 Central Document. It embodied the strategic intention of the CPC Central Committee and the State Council to set "three rural issues" (agriculture, rural areas and farmers) a top priority of the Party' work. The main contents of the policy include: to continue agricultural restructuring, broaden channels for farmers to increase their income, improve job environments for migrant workers, strengthen the construction of rural infrastructure, deepen rural reforms, provide institutional support for farmers to increase income and reduce their burden, and to do a good job in poverty alleviation and development.

At this stage, the ministries worked together to introduce a series of practical and feasible measures in supporting employment and training of migrant workers. (1) Measures on promoting migrant workers' employment. In January 2003, the General Office of the State Council issued the *Circular on Effectively Accomplishing the Work in the Administration and Service for Farmers Employed in Cities*, stipulating that support and guidance for migrant workers employed in citites should be prioritized on the agenda, and the policy guidance should be enhanced in plans of national economic and social development. According to the Circular, principles of fair treatment, proper guidance, improving administration and offering quality should be upheld, and the work in the administration and service for farmers employed in cities should be accomplished in an all-round manner. More targeted policy documents were issued subsequently to further standardize and institutionalize the employment of migrant workers. In April 2005, *the Circular of the State Council on Printing and Issuing the Key Points in the Work in 2005* was released, requesting the State Council Research Office to take the lead in "conducting in-depth research on issues concerning migrant workers employed in cities such as employment environment, vocational skills training, and guidance on proper and orderly flow of rural labor, and to formulate and improve policies involving migrant workers." In 2005, in order to further implement plans and deployments of the State Council, the Ministry of Labor and Social Security issued the *Notice on Improving Employment Services for Migrant Workers Through Spring Breeze Action* which called labor and social security departments in destination cities of migrant workers to coordinate with other departments in improving the employment environment of migrant workers as well as ensuring their access to timely and effective employment services. (2) Measures on providing vocational skills training to migrant workers. In September 2003, the General Office of the State Council issued the *National Training Program for Migrant Farmers: 2003-2010* which was jointly formulated by the Ministry of Agriculture, Ministry of Labor and Social Security, Ministry of Education, Ministry of Science and Technology, Ministry of Construction, and the Ministry of Finance, specifying goals and targets on the training of transferred rural labor. Since 2004, the Sunshine Project[1] for Transferred Rural Labor was further implemented by the Ministry of Agriculture, Ministry of Finance, Ministry of Labor and Social Security, Ministry of Education, Ministry of Science and Technology and Ministry of Construction. In April 2005, the Ministry of Construction issued the *Notice on Providing Training to Help Migrant Workers Acquire Knowledge of Law in the Field of Construction*. In August 2005, the National Security Bureau issued *Opinions on Strengthening Coal Mine Safety Training*. Policies on rural labor transfer and employment have transformed fundamentally at this stage, shifting from restriction to encouragement, from passive responses to proactively offering guidance, and from strict administration to support through service. reform and opening up was the underlying driving force for the policy change.

**Stage 4: Comprehensive promotion from 2006 to present.** Since the issue of migrant workers' mobility and employment has become a significant social problem that China must face in the process of industrialization and urbanization, as well as a comprehensive and complex issue involving a wide range of fields, the State Council Research Office organized relevant ministries, units, experts and scholars in 2005 to conduct thorough investigations and research on issues concerning migrant workers and completed the *Research Report on Migrant Workers in China*. The Report provides comprehensive, systematic and in-depth insights into existing problems on rural labor transfer and employment, including low income and poor working environment, a general lack of social security, little or no access to public services provided by city governments, and difficulties in safeguarding their rights and improving their status. The underlying causes of the above problems are: firstly, the dualistic structure featuring urban-rural divide is the root cause of migrant worker issues; secondly, the relevant laws are not sound and the legal system is not perfect, which impose institutional constraints on solving these problems; thirdly, the transformation of government administration and functions is not fulfilled, which is

---

[1] A "Sunshine Project" is a demonstration project on pre-employment vocational skills training for rural laborers transferred to non-agricultural sectors which  is supported by the government's public finance and mainly carried out in grain producing areas, labor export areas, poverty-stricken areas and old revolutionary base areas.

the mechanism obstacle; fourthly, migrant workers lack knowledge and organization, which is the practical condition that gave rise to the above problems. The Report provided a general guideline on solving migrant workers' problems (SCRO, 2006, Jin and Shi, 2016).

In January 2006, the State Council Document No.5 (*Several Opinions of the State Council on Settling Issues on Rural Migrant Workers*) was issued with milestone significance, marking a new phase of China's policies on migrant workers. It fully elaborated the importance of solving migrant worker issues, providing systematic, comprehensive and feasible guidance on matters relating to migrant workers, such as wages, labor management, employment services and training, social security, public services, protection of rights and interests, transfer and employment and leadership mechanism. Led by the State Council, a joint conference system on issues concerning migrant workers was established, composing of 31 departments and units including the General Office of the State Council and the National Development and Reform Commission. Main responsibilities, member composition, rules of procedure and the labor division plan to implement Document No.5 were also formulated. On this basis, state ministries further issued a series of supporting documents jointly, to improve the social and economic environment for migrant workers employed in cities from various aspects, and to protect their legitimate rights and interests. Since the joint conference system was set up, the Ministry of Human Resources and Social Security would issue the key points of the conference in the form of ministry documents every year, specifying overall requirements and tasks of the year for each member unit. Document No.5 represented the adoption of new policies for migrant workers. Reform of rural taxes and fees was carried out, which includes abolishing agricultural taxes and providing subsidies. In conclusion, migrant workers saw increasing benefits in this period.

Since 2008, the State has tackled the outstanding problems faced by migrant workers in a targeted and focused manner, starting with three areas: employment services and vocational skills training for migrant workers, protection of the rights and interests of migrant workers, and social insurance policies for migrant workers. On December 20, 2008, the General Office of the State Council issued the *Circular on Performing Well the Current Tasks for Migrant Workers*. On January 21, 2010, the General Office of the State Council released *Guiding Opinions on Further Fulfilling the Work on Training of Migrant Workers*, which is the first document targeted at providing training for migrant workers by the State Council, thus of far-reaching significance. On January 31, 2010, the No. 1 Central Document for 2010 issued by the State Council (*Several Opinions of the Central Committee of the CPC and the State Council on Intensifying Efforts to Comprehensively*

*Arrange Urban and Rural Development and Further Solidifying the Foundations for Agricultural and Rural Development*) used the term "new generation of migrant workers" for the first time. It called for the government to take targeted measures to solve problems "the new generation of migrant workers face" and to help them gain citizenship.

The No. 1 Central Document issued by the central government has addressed the employment of migrant workers every year since 2004, which has greatly promoted the regularization and institutionalization of their employment. In 2006 and 2007, the number of migrant workers moving to cities and towns for employment continued to rise. The state introduced a number of policy documents clearly proposing to accelerate the development of vocational education in rural areas, strengthen the construction of agricultural vocational schools and agriculture-related majors, cultivate new types of farmers who are "educated, skilled and capable of running a business." The goal is to establish a sound long-term mechanism for training talents with practical mind and scientific and technological knowledge in rural areas.

On December 3, 2013, the Political Bureau of the CPC Central Committee held a meeting, proposing to take the path of new-type urbanization with an implementation plan issued and to actively and steadily advance the reform of land management syste. In March 2014, Xinhua News Agency released the *National New-type Urbanization Plan (2014-2020)* issued by the CPC Central Committee and the State Council, which provides macro, strategic and fundamental guidelines for the healthy development of urbanization in China. The Plan has a special column for migrant workers' vocational training and skill improvement, setting up goals as follows: (1) providing employment skill training migrant workers and training 10 million workers every year, so that every migrant worker can attend at least one government-subsidized training program by 2020, and the phenomenon of starting a job without necessary skills will be basically eliminated; (2) carrying out skill improvement training for in-service migrant workers, and training 10 million workers by 2020, so that most in-service migrant workers can develop from general workers to new-type skilled workers; (3) offering training programs for high-skilled workers and entrepreneurship training programs with 1 million people trained every year, with the majority of trainees being senior workers, technicians and senior technicians; (4) providing training programs for public good in communities; (5) providing preparatory vocational training for junior and senior high school graduates in rural areas who fail to continue their studies[1].

---

[1] Jin, W. and X. Shi. Research on Policies Concerning China's Migrant Workers [M]. Beijing: Social Science Literature Press, 2016.

In 2014, in order to implement principles and decisions made on the Central Economic Work Conference and Central Urbanization Work Conference and to improve rural laborers' abilities to find a job and start a business, in accordance with the *National New-type Urbanization Plan (2014-2020)* and the State Council's *Opinions on Strengthening Vocational Training to Promote Employment,* the Ministry of Human Resources and Social Security issued the *Vocational Skill Training Program for Migrant Workers – Implementation Plan for "Spring Tide Action".* Then the "Spring Tide Action", a training program to help improve vocational skills of migrant workers was carried out across China. In October 2014, the General Office of the State Council issued *Opinions on Bringing Further Success to the Work of Providing Services to Migrant Workers,* and in June 2015 issued *Opinions on Supporting Migrant Workers and Others in Returning Home and Starting Businesses.* In August 2016, the *Notice on Implementing a Five-year Plan for Training Migrant Workers and Others to Start Businesses Back in Hometowns (2016-2020)* was jointly issued by the Ministry of Human Resources and Social Security, Ministry of Agriculture, the State Council Leading Group Office of Poverty Alleviation and Development, Central Committee of the Communist Youth League and All-China Women's Federation. In July 2017, the General Office of the National Development and Reform Commission issued the *Notice on Fulfilling the Application for the Third Batch of Pilot Areas Supporting Migrant Workers and Others in Returning Home and Start Businesses in the Context of New-type Urbanization.* In January 2018, the CPC Central Committee and the State Council issued the No. 1 Central Document, i.e., *Opinions on Implementing the Rural Vitalization Strategy,* stating that "Rural vitalization is a major strategical deployment made by the 19th CPC National Congress. It serves as a major historical task in building a moderately prosperous society in all respects and in building a modern socialist country. It is also the key in solving 'three rural issues (agriculture, rural areas, farmers)' in the new era." The document also put forward specific and feasible opinions on implementing the rural vitalization strategy. After 2021, the characteristics of poverty and major tasks of poverty alleviation in China will undergo significant changes. Alleviation policies will shift from providing welfare to promoting development. Since the evolution of poverty is dynamic and there are multiple causes of poverty, it has become harder to tackle poverty and new demands rise for poverty governance with alleviating relative poverty being the main task. Relative poverty is not a simple matter of income, but a phenomenon of poverty repeatedly being produced in the complex economic and social transformation. It is difficult to find ways to alleviate relative poverty from former programs designed for absolute poverty, and only through the restructuring of economic and social development that relative poverty can be alleviated. Therefore, when the fight against poverty turns to scenarios where the strategic design of poverty alleviation is applied after 2021, previous policies targeting individuals at the micro-level will largely fail, and macro-level adjustments of economic and social systems will become more effective. However, poverty alleviation through employment will still be the key to solving relative poverty.

## 2. Main Characteristics of Systems and Policies on Migrant Workers' Employment

### 2.1 Promoting two-way flow of integration into cities and returning home to start businesses

After the reform and opening up, China gradually abolished discriminatory regulations and restrictions against migrant workers, including administrative approval and fees on enterprises hiring migrant workers. The organization and training of migrant workers in transfer and employment were also improved. These measures created a favorable policy environment for migrant workers either to integrate into cities or return home to start businesses and thus formed a virtuous cycle of two-way mobility.

### 2.2 Paying more attention to improving institutions such as equalizing public services

The state pays more and more attention to ensuring equal basic public services for migrant workers, such as education for their children, vocational training, public health and social security. The "two mainly" policy (compulsory education for children of migrant workers is mainly taken care of by the government of destination cities and these children mainly enter public schools) of compulsory education for children of migrant workers has been established, marking the policy philosophy has shifted from "restriction" to being "human-centered". The coverage of social security is gradually expanding as well. A number of policies stipulate that all employers must apply work injury insurance for migrant workers in time and solve their in-post medical security expenses. Both a rural cooperative medical insurance system and an urban resident medical insurance system have been formed. A pension insurance system for urban and rural residents has also been initially established, enabling a part of migrant workers with low income or flexible employment to participate in pension insurance for urban and rural residents. Considering migrant workers are highly mobile, the pension insurance is allowed to transfer across provinces or between urban and rural areas, so that migrant workers' rights and interests in social security can be protected during flexible employment. For regions where local conditions permit, it is also encouraged to include migrant workers with stable jobs into the basic pension insurance system for urban employees.

*2.3 Completing the building of an efficient service mechanism for basic public employment*

A coordination mechanism on migrant worker issues has been initially established. Social management on migrant workers is shifting towards safeguarding rights and providing services. In July 2018, the Ministry of Labor and Social Security issued *Guiding Opinions on Further Promoting Services for Basic Public Employment Services in All Respects (Draft for Comments)*. Its main objectives are: to complete the building of a service system for basic public employment that integrates urban and rural areas, to establish a diversified service supply model, to improve efficiency as well as convenience of service operation mechanism, and promote the organization and application of all-round basic public employment services. Since the 18th CPC National Congress, the central government has attached great importance to solving structural contradictions in the transfer and employment of migrant workers. A new page in the history of rural labor transfer opens up as China shifts its focus onto integrating urban and rural development, onto migrant workers, onto equalizing public services and onto granting citizenship to transferred rural labor.

## 3. Issues That Still Require Attention in Improving Institutions and Policies on Migrant Workers' Employment[1]

Since the reform and opening up, rural labor mobility and employment in China has become a phenomenon of great importance in industrialization and urbanization. It brought immense impact to the original dualistic urban-rural economic structure, involving various institutions and interest relationships. The complex and deep-seated conflicts and problems regarding migrant workers are essentially contradictions related to institutions, employment policies, and structural transformation of the dualistic structure.

*3.1 Migrant workers have limited access to public services*

The discriminatory policies attached to the household registration system have been largely eliminated, but the household registration threshold remains quite high. As China has long practiced a household administration system with a separation of urban and rural areas, a household registration culture has been formed that is accepted by both urban governments and migrant workers. Such a system that collectively exclude a certain group of people is still a major obstacle blocking migrant workers from gaining citizenship. It is difficult to adjust the coverage of government public services and fiscal expenditure from the population with

[1] Jin, W. and X. Shi. Research on Policies Concerning China's Migrant Workers [M]. Beijing: Social Science Literature Press, 2016; Ji, S. Evaluation of the Social Effects of China's Migrant Workers Employment Policy Since Reform and Opening Up [J]. Economics and Management Research, 2010.

registered households to permanent residents including migrant workers. Migrant workers are included in city employment but excluded from its social management and services. This lack of access to rights undermines the protection of their rights and interests while increasing the governments cost of social management.

*3.2 Discriminations still exist against children of migrant workers to receive education in cities*

China's compulsory education policy for children of migrant workers can be roughly divided into three stages: In the first stage (1992-1997), this issue didn't receive enough attention from the government. Public primary and secondary schools in the city rejected these children through high tuition fees, causing social exclusion both physically and psychologically. Migrant workers set up simple schools funded by their own wages, which, however, were not acknowledged by the government. The dropout rate among children of migrant workers was high. In the second stage (1998-2002), the former State Education Commission and the Ministry of Public Security formulated *Interim Regulations on Schooling for Migrant Children* in 1998. This document affirmed the role of schools for migrant children, but contributed little to changing their marginalized status. Discriminatory fees in urban public primary and secondary schools were not reduced. Most private schools for migrant children failed to obtain a legal status, nor were they included in the urban compulsory education system. In the third stage (since 2003 to present), the State Council issued the *Proposals for Further Accomplishing the Work on Compulsory Education for Children of Farmers Employed in Cities* in 2003, which provided a policy framework of compulsory education for children of migrant workers and stipulated that public schools in destination cities should be responsible for addressing the schooling issues of enroll migrant children. However, currently children of migrant workers are still prevented from attending *Gaokao* (the college entrance examination) in first-tier cities.

*3.3 Difficulties in implementing policies on vocational training for migrant workers*

Institutional obstacles remain an important factor affecting the social effects of training policies. Specific and feasible plans were indeed stipulated by the state, but as we can see in the process of implementation, these plans including investment on training for migrant workers, supply of services and collocation of rights turned out to be platforms for arm-wrestling between central and local governments, between local governments of different regions and between government and enterprises. This ineffectiveness of some training policies can be attributed to the fiscal and administrative responsibilities were not specified at the policy-making level.

# III. Looking Ahead on the Grand Goal of Urbanization and Rural Vitalization

The reason why this article analyzes theories, policies and practices on rural labor mobility and employment since the reform and opening up is to provide references for the future. Looking ahead, we will continue to carry out institutional innovations while advancing reform and opening up, realize agricultural modernization, complete industrialization and urbanization, and eventually build China into a modern country. The most important task in this process would be institutional innovation. China currently is in great need of original ideas and scientific inventions that can lead the world and the future of mankind. From a long-term perspective, rural labor is the main source of China's labor market, and improving their quality and competence will bring us the most important source of original scientific ideas. Therefore, it would be the government's obligatory duty to provide high-quality public employment services for rural labor mobility and employment. Specific goals are as follows:

## 1. Looking ahead – to establish an employment system integrating urban and rural areas

Looking ahead, we should explore a path of rural labor mobility and employment with Chinese characteristics in the course of reform and opening up, eradicate the dualistic urban-rural structure and eventually achieve modernization. Two-layer connotations are embodied in resolving the dualistic structure problem: the first layer is to integrate the economic structures of urban and rural areas into one, and the second layer is to alter the original social management system affecting the dualistic economic structure, along with its consequent dualistic social structure featuring unequal rights between urban and rural residents. In order to realize urban-rural integration, the old dualistic economic system featuring urban-rural divide must be removed, with a new system of economic structure integrating urban and rural areas gradually established.

## 2. Looking ahead – to innovate the system of migrant workers gaining citizenship

How can a country with a population of over one billion realize modernization? What kind of urban-rural layout will be formed in the process of industrialization and urbanization? We cannot find answers to these questions or experience for reference in industrialized countries and we must explore on our own. It would be impossible to seek development or build a moderately prosperous society while sidestepping problems in rural labor employment and transfer. In its nature, China's development is the development of the people, and it depends on creative labor on the basis of employment. The similar philosophy can be applied to China's modernization: it is essentially modernization of the majority, which is in China's case, the rural population and rural economy.

It is based on such conditions that General Secretary Xi Jinping made his important judgment on the characteristics and pattern of China's economic and social developments at the current stage: "The essence of modernization is the modernization of people. Long-term efforts are needed to truly turn farmers into citizens and to continuously improve their competence. This cannot be done in an instant. A part of rural labor forces flowing between urban and rural areas is and will be a phenomenon in China for a long time." [1] Similarly, Xi Jinping clearly stated in his report at the 19th CPC National Congress that China will pursue a rural vitalization strategy while continuing to advance industrialization and urbanization. The Fifth Plenary Session of the 19th CPC Central Committee adopted *Proposals for Formulating the 14th Five-year Plan (2021-2025) for National Economic and Social Development and the Long-Range Objectives Through the Year 2035*, which provides guiding principles, goals, tasks and major measures of China's economic and social developments in the 14th Five-year Plan period. It depitcs a magnificent blueprint for China's development in the next five years as a programmatic document for economic and social work. After 2021, the characteristics of poverty and major tasks of poverty alleviation in China will undergo significant changes. Alleviation policies will shift from providing welfare to promoting development and alleviating relative poverty will become the main task. Therefore, when the fight against poverty turns to scenarios where the strategic design of poverty alleviation is applied after 2021, previous policies targeting individuals at the micro-level will largely fail, and macro-level adjustments of economic and social systems will become more effective. However, poverty alleviation through employment will still be the key to resolving relative poverty.

## 3. Looking ahead – to deepen reform in key areas of agricultural modernization

### 3.1 Improving the rural land system

The rural land system plays a pivotal role in the transfer and employment of rural labor. Practices of reform and opening up show that the contracted land of farm households is not only a support for their proactive exploration of the depth

---

[1] Xi Jinping's Speech at the Central Urbanization Work Conference on December 12, 2013. Selected Documents Since the 18th National Congress of the Communist Party of China (Part 1) [M]. Beijing: Central Literature Publishing House, 2014: 594-595.

and breadth of agriculture, but also an important source of original accumulation gained through non-agricultural employment opportunities created by themselves on the basis of their agricultural operation. This also serves as a kind of social security which offsets risks in employment transfer and urban-rural migration. Having farmers hold the right to transfer land voluntarily, rather than having external forces hold such right and force farmers to transfer, is more conducive to reducing the costs and risks of structural transformation.

### 3.2 Protecting rural laborer's employment rights and interests according to law

The development of China's labor market is based on the employment transfer of surplus rural labor. Now the employment in urban and developed areas tends to be saturated, and with the implementation of economic regulation and other measures by the state, the flow has slowed down. Therefore, we should endeavor to establish a good market order that safeguards farmers' legitimate rights and interests in employment. The government should provide quality public employment services and form a network of information, intermediaries and training services, to reduce rather than increase the cost of rural labor mobile employment. The legal system of the market should also be strengthened to safeguard the legitimate rights and interests of rural labor forces in mobile employment, and to reflect social justice.

### 3.3 Innovating the policy system supporting migrant workers in returning home and starting businesses

In recent years, the flexible employment of migrant workers witnessed new changes. Returning home and starting businesses have become a new trend, resulting in a chain reaction involving rural industries, employment, wage increase and poverty alleviation. Utilizing this trend has become a key factor in tackling rural poverty at this stage. It is necessary to grasp the new situation and understand new requirements, and the government should improve the policy system that supports migrant workers in returning home and starting businesses by (1) providing targeted and detailed supporting policies on financing, fees & taxes and land use; (2) creating physical support platforms such as entrepreneurial parks, incubation bases, workshops and factories; (3) providing non-physical support platforms such as skill training and talent cultivation; (4) increasing investment in infrastructure such as transportation and Internet facilities. "One-stop" business services for startups should be pushed forward to provide good conditions for migrant workers to up businesses in their hometowns.

### 3.4 Unblocking channels for mobile rural labor to obtain citizenship

Unimpeded and low-cost institutional mechanism and policy system for the mobility and employment of rural labour and for the agricultural population to gain citizenship should be established the *hukou* system should also be further reformed, so that agricultural population who have the will and qualifications to settle in cities can obtain citizenship and transform into citizens successfully. A system of residence permits should be widely implemented in cities and towns so that migrant workers and their families can enjoy the same rights and obligations as local citizens. Efforts should be made to improve living conditions in rural areas, and the equalization of public infrastructure, basic public services and basic social security systems between urban and rural areas should be accelerated. The transfer and employment of rural labor across regions will undoubtedly run through the entire process of building a moderately prosperous society in all respects, basically achieving modernization and turning China into a modern socialist country. The situation of migrant workers and their families will also become an important indicator of China's economic and social development and overall social progress. In the course of reform and opening up, as urbanization and rural vitalization is advanced in a coordinated manner, the special title of "migrant workers" will increasingly reflect its unique historical significance and contemporary value in the integration of urban and rural development.

## References

[1] Du, R. Essay Collection on China's Rural Reform and Development [M]. Beijing: China Yanshi Press, 2018.

[2] Zhao, S. Farmers' Revolution [M]. Beijing: The Commercial Press, 2016.

[3] Johnson, D.G., Y. Lin. & Y. Zhao. Agriculture, Rural and Farmer Issues in Economic Development [M]. Beijing: The Commercial Press, 2017.

[4] Jin, W. & Shi, X. Research on Policies Concerning China's Migrant Workers [M]. Beijing: Social Sciences Academic Press, 2016.

[5] Cui, C. Transfer and Employment of Chinese Farmers and Modernization [M]. Taiyuan: Shanxi Economic Publishing House, 2017.

[6] Lewis, A. Dual Economy [M]. Beijing: Beijing College of Economics Press, 1989.

[7] Schultz, T.W. Human Capital Investment [M]. Beijing: Beijing College of Economics Press, 1990.

[8] Pan, Z. "Process Analysis, Theoretical Judgment and Policy Thinking of the State in Adjusting Policies on Migrant Workers" [J]. Theory and Reform, 2008(5) : 59-61.

[9] State Council Research Office (SCRO). Research Report on Migrant Workers in China [M]. Beijing: China Yanshi Press, 2006.

[10] Research Group on Migrant Wokers of the State Council. Research on the Development of Chinese Migrant Workers [M].Beijing: China Labor and Social Security Press, 2013.

[11] Ji, S. Early Warning on Unemployment in China – Theoretical Perspective and Research Model [M]. Beijing: Capital University of Economics and Business Press, 2008.

# Labor Relations

- A Review of China's Labor Relations Research over the Past 70 Years and an Outlook for Its Development

# A Review of China's Labor Relations Research over the Past 70 Years and an Outlook for Its Development[*]

*Liu Xiangbing, Wen Xiaoyi, Pan Taiping, Dou Xuewei[**]*

**Abstract:** Research in labor relations in China is rooted in the country's practices in handling labor relations and national and social conditions. After seven decades of development at five stages, a theoretical system of labor relations with Chinese characteristics has been established, which is based on the Western labor relations system, but abandons the idea of treating labor relations as purely economic relations and only using property rights rules to solve labor disputes. According to Chinese theoretical system, labor relations include political relations, and the two parties of labor relations have the same fundamental interests. Given this, conflicts in labor relations are problems among the people, as they reflect the differences of the disputing parties in certain specific interests in the context of the alignment of fundamental interests. On this basis, the pillars of the state-led governance system of China's labor relations have been well established. At present, the structure of Chinese labor force is undergoing profound changes, and the economy is in a transition from a phase of rapid growth to a stage of high-quality development. Meanwhile, the rapid development of the Internet platform economy has led to the emergence of various new employment forms and opportunities. These changes will inevitably promote the evolvement of labor relations and bring new topics to labor relations research.

**Keywords:** labor relations; trade unions; labor issues; Chinese characteristics

[*] This paper was published in *Journal of China University of Labor Relations*, Issue. 1, 2020.

[**] Liu Xiangbing, PhD in management, Secretary of Party Committee, fellow researcher of China University of Labor Relations, specializes in higher education management, university strategic management, and ideological and political education. Wen Xiaoyi, PhD in economics, Professor and Dean of the School of Labor Relations and Human Resources, China University of Industrial Relations, specializes in labor relations. Pan Taiping, PhD in economics, Professor and Associate Dean of the School of Labor Union, China University of Industrial Relations, specializes in labor relations. Dou Xuewei, PhD in law, lecturer of the School of Labor Relations and Human Resources, China University of Industrial Relations, specializes in labor sociology and labor relations.

General Secretary Xi Jinping has pointed out that building harmonious labor relations with Chinese characteristics is a part of the efforts to uphold the socialist path, put the theory of socialism into practice and improve the socialist system with Chinese characteristics, and therefore has great and far-reaching economic, political and social significance. There is a proposition of "historical cycle" in the history of Western industrial development and labor relations research. This means, under the market economy, the development of industrialization resulted in huge industrial capital and a large number of workers, which in turn caused serious outbreaks of labor conflicts. With the continuous expansion of workforce, large-scale and radical workers' movements constantly broke out, opposition parties appeared, and finally the social system and structure were reorganized. It took the western countries over 100 years to achieve industrialization, while China has instituted a full-fledged industrial system in just 40 years after the establishment of its socialist market economy. China has both the world's largest manufacturing industry and the biggest number of workers. Naturally, there are also potential great risks of labor conflicts. However, the country has largely maintained stable and harmonious labor relations, minimizing the impact of labor conflicts emerging in the process of industrialization on social stability and greatly supporting the healthy development of China's economy and society. It has broken the so-called "historical cycle" in managing labor relations and coordinated industrialization and national governance in a sound way, and its experience has contributed "Chinese wisdom and solutions" to the world. The development of the research on labor relations in China is built on the evolvement of Chinese labor relations and the valuable experience and lessons gained in this process.

## I. The Start of Labor Relations Research: Solving Labor Problems

Keith Whitefield, a famous British scholar in labor relations, pointed out that "in social sciences, people accept something as an independent discipline because it must prove that it is better than other approaches in explaining or solving a certain kind of problem." (Keith and George, 2005) As a branch of social sciences, research in labor relations is committed to studying and solving labor problems after the establishment of labor relations. The labor market serves as a mechanism connecting labor demand and supply, where employers and employees can trade what they can provide and finally reach a labor contract with wage at the core. However, the market mechanism presents a strong externality in the process of performing contracts. Labor capacity, as a special commodity of laborers, is highly uncertain as labor time, labor intensity and laborer's willingness are all full of uncertainty, which may cause problems between employers and employees in the workplace. The problems will lead to negative consequences, such as loafing on the job, high turnover rate, low production efficiency, and serious labor conflicts. If they are not addressed properly, the healthy operation of the labor market or even social stability will be adversely affected. In this sense, labor problems and their solutions have become the "core issues" of labor relations.

To address labor problems, researchers from different disciplines provide their insights from different perspectives, and so far three research paradigms have been established. The first paradigm stresses monophyletic study. It believes that an enterprise is an organization where every member shares the same goals and values. Labor problems in such organizations are a kind of operation frictions, which are not caused by conflicts of interests, but by poor management or communication. Therefore, the solution requires the optimization of communication mechanisms which feature in sharing goals among employees, flexible management policies and participation of employees. The second paradigm focuses on pluralistic study. Under this paradigm, employers and employees are different interest groups with different values and positions, and labor problems originate from conflicts between the two groups. To solve the problems, the two sides need to seek a compromise. By collective bargaining, they can reach consensuses and build a regulation system recognized by both sides. The third paradigm emphasizes studies on class relations. It believes that the employer-employee relation is a class relation in essence, and labor problems result from irreconcilable structural labor conflicts. Only by reforming the social system can the problems be solved. Meanwhile, different cognitions of labor relations and different stages of development in countries lead to different adjustment approaches to labor relations, thus forming different development paths of labor relations governance.

## II. A Brief Review of Labor Relations Research in China

In the process of China's industrialization and modernization, labor relations have gradually become one of the most important and fundamental social relations because of the emergence and impacts of labor problems. The research in labor relations in China keeps in line with the development of labor relations with Chinese characteristics and is carried out in a systematic and scientific manner.

### 1. The Study of Labor Relations in the Republic of China (ROC)

Since modern times, a large working class has come into being with China's industrialization, and with it came the countless labor problems (Ma, 1927;

Zhang, 2011; Liu, 2006). Due to the emerging labor problems and social pressure, scholars at that time conducted numerous empirical studies with laborers as the subject. According to Pan Jintang's statistics, more than 100 works on labor issues were published between the 1920s and 1940s, covering work, life, welfare, labor organization and labor movement, etc. (Pan, 1992; Wen, 2018). Some of the well-known ones include the joint study on workers' life by Tao Menghe and the Peking Social Investigation Institute (Tao, 2005; Wang et al.; 1928, Xin et al., 1932), the joint comprehensive survey and interview on labor issues by Tao and Tsinghua University's Institute for Contemporary China Studies (Chen, 1929), the ethnographic community research on factories by Fei Xiaotong and his research group "Kuige" (Shi, 1946; Tian, 2014), and the study on labor movement by Deng Zhongxia (Deng, 2016).

In addition to the empirical research on labor issues, some scholars, from the perspective of system design or legislation and on the basis of the Western experience, attempted to build a coordination system for labor relations. Regarding labor law, Li Jianhua, Cao Jianguang, Luo Yunyan, Shi Taipu, Xie Fumin and other scholars all published relevant works to discuss the formulation of laws for protecting laborers' rights and interests (Tian, 2011; Li, 1928; Li, 1934; Cao, 1929; Luo, 1939; Shi, 1945; Xie, 1937) . In their work *Comparative Study on Labor Policies*, Ma Chaojun and Yu Changhe examined labor policies and laws by a comparative approach. Their study is praised as the highest level of labor law research during the ROC period (Ma and Yu, 2012). The above research not only closely followed the frontier Western research on labor relations with an international view, but also focused on practical problems in China. Therefore, they are still of great academic value in current times.

## 2. The Study of Labor Relations in the Planned Economy Period of the People's Republic of China (PRC)

After the founding of the PRC, especially after the completion of socialist transformation in 1956, China established a labor administrative system compatible with the socialist planned economy. It was a governance system for labor relations, featuring workplace as a basic unit and redistribution as a supporting mechanism (Lu, 1993). Under this system, the state, as the representative of social benefits, was responsible for the distribution of benefits for country, enterprises and workers. The characteristics of such a planned and administrative labor relationship included a labor employment system based on overall planning and distribution and permanent employment, a wage system with a low and averaged level, and a comprehensive welfare system.

Labor relations theory and research in this period were basically transplanted from those of the Soviet Union, focusing on the idealized description of labor relations and the interpretation of policy and management models. The management of labor relations was mainly for supporting the country's socialist transformation and organizing and motivating workers to actively participate in the production of enterprises. The major problem that need to be solved was mainly the increasingly serious bureaucracy in state-owned enterprises (SOEs), which resulted in the infringement of employees' interests and rights. Against this background, four important theories came into being:

(1) Theory of public-private conflict. This theory states that there are conflicts between public and private sectors instead of between employers and employees in the national economic system. Enterprises represent the public side, while employees represent the private side. The public-private conflict manifested itself in employee's living and working conditions, which also reflects the conflicts between overall interests of working class and individual workers' interests, and between long-term and immediate interests. This type of conflicts can be found in almost every specific problem in factories and enterprises (Chinese Workers' Movement Institute, 1987).

(2) Theory of specific positions. This theory holds that the "general positions" of employees and employers are the same, but the "specific positions" can be different due to their different tasks and responsibilities (Shanghai Municipal Party School and Shanghai Federation of Trade Unions,1992).

(3) Theory of internal problems. This theory acknowledges the conflicts between public and private sectors, but such conflicts are problems among the people and not confrontational, which can be resolved through coordination. Trade union is an important organization to solve such problems (Zhang and Liu, 1985).

(4) Theory of homology. This theory suggests that both trade union and the Communist Party of China (CPC) are organizations of working class. The former is the mass organization of the working class, while the latter is the vanguard of the class. The unique function of trade union is to unite all the working class people, protect their special interests and rights, educate them with Communist principles, and strengthen the close ties between the Party and the people (Chinese Workers' Movement Institute,1987).

## 3. The Study of Labor Relations in the Initial Period of Reform and Opening Up

After the Third Plenary Session of the 11th Central Committee of the CPC, the research in labor relations has been more active than ever since it shattered mental shackles of the "left" ideology. A large number of famous scholars such as Yuan Fang, Zhao Lukuan, Ren Fushan and Guan Huai made studies on labor issues from different disciplinary perspectives. During this period, significant changes took place in the labor system under the planned economy where the interests of the state, enterprises and employees were integrated. Meanwhile, the labor system under the market economy was established step by step, which was based on market rules and the separation of property rights, management rights and labor rights (Chang, 2008). Both theory and research about labor relations at this stage paid attention to the market-oriented transformation of labor relations. The transformation means efforts to set up a market-oriented labor relations system, shatter the "iron rice bowl"[1] to promote the free flow of laborers, abandon the practices of "iron wage"[2] to advance the independent distribution by enterprises, and break the "iron chair"[3] to motivate the officials at all levels. The main tasks of labor relations management were to support the state to reform the fixed labor system, improve labor efficiency, fully implement the labor contract system and the system of linking workers' pay with their performance, and implement the system that enterprises' leaders should assume responsibility for business performance. The labor relations problems to be solved included the different treatments of contract workers, the arrangement of surplus workers in SOEs, the widening income gap in enterprises and so on. The release of the Interim Provisions on the Implementation of the Labor Contract System by the Ministry of Labor in 1986 was a milestone in the early period of labor relations reform.

Theoretical research in this period mainly focused on the organization function of trade unions. With the establishment of the market economy system, transformation of trade unions became an urgent task. Scholars had heated discussions over the function of trade unions. Some of them held that trade unions have a single function: to represent workers and safeguard their interests. However, more scholars agreed with the dual function theory, that is, trade unions safeguard the overall interests of all people and the specific interests of the workers. Furthermore, a large majority of those who advocated multiple functions believed that the most important function of trade unions was protecting the interests of workers (Sun et al. 1997). The contents of this discussion were reflected in the Initial Plan for Trade Union Reform adopted by All-China Federation of Trade Unions (ACFTU) in October 1988. The 11th National Congress of Trade Unions held in the same year identified the functions of trade unions as "protection, education, construction and participation". The Initial Plan

---

[1] Iron rice bowl refers to a guaranteed job many Chinese people dreamed of getting during the era of the planned economy–translator's note.

[2] Iron wage refers to a relatively fixed wage of the workers in the SOEs in China during the era of the planned economy–translator's note.

[3] Iron chair refers to the stable positions of officials in government and SOEs in China during the era of the planned economy–translator's note.

proposed to added "protection" and "participation" to the functions of trade unions. This indicates that with the deepening of reforms on economic system, SOEs and labor system, Chinese trade unions began to explore new functions meeting the need of the market economic system (Zhang, 2004).

## 4. The Study of Labor Relations in the Period of Market-oriented Transformation of Labor Relations

The reform of labor relations and labor system was further deepened after Deng Xiaoping's southern tour speeches in 1992 and the release of the decision announced at the Party's 14th National Congress that "China's economic reform aims at establishing a socialist market economy". On the one hand, focusing on fostering and developing the labor market, the state vigorously deepened reforms on labor, training, wages and social insurance, while enterprises had bigger autonomy on employment and wages. On the other hand, the broad reform of the SOEs and the increase of foreign investment brought about a large number of laid-off workers and rural migrant workers and caused concerns about rights and interests protection. During this period, the research on labor relations moved forward quickly. The focus was how to systematically make use of the labor relations theories and methods of market economy, and how labor relations can play an important role in improving the relationship among "reform, development and stability", especially the role in promoting stability.

The labor system reform was deepened in this period. Specifically, the market mechanism began to play a fundamental role in allocating and utilizing labor resources. In terms of employment system, the state gradually established a new model characterized by "macro-control by the state, flexible employment policies by enterprises, coexistence of various employment forms and full application of labor contracts". In terms of workers' pay, market would play a decisive role, enterprises would determine the distribution schemes by themselves, and government would be responsible for supervision and regulation. In terms of labor insurance, the coverage of old-age pension scheme and unemployment insurance were expanded. In terms of labor legislation, a more complete system of labor laws was established to put work related labor relations on the right development track. It should be noted that the Labor Law promulgated in 1994 stipulated two systems of protecting workers. One was to set legal labor standards and clarify the legitimate rights and interests of workers (including labor contracts, wages, holidays and social insurance). The other was the collective bargaining and the collective contract systems, which provided that "the employees of an enterprise can sign collective contracts with the enterprise on matters such as labor remuneration, working hours, holiday and vacation, labor safety and health, insurance and welfare, etc." These two systems formed the basis of China's labor laws and policies. On this basis, ACFTU put forward the general idea of trade union's work, "Following the enactment of the Labor Law, trade unions around the country should further highlight their function of safeguarding rights and interests, and prioritize the work related to equal negotiation and collective contracts", with an aim to put the collective labor relations system into practice.

Study on labor relations in this period tended to be more systematic. Centering on the market-oriented transformation of labor relations, many scholars conducted in-depth studies and theoretical research from the perspectives of labor law, history, political science, sociology and other disciplines. A group of scholars represented by Chang Kai, Feng Tongqing and Qiao Jian emerged in this period. On the basis of respecting Chinese experience in transformation and introducing classical Western theories on labor relations, China gradually established the knowledge framework of China's labor relations research and began to turn their eyes towards a range of far-reaching issues.

Chang Kai and other scholars from the Chinese Labor Movement Academy (predecessor of China University of Labor Relation) began to systematically study China's labor relations during this period, whose theoretical achievements were reflected in the book *Labor Relations, Laborers, and Labor Rights*. The book proposed for the first time to "study China's labor issues with a focus on labor rights, and then establish a labor legal system for protecting workers' rights and interests". It marked that the study areas of labor relations had started to shift from the phenomena to the essential issues like sound governance and system design, indicating that the discipline of labor relations came into being and was developing into an inter-discipline that interacts with economics, law, management, sociology and political science. During this period, a large number of research results emerged in the fields of labor relations, such as labor law, trade union organization, collective bargaining, democratic management of workers and international labor standards. This was evidenced by the publication of many research works about other market economy countries' mature experience on labor relations governance. These works not only became important reference for the establishment of China's labor relations system, but also further promoted the rapid development of labor relations research in the country.

## 5. The Study of Labor Relations in the 21st Century

Since the beginning of the 21st century, the market-oriented labor relations have taken shape, and several systems have been initially established, including contract system, the tripartite mechanism for settling disputes, and the collective bargaining system between trade unions and enterprises. These systems have played a key role in promoting the stability of labor relations. However, the expansion of economic aggregate and the decline of the "demographic dividend" during this period have brought about a persistent shortage of labor supply. China has been considered a country with unlimited labor supply for a long time, as it seems that the country has endless surplus labor to transfer from agricultural sector to other sectors and support its development mode based on the labor-intensive and export-oriented industries. In fact, after the launch of reform and opening up, China's rapid economic growth for many years benefited from this mode. However, the increasingly shortage of labor supply since 2004 has indicated a reversal of supply-demand relation in China's labor market and a smaller rural surplus labor pool. This is known as the "Lewis turning point", meaning that capital has become relatively abundant while labor force relatively scarce, and the "demographic dividend" that used to drive growth through the comparative advantage of low labor costs has been disappearing (Cai, 2010). The workers are no longer the passive party in the labor market, but gain structural power from the "tight labor market" (Shen, 2006). This power has not only helped them improve their bargaining power in the market, but also promoted their awareness of rights and demands and given them stronger capability in collective actions. Scholars defined this change as a shift from rights disputes to interest disputes (Chang, 2013) or from requiring "bottom-line" interests to asking for "satisfying" interests (Cai, 2010). The worker's appeal is no longer to meet the legal minimum wage, but to gain interests above the legal standards, including raising wage standards, improving working conditions, shortening working hours, paying overtime wages, etc. Most of the appeals are made because of the intention of "gaining more interests". What's more, workers' awareness of carrying out organized activities have got stronger, and they began to express their demands by organized means with Internet as the tool instead of traditional government bodies, which has posed a challenge to the stability of workforce and society. The research in labor relations is faced with new situation and challenges in paradigm, theory and method, but the challenges are also a thrust to innovation.

During this period, one focus of the research on labor relations was whether China had entered a stage of collective labor relations. Professor Chang Kai examined the theory of collective transformation of labor relations in a comprehensive manner. According to his findings, the transformation from individual to collective labor relations is a significant historical process commonly seen in other countries. In China, such a transformation is based on the adjustment of individual labor relations and realized through the synergy of two paths, i.e. the "top-down system led by the government" and the "active bottom-up support from workers". In response to this collective transformation, China needs to promulgate and improve laws on collective labor relations as soon as possible and establish an adjustment system accordingly (Chang, 2013). Despite the controversy it aroused in the academic circle (You, 2014; Dou, 2016), this viewpoint has become a focus of labor relations research at that time (Qiao et al, 2011).

The Guidelines on Building Harmonious Labor Relations issued by the CPC Central Committee and the State Council in April 2015 proposed to develop harmonious labor relations with Chinese characteristics, which is of guiding significance for the theoretical research in the new era. Among the major issues mentioned in the Guidelines, the influence of a harmonious trade union system with Chinese characteristics on labor relations has become a trending research topic. There are many stereotypes about trade unions whether in the West or in China. However, through comparative studies on a lot of data, many economists found that China's trade unions have played a positive role in improving welfares such as wages and social insurance (Yang and Yang, 2013). They have contributed to the income growth of workers in private enterprises (Chen and Zhang, 2019), the increase of the long-term employment proportion, the decline of short-term employment proportion, and the stability of labor relations (Wei et al., 2015). In addition, trade unions have produced a macro social impact, as they play a major role in protecting labor rights and interests of the floating population (Ji and Lai, 2019) and promoting production expansion, R&D of new products, and technology innovation of enterprises, thereby supporting the country's innovation-driven development strategy (Wei et al., 2018). These findings further enrich and support the connotation of harmonious labor relations with Chinese characteristics and are important theoretical achievements of labor relations research in China.

The research on labor relations in Western countries have dropped significantly due to the declining trade union density and collective bargaining coverage. China, however, has shown a dynamic and thriving trend in labor relations research. A large number of influential works have been published, and the discipline construction has also been improved. Scholars have developed labor relations theory with Chinese characteristics and published relevant textbooks to meet the practical needs (Chang, 2005; Li, 2008). During this period, labor relations were established as an undergraduate major by the Ministry of Education for the first time, and China University of Labor Relation became the first university in the country to formally introduce the major of labor relations. Renmin University of China has formed a complete education system from undergraduate to doctoral degrees for this major. Thanks to these efforts, labor relations have been established as a discipline in China, with constantly improved theoretical paradigms and broadened research areas.

## III. Labor Relations Research with Chinese Characteristics

China's labor relations research has achieved significant progress over the past seven decades. With distinctive Chinese characteristics, it differs from the Western studies in theoretical hypothesis and research logic. The Western scholars assume that labor relations are economic relations and propose to settle labor disputes with property rights rules, while the Chinese scholars think that labor relations are not just economic exchanges between labor and pay, but also a kind of political relations. This is the largest difference between the Western and Chinese studies. The "political relations" in the Chinese research mean that the two parties of the labor relations have same fundamental interests, and their disputes stem from differences in some specific interests and therefore are problems among the people. It is because of such political relations that Chinese researchers emphasize the fundamentally interdependent relation between the two parties of labor relations. Understanding the interdependence could help us find a path to solve labor disputes, establish a mediation system, and change the confrontation between employers and employees to cooperation. From a monophyletic perspective, Chinese researchers are committed to deepening labor relations studies by basing themselves on the nation's reality and institutions and highlighting those features in a socialist country. On the basis of respecting China's history, culture and political system, they carry out their studies to serve the country's economic and social development.

The research on  labor relations in China, to a large extent, is about a summary of the practical experience that the country has accumulated in handling labor relations. So far, four consensuses have been reached. Firstly, due to the nature of China's labor relations, in the process of developing harmonious labor relations, we must uphold the CPC's leadership, stay on the path of socialism with Chinese characteristics, and follow the general laws of labor relations on the basis of taking into account our fundamental political system, economic system and other national conditions. Secondly, as a result of the Confucian culture's influence, Chinese people believe that harmony is one of the most important social norms, and disputes and confrontations are often the consequences of social disharmony. Therefore, all parties of labor relations have an innate cultural belief to promote interpersonal harmony, and thus compromise and inclusiveness become the basic values of the labor relations system in China. Thirdly, affected by the interpersonal factors in labor relations, the related rights and obligations in China are not rigid or rational like those in the West, but more variable and flexible. And there is no unified law to settle the varying relations of rights and obligations. Therefore, to establish a long-term relation of mutual trust, consultation based on specific conditions is more important than negotiation, and the settlement of problems mainly depends on mediation rather than arbitration or judgment. Fourthly, and most importantly, the Party and the state have a deep influence over the parties in labor relations and play a key role in maintaining harmonious relations. They keep adjusting or stabilizing labor relations through formulating rules, procedures and norms, thereby bringing distinct institutional characteristics to the nation's labor relations system. These characteristics and consensuses have shaped the pillars of China's state-led governance system for labor relations .

At the political level, the Party Central Committee and the State Council attach great importance to labor relations issues. General Secretary Xi Jinping has expounded the position and role of labor relations in the cause of socialism with Chinese characteristics, pointed out the social nature of Chinese labor relations, and set forth the basic requirements and missions for the work of labor relations in the new era. The Guidelines on Building Harmonious Labor Relations requires Party committees and governments at all levels to maximize the factors that contribute to social harmony, and minimize the ones that undermine it, so as to develop a governance system led by the Party committees, implemented by the government, based on consultation and coordination, participated by enterprises and employees, and guaranteed by the rule of law. As the most important political groups of labor, trade unions have established a large organization system involving enterprises and the state. Guided by the concept of "promoting enterprises' development and safeguarding workers' rights", trade unions encourage enterprises and workers to find the middle ground between partial and overall interests, and between short-term and long-term interests, and then become a central pillar of strength for maintaining harmonious labor relations.

At the legal level, China focuses on the most pressing, most immediate issues that concern the workers the most and takes solid measures to protect their rights and interests, which has been considered the ultimate goal of all the endeavors to build harmonious labor relations. To this end, the nation has been actively promoting the formulation of laws and regulations in labor, economic, social and other fields closely related to the interests of workers. Since the enactment of Labor Law in 1994, China has gradually established a labor law system with Chinese characteristics by formulating and revising dozens of laws. Those laws include Enterprise Bankruptcy Law, Corporate Law, Property Law, Labor Contract Law, Employment Promotion Law, Social Insurance Law, Labor Dispute Mediation and Arbitration Law, Prevention and Control of Occupational Diseases Law, Regulations on Work-Related Injury Insurances, Regulations on Labor Security Supervision, Regulations on the Implementation of the Employment Contract Law, Special Rules on the

Labor Protection of Female Employees, etc. As a result of these efforts, a labor rights protection system covering working hours, overtime work, labor protection, minimum wage, social security, decent work and so on has been established.

At the public level, educational outreach has been conducted to inform them of the significance of building harmonious labor relations, the Party and the government's policies, the laws and regulations on labor security, and the examples contributing to the harmonious relations. These efforts aim to maintain the right tone in public communication, strengthen the influence of public outreach, guide enterprises and workers to foster a sense of shared interests and develop a vision of win-win cooperation and common development, and create a social atmosphere of following, supporting and participating in the building of harmonious labor relations (Yin, 2015). At the same time, China has set up a large number of labor dispute mediation organizations and mechanisms at the levels of enterprises, towns and townships and communities. A labor dispute settlement mechanism of "mediation-arbitration-litigation" has been completed to appropriately resolve labor disputes through mediation and arbitration, supplemented by the use of judicial means.

As enterprises are the cornerstone of harmonious labor relations, the core goal of building a system of harmonious labor relations is raising the awareness of enterprises and employees about inclusiveness and common development. On the one hand, under the principle of "harmonious co-existence", efforts will be made to create material conditions for harmonious labor relations by promoting high-quality development of enterprises and economy and increasing employment. On the other hand, enterprises are encouraged to pay close attention to the needs of their employees, promote decent work, and conduct collective wage negotiations in accordance with relevant laws. Enterprises are also supported to establish and improve democratic management systems such as employees' conferences, system for transparent management, boards of directors, and supervisory committees. These efforts aim at pushing employers and employees to jointly implement consultation practices, establish working mechanisms, improving performance, and sharing benefits.[1]

## IV. Outlook for the Development of Labor Relations Research in China

China is undergoing profound changes in social and economic situation, which will inevitably affect labor relations and bring about new topics to research in this

---

[1] Guidelines of the CPC Central Committee and the State Council on Building Harmonious Labor Relations [EB/OL]. (2015-03-21) [2020-01-14]. http://www.gov.cn/guowuyuan/2015/04/08/content_2843938.htm.

regard.

## 1. Changes in Population Structure Will Affects Laborer's Bargaining Power and Interests

The development of labor relations is shaped by the evolvement of labor market. Since the start of the 21st century, China's labor supply has seen significant changes as the working-age population continues to decline, while the new generation workers become the main force in the labor market. The change in labor market structure will lead to a different power balance between players of labor relations and affect the background and focus of labor relations research.

*1.1 The declining working-age population and the growing bargaining power of workers*

At the beginning of the 21st century, many Chinese scholars began to study the relationship between Chinese changing demographic profile and its economic growth. They started to discuss whether China's economic development had reached the "Lewis turning point" and whether its "demographic dividend" was diminishing. Since 2012, the total number of working-age population between 16 and 59 in China has dropped rapidly, leading to a shortage of labor supply. Meanwhile, labor force participation rate has kept declining, while wage has been rising (Du and Jia, 2018). Driven by the two factors, China is turning from a labor surplus to a labor shortage economy, which has changed the weak position of workers in labor relations – their bargaining power in the market is increasing, their sense of rights and interests has become clearer, and their expectation for higher wages, better working conditions and sharing more the fruits of development.

*1.2 Changes in labor force structure and the workers' pursuit of diverse interests*

China's labor force structure has changed tremendously over the past decade. The first change is the increase of younger laborers. From 1996 to 2015, the laborers born before the 1980s decreased from 800 million to 600 million and their percentage in the total labor force dropped to 61.0% from 95.6%, while the laborers born after the 1980s kept increasing and their percentage increased to 39.0% from 4.4%. The second change is the education levels of laborers become higher. From 1996 to 2015, the percentage of people with high school degree or below in the entire employed population decreased from 97.2% to 82.6%, while the percentage of those with college education or above increased from 2.8% to 17.4%. Overall, the proportion of manual laborers dropped quickly while that of knowledge workers rose fast (Jiang et al., 2018). The third change is the stable growth of migrant workers. According to a report about the conditions of migrant workers, their total number has steadily increased in recent years, reaching nearly 300 million. The new generation migrant workers who were born after 1980 and beyond, accounting for more than half of the total, have become the mainstay of migrant workers and an important part of China's labor force. As a result, profound changes have taken place in the structure of China's working population. The new generation laborers who were mainly born in the 1980s are young and high-caliber workers with distinct personalities and strong awareness of legal rights. In addition, they are eager to be acknowledged and prove their self-worth from achievement. In this sense, research on the characteristics and needs of the new generation laborers, especially the new migrant workers, should be enhanced to promote the stability of labor relations.

## 2. The Shift of Economic Growth Modes Will Weigh on the Stability of Labor Relations

With China's economy entering a new normal state, labor relations present some new features. Overall, the number of labor disputes will increase, and collective labor disputes and collective labor movements will rise significantly. Accordingly, potential risks will grow and new problems will emerge .

*2.1 Slowing economic growth adding risks to labor relations*

According to the forecast of the Laboratory of Macroeconomics of the Chinese Academy of Social Sciences, China's GDP growth will remain stable at rates between 5.4% and 6.3% from 2021 to 2030, indicating that economic growth will continue to slow down (Tian, 2018). In this context, some industries and enterprises may face the challenges of receiving less orders, running below capacity and getting smaller profits. They have little room to improve working conditions and raise wages, and are confronted with the risks of layoffs and failure to pay wages, which may undermine the workers' rights and interests and the stability of the workforce and then further increase risks in labor relations. The labor-intensive industries have suffered the most, because their competitive advantages brought by lowering wages and labor costs cannot be sustained. Low wages and poor welfare of workers in many labor-intensive enterprises have become the root cause of labor disputes and conflicts. In addition, economic structural adjustment and transformation have posed threats to some businesses, such as bankruptcy, relocation, merging and reorganization. These unfavorable factors, coupled with the uncertainty brought by China-US trade frictions, will weight on the stability of labor relations. As a result, regulations over enterprises' failure to pay wages, assistance to the affected employees and training for the unemployed will become important research topics.

*2.2 New highlights in labor relations research in the era of high-quality economic development*

China's economy is transitioned to a stage of high-quality development, which means changes in both development philosophy and growth model, and more attention to people's livelihood (Zhao et al., 2019). On the one hand, to pursue high-quality economic development, we need to promote the construction of a modern industrial system and the upgrading of industrial structure. The scientific and cultural literacy, skills, and innovation capability of laborers are important factors to promote the optimization and upgrading of industrial structure. In other words, the improvement of workforce's competence is critical for the upgrading of industrial structure. Given this, how to improve the skills and innovation ability of workers, how to promote their all-round development, and how to establish a high-caliber labor team become the key topics in labor relations research in the era of high-quality development. On the other hand, high-quality development is also people-centered development. "People-centered" means that people can achieve high-quality employment and share the benefits of economic growth (Sun and Chen, 2019). Only when laborers are employed, can there be labor relations; and only when laborers have high-quality jobs can there be stable and harmonious labor relations. In the process of advancing high-quality development, structural unemployment caused by the upgrading of industrial structure will be inevitable, and the structural contradiction of employment will be more prominent. Therefore, how to promote employment and achieve high-quality employment is also a focus of labor relations research.

### 3. New Research Topics Inspired by the Growth of Platform Economy and the Emergence of New Employment Forms

With the growth of platform economy, a variety of new forms of employment have appeared, including delivery men, couriers, online shop owners and so on. Since these forms have completely different features from the traditional ones, those people work in platforms cannot be categorized into labor relations according to the existing laws, and thus their social insurance and the basic rights and interests cannot be guaranteed. These new employment forms are very flexible in terms of working schedule and time, but they also face challenges like unstable earnings, lack of social insurance, etc. Hence, new labor relations problems arising from platform economy will be a hot spot of labor relations research.

*3.1 Identifying labor relations in the context of new forms of employment*

Different from the traditional ones, the new employment forms are Internet-based, informal and flexible production activities with non-fixed workplaces. These characteristics make the standards of existing labor relations not applicable to them. At present, there are still debates about identification standards for new employment forms, and thus laws and regulations in this regard have not been in place yet. Some scholars have studied the identification of "gig workers" and believe that the criteria for the labor relations of new employment forms should be flexible, that is, both the standards of typical and non-typical labor relations should be taken into consideration, and "gig workers" fall into the category of non-typical labor relations (Wang and Wang, 2018). Some scholars believe that there are three forms of employment under the sharing economy and three identification standards: the informal and non-fixed gig work can be identified as service relations, the full-time and fixed gig work as gig relations, and the full-time and fixed work as labor relations (Yu, 2018). Some scholars think that the identification of labor relations for online platform workers should take into account the actual conditions of specific workers and platforms. That is to say, researchers need to analyze on a case-by-case basis, focus on the essence of labor relations and attach importance to other factors such as working time, source of income and the necessity of social protection (Xie, 2018). For a rather long time in the future, labor relations research will concentrate on how to identify the legal status of workers in new employment forms in order to effectively protect their rights and interests and how to promote the sustainable and healthy development of platform economy.

### 3.2 Protecting rights and interests of workers' in new forms of employment

Current labor laws and policies in China are mainly to protect workers in labor relations. As the legal status of workers in new forms of employment have not been clearly defined, their rights and interests have not yet been fully covered by law. Firstly, there is no social insurance for platform workers. Due to the vague identification criteria for their labor relations, many of them are still excluded from the social insurance system. Secondly, there is no minimum wage guarantee for platform workers. Since their working time is flexible, the platforms do not pay them according to the working time, but to the tasks completed. Since the calculation standards of minimum wage have changed drastically, it is difficult to set the minimum wage standards (Wu et al., 2019). Finally, working hour standards are not applicable. The flextime of platform workers makes it difficult to implement the overtime regulations and vacation policies based on traditional working hour systems. With the rapid development of platform economy, the number of gig workers is large and continues rising, and employment forms get even more complex and diverse. Against this backdrop, identifying labor relations in platform economy and protecting the rights and interests of the new types of workers has become a complicated and important issue.

In conclusion, labor relations have undergone significant changes at different stages of the PRC, but the socialist nature of China's labor relations and the position of the working class as the country's master remain unchanged, and the two parties of labor relations still have the same fundamental interests. The research in labor relations focus on the problems and conflicts in different periods, but its mission is contributing to the improvement of the policies and systems for labor relations that benefit both workers and enterprises, and promoting the building of stable and harmonious labor relations. With this mission in mind, our scholars have examined the country's practices of building labor relations with Chinese characteristics over the past 70 years and gained valuable findings. They have played an important role in promoting the development of Chinese labor relations, and are committed to forming labor relations theories with Chinese characteristics and providing Chinese wisdom and solutions to the international research.

## References

[1] Keith Whitefield, George Strauss. Translated by Cheng Yanyuan et al. Research Methods in Industrial Relations(Chinese version) [M]. Beijing: China Labor and Social Security Press, 2005.

[2] Ma Chaojun. Labor Issues in China [M]. Shanghai: Minzhi Publishing House, 1927.

[3] Zhang Jinfen. The Labor Sociology [M]. Taipei: National Chengchi University Press, 2011.

[4] Liu Aiyu. Labor Sociology (2nd edition) [M]. Beijing: Peking University Press, 2006.

[5] Pan Jintang. The Origin and Development of Labor Sociology [J]. Social Science, 1992(1):68-71.

[6] Wen Xiang. Sacred Labor: The Vision of Early Sociology in China [M]. Beijing: The Commercial Press, 2018.

[7] Tao Menghe. Analysis of the Cost of Living in Beijing// Li Wenhai, Xia Mingfang and Huang Xingtao. Social Survey Series of the Republic of China: Urban (Labor) Life Vol. I [M]. Fuzhou: Fujian Education Press, 2005.

[8] Wang Qingbin, Wang Shumeng, Lin Songhe et al. The First Labor Yearbook of China [M]. Beijing: Peking Social Investigation Department, 1928.

[9] Xing Bixin, Wu Duo, Lin Songhe et al. The Second Labor Yearbook of China [M]. Beijing: Peking Social Investigation Department, 1932.

[10] Chen Da. Labor Issues in China [M]. Beijing: The Commercial Press, 1929.

[11] Shi Guoheng. Labor in Kunming Factory [M]. Beijing: The Commercial Press, 1946.

[12] Tian Rukang. Female Workers in Chinese Mainland // Li Wenhai, Xia Mingfang and Huang Xingtao. Social Survey Series of the Republic of China: Urban (Labor) Life Vol. II [M]. Fuzhou: Fujian Education Press, 2014.

[13] Deng Zhongxia. A Brief History of Chinese Workers' Movement [M]. Zhengzhou: Henan People's Publishing House, 2016.

[14] Tian Tong. Review and Reflection on the Study of the History of Labor Relations in the Republic of China [J]. Historical Research, 2016(1):173-189.

[15] Li Jianhua. Labor Issues and Labor Law [M]. Shanghai: Pacific Bookstore, 1928.

[16] Li Jianhua. Labor Law [M]. Shanghai: Shanghai Law Compilation Press, 1934.

[17] Cao Jianguang. Research on Labor Law [M]. Shanghai: South China Book Bureau, 1929.

[18] Luo Yunyan. Labor Legislation in China [M]. Shanghai: Zhonghua Book Company, 1939.

[19] Shi Taipu. Study on the Law of Trade Unions in China [M]. Nanjing: Zhengzhong Book Company, 1945.

[20] Xie Fumin. Legislation History of the Republic of China [M]. Nanjing: Zhengzhong Book Company, 1937.

[21] Ma Chaojun and Yu Changhe. Comparative Labor Policy [M]. Beijing: The Commercial Press, 2012.

[22] Lu Feng. The Origin and Formation of China's Company System [J]. China Social Sciences Quarterly, 1993(5):66-87.

[23] Chinese Workers' Movement Institute. Li Lisan and Lai Ruoyu's Views on Trade Unions [M]. Beijing: Archives Publishing House, 1987.

[24] Shanghai Municipal Party School and Shanghai Federation of Trade Unions. Selected Documents on Socialist Trade Unions [M]. Beijing: History of the Communist Party of China Press, 1992.

[25] Zhang Baoshan. Liu Shaoqi's Theoretical Guides on Internal Conflicts of State-owned Factories and Trade Union Work//Liu Shaoqi Research Group, Literature Research Office of the CPC Central Committee. Selected Works of Liu Shaoqi, vol. 2, study and research[M]. Beijing: Central Party School Press, 1985.

[26] Chang Kai The Evolution of Labor Relations in the Past Thirty Years [J]. China Business (the first half of the month), 2008(6):39-41.

[27] Sun Zhongfan, An Miao and Feng Tongqing. Trade Union Theory Outline and Review in the Transition Period to Socialist Market Economy [M]. Beijing: People's Publishing House, 1997.

[28] Zhang Yingshuo. Changes of Contemporary Chinese Labor System and Labor Union Functions [M]. Baoding: Hebei University Press, 2004.

[29] Cai Fang. Report on China's Population and Labor Issues [M]. Beijing: Social Sciences Academic Press, 2010.

[30] Chang Kai. Collective Transformation of Labor Relations and the Improvement of Government Labor Policy [J]. Social Sciences in China, 2013(6).

[31] Cai He. From "bottom-line" Interests to "satisfying" Interests: The Changes of Migrant Workers' Interest Appeal and the Order of Labor Relations [J]. Open Era, 2010(9): 37-45.

[32] You Zhenglin. Another Interpretation of the Transformation of Labor Relations in China: A Discussion with Professor Chang Kai [J]. Chinese Social Sciences, 2014(3):167-170.

[33] Dou Xuewei. "Collective Labor Relations" or "Company-like System"? Two Directions of Chinese Labor Relations Reform [J]. Social Sciences of Gansu Province, 2019(3):210-214.

[34] Qiao Jian, Zheng Qiao, Yu Min et al. Current Situation and Policy Orientation of China's Labor Relations in the 12th Five-year Period [J]. Journal of China University of Labor Relations, 2011(3):14-19.

[35] Yang Jidong and Yang Qijing. Trade Unions, Political Connections and Wage Decisions: An Analysis Based on the Data of Chinese Enterprises [J]. World Economic Literature, 2013(2):36-49.

[36] Chen Zongshi and Zhang Jianjun. Trade Unions, Regional Regulation and Wage Rates of Private Enterprises [J]. Sociological Research, 2019, 34(4):50-72.

[37] Wei Xiahai, Dong Zhiqiang and Jin Zhao. Have Labor Unions Improved Enterprise Employment Term Structure? Empirical Evidence from a Sample Survey of Private Enterprises in China [J]. Management World, 2015 (5):60-70.

[38] Ji Wenwen and Lai Desheng. Can Labor Unions Safeguard the Rights and Interests of Floating Population Labor? [J]. Management World, 2019(2):88-101.

[39] Wei Xiahai, Jin Zhao and Sun Zhongwei. Trade Unions, Labor Protection and New Investment of Enterprises [J]. World Economy, 2018(5):175-194.

[40] Chang Kai. Labor Relations [M]. Beijing: China Labor Social Security Press, 2015.

[41] Li Qi. An Introduction to Industrial Relations [M]. Beijing: China Labor Social Security Press, 2008.

[42] Yin Weimin. Striving to Build Harmonious Labor Relations with Chinese Characteristics [N]. People's Daily, 2015-04-09(12).

[43] Guidelines of the CPC Central Committee and the State Council on Building Harmonious Labor Relations [EB/OL].(2015-03-21)[2020-01-14].http://www.gov.cn/guowuyuan/2015-04/08/content_2843938.htm.

[44] Du Yang and Jia Peng. Labor Supply and Economic Growth [J]. Labor Economics Research, 2018 (3): 4-22.

[45] Jiang Juan, Yang Huafeng, Yang Ligao et al. An Empirical Study on the Impact of Labor Structure Change on the Upgrading of Manufacturing Structure [J]. Scientific Decision Making, 2018(8):73-94.

[46] Tian Litao. Discussion on China's Economic Development and Reform Based

on the Background of Economic New Normal [J]. Commercial Economics Research, 2018(23):187-190.

[47] Zhao Jianbo, Shi Dan and Deng Zhou. Research on the Connotations of High-quality Development [J]. Economics and Management Research, 2019(11):15-31.

[48] Sun Zhijun and Chen Min. Xi Jinping's Thought of High-quality Economic Development in the New Era and Its Value [J]. Shanghai Economic Research, 2019(10): 25-35.

[49] Wang Quanxing and Wang Qian. The Identification of Labor Relations and Protection of Rights and Interests of "Online Platform Workers" in China [J]. The Study of Law, 2018(4): 59-74.

[50] Yu Ying. Identification and Laws and Regulations of Employment Relations in the Sharing Economy: Starting from Understanding the Current Register of "Sharing Economy" [J]. East China University of Political Science and Law Report, 2018(3): 49-60.

[51] Xie Zengyi. Identification of Labor Relations on Internet Platforms [J]. Chinese and Foreign Law, 2018, 30(6):148-171.

[52] Wu Qingjun, Zhang Yiyuan and Zhou Guangsu. The Development Trend of Employment and Labor Policy on the Internet Platform: An Analysis Based on the Identification of Laborers [J]. Chinese Administration, 2019(4):118-125.

[53] Shen Yuan. Social Transformation and the Re-formation of the Working Class [J]. Sociological Research, 2006(2):13-36.

# Collective Labor Relations

■ Trends and Characteristics of China's Trade Union Reform since Reform and Opening Up

■ From "State-led" to Multiple Drivers: New Trends and the Typology of the Collective Consultation in China

# Trends and Characteristics of China's Trade Union Reform Since Reform and Opening Up[*]

*Wu Jianping*[**]

**Abstract:** There are four systematic reforms of China's trade unions to adapt to the political and economic changes since the reform and opening up. In this process, China's trade unions have clarified their role of representing workers and safeguarding their rights and interests. Their responsibility has transformed from focusing on production to safeguarding and serving workers. To perform their duties, they drew lessons from international experience, and put more emphasis on returning to and developing domestic socialized safeguarding and serving mode dominated by the Party and government. In addition, local trade unions and grassroots trade unions have gradually presented differentiated functions. Grassroots trade unions tended to get "downsized and unloaded", while local trade unions tended to "take the role of grassroots trade unions", to fulfill their duties of safeguarding and serving workers by integrating various resources.

**Keywords:** trade union reform; local trade union; grassroots trade union; reform and opening up

## I. Introduction

Since the reform and opening up, China has experienced rapid economic growth. It was considered as a "miracle" for the high-speed growth in a quite long period. However, since the global financial crisis in 2008, the Chinese economy has been greatly affected and entered a "new normal" phase, which was characterized by steady growth and structural adjustment. Even so, China remains a medium-high

---

[*] This paper was published in *Journal of China University of Labor Relations*, Issue. 1, 2018. It was abridged when included in this report.

[**] Wu Jianping, professor at the School of Social Work, China University of Labor Relations.

rate of growth. Economic growth is always accompanied by social differentiation and contradictions. One of the most significant manifestations is in the field of labor relations, namely conflicts between workers and employers. As the only legitimate organization that represents workers, trade union attracted the whole society's attention. China's trade union reform has also become a hot issue, since the CPC Central Committee Conference on the Work of the Party's Mass Organizations was held and *Opinions of the CPC Central Committee on Strengthening and Improving the Work of the Party's Mass Organizations* was released. In such a situation, the All-China Federation of Trade Unions (ACFTU) also began to promote top-down pilot reform, and made some achievements.

In a sense, such a top-down reform indirectly indicates that China's trade unions are different from trade unions in the western countries. They serve as a bridge between the Party and workers. On the one hand, they adopt the top-down approach to carry out the will of the Party and the state; on the other hand, they adopt the bottom-up approach to express the demands of workers. However, the dual function of trade unions may easily lead to conflicts, while the trade union may be partial to either side of the conflict. From the perspective of historical development, China's trade unions have always adhered to the leadership of the Party, but broken away from the masses to a certain extent for they couldn't perform their duties well in representing workers and safeguarding the legitimate rights and interests of workers (Chen, 1999). This can reduce the satisfaction and recognition of workers to trade unions. Therefore, the CPC Central Committee has been promoting reforms of trade unions, so as to make them closer to the masses, thus consolidating the governing foundation of the Party.

In fact, since the reform and opening up, China's trade unions have explored different approaches of reform, in order to better represent workers and safeguard their legitimate rights and interests. Experience had been gained in different phases of the reform. However, the survey on China's workers carried out by ACFTU every five years shows that workers are not satisfied with the trade unions. For example, the survey in 2017 showed that only 30% of selected workers would seek help from the trade union when they encountered difficulties. Why would this happen? In order to figure it out, we should review systematically the trade union reform in China: to find out the aspects in which the previous reform started from, and problems solved and yet to be solved. Only in doing so can we learn the trend and characteristics of the trade union reform in China, and put forward appropriate future reform direction. In general, since the reform and opening up, there have been reforms initiated by trade unions to adapt the development of China's economic reform in different periods. China's trade union reform has gone through four stages.

## II. Develop a Planned Commodity Economy (1978-1992): Basic Assumptions of Trade Union Reform

The first reform of China's trade unions after the implementation of the reform and opening up was driven by many factors. The first and the most direct factor is workers. In the early 1980s, workers started to be dissatisfied with the trade union. They slacked off at work. The reasons could be as follows. Workers might feel unfair due to the uneven distribution of benefits and social opportunities. Some of them even experienced mental breakdown. The process of the reform was full of ideological contradictions. The market-oriented reform and competition gradually made some people get rich first, while many enterprises went bankrupt, and the employment system was reformed. The first-line workers felt generally unbalanced because the salary was low and did not reflect the difference between first-line workers and second-line workers. In addition, due to the formalism in democratic management, workers generally had a low perception of their own social status and had no voice in housing distribution, bonus allocation, production task arrangement and many other aspects. Meanwhile, as the autonomy of enterprises strengthened, many cadres came to compete for benefits with the masses, abuse power for personal gains, abuse punishment towards workers and force workers to work overtime, which worsen the relationship between the masses and cadres in enterprises.

The second factor is the economic reform. In 1984, the Third Plenary Session of the 12th CPC Central Committee approved *Decision of the CPC Central Committee on Economic Reform*, which focused on the economic reform in cities. The reform required the transition of economic system from planned economy to the socialist commodity economy. The key task of the reform was to stimulate the vitality of enterprises. Under the circumstances, the trade union reform was put on the agenda officially. Trade unions would have to consider how to adapt to the trend.

The third factor is the international influence. It did arouse the attention of the state to trade unions and issues related to workers, although it affected the reform in an indirect manner. In the early 1980s, Polish workers went on nationwide strike. It led to the formulation of Solidarity, which then became an opposite force of the state. In light of this movement, the secretariat of ACFTU immediately held a meeting. He stressed that ACFTU should learn from it, and pointed out that "breaking away from the masses has become the main danger of China's trade unions, which should be faced up to." In March 1983, during a meeting about the work report outline of the 10th Congress of ACFTU, the Secretariat of the CPC Central Committee pointed out that the work of trade unions had been disturbed by the "leftism". He also stressed that, it was necessary that trade unions upheld the Party's leadership; but neglecting the truth that the trade union was a mass organization of the working class, made it become an administrative organ to a certain extent and broke away from workers.

The last and most important factor is the political reform proposed by the Central government in 1986. At that time, Deng Xiaoping underlined in several important speeches that economic reform should be guaranteed and promoted by political reform. He also put forward three objectives of the political reform, one of which was to decentralize power to the grass-roots level. It requires workers and intellectuals to engage in the management of enterprises, achieving the democratization of management. Therefore, it was essential to consider how to improve the Party's leadership in trade unions, and how could trade unions autonomously work to motivate workers under the Party's leadership.

In view of the above factors, in October 1988, the 6th Meeting of the 10th Executive Committee of ACFTU approved *Basic Assumption of Trade Union Reform* (hereinafter referred to as the "*Assumption*"). It was the most systematic "assumption" of the work of trade unions, as it pointed out the roles and responsibilities of trade unions in socialist countries, that is, to represent workers in the presence of the government and enterprises, and fulfill their responsibilities of safeguard, construction, participation and education. It also explained how to deal with two basic relations. One is the relations between trade unions and the Party as well as the government. It stressed that trade unions should operate autonomously under the leadership of the Party and in accordance with law. Trade unions should unswervingly uphold the political leadership of the Party. The will of the Party's should be carried out in the work of workers through the exemplary role of the Party and Party members in trade unions, and the democratic procedures in trade unions. In terms of the relations between trade unions and the government, trade unions should be an organized democratic channel for workers to participate in the administration and the discussion of state affairs. They should also function as a supervisor in the process of exercising power of the government. The other is the relations between trade unions and workers. It emphasized that the work of trade unions should focus on workers, and should be democratic. This could be achieved when they would be set up by workers. It should enhance the vitality of grassroots trade unions, prevent the tendency of administerization. In addition, it proposed that the system of trade unions should gradually transform to associated and representative system. Thus, leading organs of trade unions at all levels could be composed of representatives from grassroots trade unions or lower-level trade unions. In this way, trade unions could represent workers.

The proposition of reforming personnel system of trade union cadres is the most remarkable point in the reform. It required trade unions to self-manage their cadres in accordance with their own rules and regulations. So, the trade union's supervision system advanced in this direction as well, which means that cadres were no longer supervised by the Party committee and co-managed by the union. Some provincial trade union federations even formulated measure to self-manage their cadres, which was approved by the Provincial Party committee (Chen, 1999). This could prevent the disconnection between "people management" and "task management". In addition, the election system should also be improved, so that the existing delegating system could be changed.

For China's economic reform was still in the early exploration stage, and the labor relations system had not been market-oriented, the *Assumption* was still facing a fact that it was public ownership dominated. So it had not emphasized that the primary role of trade unions was to coordinate the relationship between workers and their employers, and protect legitimate rights and interests of workers. Nevertheless, the *Assumption* was still significant, as it did not only clarify the role, status and four responsibilities of trade unions, but also illuminated the relationship between trade unions and the Party as well as the government, and the relationship between trade unions and workers. In particular, it dared to propose reform of cadre personnel system. However, *Notice of the CPC Central Committee on Strengthening and Improving the Party's Leadership in Trade Unions, the Communist Youth League and the Women's Federations*, which was issued in December 1989, reiterated that personnel management should be led by the Party committee and the trade union, with the leadership of the Party committee of the same level at its core.

## III. Build a Socialist Market Economy (1992-2003): General Guidelines of the Work of Trade Unions

Deng Xiaoping commended the achievements of the reform and opening up in his speeches delivered during his famous tour of southern China. The 14th National Congress of the CPC made an important strategic decision to establish a socialist market economy. All of these deepened the reform. The working situation of trade unions also changed significantly, which urged trade unions to undertake new reform.

First, the reform of state-owned sectors led to a large number of workers in unemployment and poverty. Since the early 1990s, economic losses in state-owned enterprises had continued to increase. In 1994, in 39 major industrial categories, 13 of them saw industry-wide losses in state-owned independent accounting industrial enterprises, and the number increased to 25 in 1997. In addition, under the policy of "invigorating large enterprises and relaxing control over small ones", local governments actively promoted the merger, reorganization, restructuring or bankruptcy of small state-owned enterprises, which brought out large-scale job loss. In terms of the state-owned large and medium-sized enterprises, China launched the "off-the-hook in three years" reform in 1997 to encourage mergers, standardize bankruptcy, get the layoffs re-employed elsewhere, increase efficiency by downsizing and implement re-employment project. During 1998-2000, nearly 19 million workers were laid off, and about 14 million workers during 2001-2005. These laid-off workers fell into poverty or even absolute poverty.

Second, non-public enterprises developed rapidly. Since the early 1990s, township enterprises had been successively restructured, which made the original relationship of community with shared interests gradually transformed into the relationship between worker and employers. In 1988, the First Session of the Seventh National People's Congress passed a constitutional amendment to give the private sector a clear legal status. Since then, the private sector had developed rapidly. Foreign-funded enterprises had experienced a rapid growth since 1992. In that year, the number of foreign-invested projects and the amount of foreign capital in China exceeded the total amount of that from 1979 to 1991. The rapid expansion and the growing social influence of non-public enterprises made the terrible labor relations in these enterprises become a public issue that attracted a wide attention. Some researchers even described the factory system at that time with "chaos of the tyranny" (Lee, 1999). Data from the National Bureau of Statistics shows that, during 1996-2005, the number of labor disputes rose from 48,000 to 314,000, with an average annual growth rate of 23.6%; the number of people involved increased from 189,000 to 744,000, with an average annual growth rate of 18.4%. Among these cases, the number of cases of collective labor disputes increased from 3,000 to 16,000, and the people involved increased from 92,000 to 410,000, representing an average annual growth rate of 23.5% and 22.1% respectively.

It can be seen that since the early 1990s, China's labor relations had undergone an important change in nature, from the administrative relationship between the state and state workers to the market relationship between enterprises and their employees. The former relationship had both administrative and certain ideological features, which made it hard for trade unions to clarify their duties of representing and safeguarding workers in coordinating or managing  labor relations. The latter turned labor relations into market relationship with exchange of interests, which provided the possibility of admitting interest differentiation and conflicts, then clarifying trade unions' duty of representing and safeguarding workers.

It is in such a situation, China's trade unions began to reform, in response to the problem of labor relations brought about by the socialist market economic reform. The trade union reform in this phase focused on the "general guidelines of the work of trade unions", which was originally proposed at the 2nd Meeting of the 12th Executive Committee of ACFTU in 1994. The main task was to "take the implementation of *Labor Law* as an opportunity and the breakthrough point to promote the work of trade unions and the reform and development, strive to improve the work of trade unions to a new level, and play a better role in the process of reforming and developing."

The reform clarified and highlighted first that safeguarding the rights and interests of workers is the basic responsibility of trade unions. Wei Jianxing, the then chairman of ACFTU said at the 2nd Meeting of the 12th Executive Committee of ACFTU, "safeguarding the rights and interests of workers is the main means of trade unions in the service of the Party's central task". It was included in Article 6 of *Labor Law (Amendment)* in 2001, which states that "safeguarding legal rights and interests of workers is the basic responsibility of trade unions."

Regarding how to perform the duty of safeguarding the rights and interests of workers, China's trade unions began to actively learn from international labor standards and advanced experience (Qiao, 2017), including the collective contract. In fact, the collective contract is not a new thing for China's trade unions. However, it focused more on ensuring the production in the past, only a few of which was about workers' rights and interests. It then kept with the international practice, focusing on the labor provisions about workers' vital interests, such as wages, working hours and labor security. To adopt the collective contract, it is necessary to promote the establishment of trade unions, and the implementation of democratic management system in enterprises with the workers' congress as its basic form. Therefore, no matter from the content or the form, the collective contract could indeed be considered as the key to coordinating labor relations. China's trade unions had also introduced the worker-employer-government tripartite mechanism for the first time. Then the tripartite consultation mechanism was gradually established at all levels. In addition, another important reform initiative during this period was the participation in the formulation or amendment of laws, regulations and policies, which was an important channel for performing the duty of safeguarding workers. Moreover, grassroots labor relations coordination system, workers' democratic management system, labor law supervision system, labor dispute early warning and settlement system, which consist the current system and mechanism of trade unions, began to develop in this period.

In addition, it actively promoted the establishment of trade unions in non-public enterprises during this period, which can also be seen as an important reform measure. Although it was proposed in the 1980s to establish trade unions in non-public enterprises on a pilot basis, few non-public enterprises had trade unions until the middle and late 1990s. It was only at the end of the last century that trade unions were generally established in non-public enterprises due to the "trade union establishing movement" launched by ACFTU. It can be seen as a part of the reform, not only because China's grassroots trade unions expanded from the public sector to the non-public sector. More importantly, it created "the work pattern of trade unions of newly-established enterprise, which were led by the Party committee, supported by the government, and operated under the cooperation of all parties", which indicated the direction of the future reform of trade unions in terms of the system and mechanism.

## IV. Improve Socialist Market Economy (2003-2012): Development Path of Socialist Trade Unions with Chinese Characteristics

Since the beginning of the 21st century, China's domestic and international situations had undergone important changes. First, in 2004, the central government put forward in building a harmonious socialist society, which was included in the governance capacity of the Party. It then put forward the concept of Scientific Outlook on Development, which not only corrected the past growth pattern of local governments which only focused on the economic growth, but also let local governments recognize the importance of labor relations, and regard it as one of the breakthrough points of implementing scientific development and building a harmonious society.

Second, economic globalization and the development of Internet technology were accompanied by the inflow, collision and spread of various thoughts, including those about international labor movements and social movements, which would have a certain impact on China's political, economic and social stability. Besides, the awareness of laws and rights gradually rose in these years. People had a better understanding of their rights, and learned to protect their rights and interests through legal means. Furthermore, the global financial crisis and the "new normal" of China's economy would also cause many economic and social problems. All these changes had brought about new challenges to the work of China's trade unions: it should consider how to respond to these changes in order to better represent and safeguard the legitimate rights and interests of workers.

To some extent, it is not only a response to the current challenges, but also a reflection on the work of trade unions since the reform and opening up. At the beginning of the new century, ACFTU began to explore the major issues of "how to develop trade unions, and what kind of trade unions to build". It decided to choose the working mode and development path in line with national conditions. That is, trade union workers should pay attention to the fundamental differences between Chinese trade unions and western trade unions, and should not simply copy the experience of foreign trade unions. This idea was directly included in *Resolution on Adhering to the Development Path of Socialist Trade Union with Chinese Characteristics* adopted at the Sixth Plenary Session of the Presidium of the 14th Executive Committee of ACFTU in July 2005. The *Resolution* systematically elaborated the guiding ideology, political guarantee, fundamental task, functional role, organizational system, foreign relations, internal motivation and other aspects of the development path of socialist trade unions with Chinese characteristics. The key points are as follows. First, it should uphold the Party's leadership, which is the fundamental political guarantee of the work of trade unions. Second, it should adhere to the overall work plan of the Party and the state, and deploy the work of trade unions in a big picture. Third, expressing and safeguarding the legitimate rights and interests of workers is the basic duty of trade unions. Finally, it should learn from the experience of foreign trade unions, but should not copy their development patterns.

In December 2005, the 3rd Meeting of the 14th Executive Committee of ACFTU adopted *Decision on Strengthening Coordination of Labor Relations, Effectively Safeguarding the Legitimate Rights and Interests of Workers and Promoting the Construction of a Harmonious Socialist Society*. It put forward seven basic tasks: safeguarding workers' right to employment, right to remuneration, right to occupational safety and health, right to social security, democratic rights, social rights, and spiritual and cultural rights. It also summarized six systems and mechanisms: macro-level participation of trade unions, coordination of labor relations in enterprises, democratic management of workers, labor law supervision, early warning and settlement of labor disputes, and assistance for workers in difficulties.

It can be seen that, on the one hand, China's trade unions had been developed, improved and integrated under the preliminary exploration of various systems and mechanisms, and became more systematic; on the other hand, they re-stressed the political premise of these systems and mechanisms, namely to highlight the uniqueness of Chinese trade unions, not to simply copy foreign trade union mode. This uniqueness is reflected in its specific operation mode, that is, the "socialized mode of safeguarding rights" under "the leadership of the Party committee, the support of government, the cooperation of all parties, the operation by trade unions, and the participation of workers".

However, this mode was mainly carried out by local trade unions. In essence, local trade unions assisted the local governments to manage and coordinate labor relations under the approval, supervision and support of the local Party Committee and local government, and in accordance with the need of their functional goals. Local trade unions provided a platform to coordinate and integrate different parties related in order to help local government to manage and coordinate labor relations.

For example, they promoted industrial or regional collective bargaining or collective contracts through the Industry and Commerce Bureau, the (Management) Office of Industry or the Industry and Commerce Association; in the case of legal litigation, they seek help from the judicial department, enabling the legal aid of the trade union to be integrated into the local legal aid system; in terms of the supervision of the implementation of labor laws and regulations, they cooperated with law enforcement supervision departments such as the National People's Congress (NPC) and the Chinese People's Political Consultative Conference (CPPCC), to carry out joint inspections,, for example, the supervision and inspection of the safety of migrant workers in production with the safety supervision bureau. In this way, local trade unions could cooperate with different departments of the local government to achieve their goals, while reduce the social risks that labor conflicts may cause when local trade unions intervened in the labor relations governance (Wu, 2017).

Local trade unions had made great achievements in representing and safeguarding the legitimate rights and interests of workers through this mode of socialized rights protection. According to the information released by the News Center of ACFTU, during 2005-2014, ACFTU mainly participated in the formulation and amendment of more than 20 laws, regulations and rules concerning the major rights and interests of workers, including the Labor Contract Law, Law on Mediation and Arbitration of Labor Disputes, Employment Promotion Law, Safety in Production Law, Company Law, Social Insurance Law, Law on the Prevention and Cure of Occupational Diseases, Bankruptcy Law, and Regulations on Work-related Injury Insurance. Besides, trade unions at the provincial and prefectural (municipal) levels participated in the formulation of more than 1,600 local laws and regulations, and nearly 4,800 local standards (excluding laws and regulations), covering democratic management in enterprises, wage payment, collective consultation, labor law supervision, protection of trade unions' rights and interests and other issues (News Center of ACFTU,2015). During 2008-2012, labor dispute mediation committees of trade unions at all levels delt with a total of 2.934 million labor disputes, 839,000 of which were successfully mediated and settled. Among all labor disputes, 154,000 were collective labor disputes, 39,000 of which were successfully mediated and settled. During these five years, a total of 5,503 trade union cadres were qualified as arbitrators of labor disputes;134,000 cases of labor dispute were arbitrated and settled with the participation of  trade unions (Legal Affairs Office of ACFTU, 2013). In addition, China's trade unions had also carried out a series of innovations about the system and mechanism in the areas of helping workers in difficulties, mutual medical assistance for workers, collective consultation and signing of collective contracts, and legal aid services.

Still, this mode saw limitations. First of all, the extent and effect of the cooperation among local trade unions and others directly depended on the balance of multiple objectives of local governments. Therefore, if the local government attached less importance to the governance of labor relations than to the regional economic growth, it was difficult to have this kind of mode, or even if it adopted this mode, it would be fragile. Second, this mode required a high level of cooperation with other parties and governmental departments, so local trade unions tended to adopt it for the key tasks rather than the daily tasks. In other words, the mode was mainly adopted in the construction of institutions at the macro level or policy making rather than safeguarding workers' rights and interests at the micro level. This could avoid direct conflict with the enterprise or the local government. However, as a result, local trade unions would pay less attention to the protection of the rights and interests of specific individual workers at the micro level, but mainly to the protection of the rights and interests of workers as a whole at the macro level. Finally, the trade union of enterprise would be mainly restricted by the enterprise (owner of enterprise), which led to the lack of close contact between the trade union of enterprise and local trade unions. The efforts of local trade unions at the macro level would be difficult to have effective outcomes in enterprises due to the lack of cooperation with trade unions of enterprises (Wu, 2017).

In a word, compared with the first phase of reform, the reform in this phase did not touch on the organizational institution and the cadre and personnel system of trade unions, or how to straighten out the relationship between trade unions and the Party and the government, but focused more on the innovation of the system and mechanism. Compared with the second phase of reform, it put more emphasis on the leadership of the Party and the government. Compared with the international experience of self-coordination between workers and employers, it was the most effective way of protecting the rights of workers that the present Chinese trade unions could adopt, because there was neither a bottom-up social mobilization, nor a top-down administrative power. Therefore, it could only standardize the rights and obligations of both sides of the labor relationship by maximizing the use of administrative power, promoting labor legislation and strengthening law enforcement (Qiao, 2010).

## V. Socialism with Chinese Characteristics in the New Era (2012-): Strengthening the political consciousness, becoming more advanced, and better representing the people; while avoiding the tendency of bureaucratism, administerization, being aristocratic and entertainment

As the socialism with Chinese characteristics entered a new era, trade unions launched the reform for the fourth time. With the guiding principles of General Secretary Xi Jinping embodied in a series of important speeches about working class and the work of trade unions and at the CPC Central Committee Conferences on the Work of the Party's Mass Organizations, trade unions set their goal of strengthening their political consciousness, becoming more advanced, and better representing the people; while avoiding the tendency of bureaucratism, administerization, being aristocratic and entertainment, in order to better serve as the bridge between the Party and workers. Thus, the reform is partly a top-down political imperative.

China's trade unions had made progress and achievements in the previous three phases of reform. It is now essential to enhance mass participation. Due to the specific system, the major weakness of China's trade unions laid in enterprises and entities. It was hard to establish trade unions in enterprises and other entities, while it was difficult for workers to join. Even if there were trade unions in enterprises and other entities, it was difficult to effectively representing workers and safeguarding their rights and interests as well. Eventually, grassroots trade unions would be lack of vitality, and lack of recognition among workers. Thus, China's trade unions appeared to break away from workers to a certain extent (Qiao, 2017).

Some researchers explained this predicament of grassroots trade unions. First, in order to promote the establishment of trade unions in private enterprises, ACFTU initiated a campaign. To accomplish the task of the campaign within a limited time, the trade unions at all levels only focused on persuading enterprises to agree to establish trade unions, no matter how they were established. In some cases, even the nomination of the chairman of the trade union, the implementation of specific works of the trade union, and the use of trade union dues were dominated and approved only by the enterprises. This kind of top-down mode would inevitably blur the nature of trade unions of enterprises, and lead to the weak consciousness of trade union members. Second, trade unions of enterprises were highly dependent on enterprises, both economically and politically. The chairman of the trade union was usually the leader of the Party committee of the same level, while the business owner or his agent often served as the leader of the Party committee of the enterprise. Finally, the existing trade union system also had some restrictive factors. For instance, the legitimate rights and interests of cadres of the trade union of enterprise could not be effectively protected by the law or superior organizations. For another example, due to the constraints of existing laws, trade unions lacked necessary mechanism. They could only put forward requirements, opinions or suggestions to the enterprise to protect workers' rights (Qiao and Qian, 2010).

Therefore, how to stimulate the vitality of grassroots trade unions was the main point of the new round of trade union reform. In fact, *Opinions of the CPC*

*Central Committee on Strengthening and Improving the Work of the Party's Mass Organizations* released in 2015 clearly pointed out that "grassroots organizations are the basis of and the key to the work of the Party's mass organizations". However, the major problem was "the weak foundation of the Party's mass organizations, insufficient effective coverage and insufficient attraction and cohesion. In particular, their influence in organizations of non-public sector, social organizations and various emerging groups urgently needed to be enhanced."

So how to reform the grassroots trade unions? There had been three common ideas or attempts. The first was to adopt the direct election system of grassroots trade union cadres, that is, to let trade union members elect their own cadres. Although this practice appeared as early as the mid-1980s, and was adopted in the coastal areas where there were more labor conflicts, it had not been systematically developed or promoted. Moreover, the assumption of such a measure is that the way how trade union cadres are elected would determine their actions or whom they are responsible for. However, under the existing trade union system, especially in non-public enterprises, as long as the union cadres were part-time cadres, it would be difficult for them to really think and act out of the attachment to the enterprises.

Perhaps it was due to this predicament of trade union cadres of the enterprise, or the reference to foreign experience of trade unions, the second point of view appeared. That is, the lack of vitality of grassroots trade unions should be addressed by developing industrial trade unions. In particular, the advantages of industrial trade unions in setting industrial standards and collective consultation on wages should be given full play. However, in order to maintain the stability, although the system reform of industrial trade unions had been put on the agenda, there was no substantial changes.

The third point of view also aimed at the predicament of trade union cadres in enterprise. It proposed to change the existing management system of trade union cadres, that is, from the current dual leadership of the Party committee at the same level and the trade union at the higher level with the former as its core, to that with the latter as its core, so as to achieve the unity of appointing officials and task management. This point of view, at least at this stage, was not feasible. In fact, "*Opinions of the CPC Central Committee on Strengthening and Improving the Work of the Party's Mass Organizations*" released in 2015 reiterated that "the Party's mass organizations should be managed at different levels, with the Party committees at the same level as the main leader."

In a word, the above viewpoints tried to reform the existing organization system or personnel management system, but there were obstacles which made it hard to put into practice. However, it also showed that a new round of trade union reform must be carried out in a different approach. It should maximize the efficiency of the reform while remain the existing system almost the same, to stimulate grassroots trade unions. The reform during this period could be summarized as follows: grassroots trade unions got "downsized and unloaded", and the higher-level (local) trade unions tended to "take the role of lower-level (enterprise) trade unions", with the former as the main innovation point. This experience came from the Gucun Town Federation of Trade Unions in Baoshan District of Shanghai, and had been commended and vigorously promoted by ACFTU.

## 1. Grassroots Trade Unions Get "Downsized and Unloaded"

The characteristics of existing trade union management system, and the fact that grassroots trade union cadres were usually part-time cadres and the duties of trade unions were "general and comprehensive", which caused that grassroots trade union cadres, especially those in non-public enterprises, were dependent to the enterprise and "dare not", "could not" and "did not want to" do anything. It is necessary and urgent for the trade unions to solve this problem. Gucun Town Federation of Trade Unions in Baoshan District of Shanghai adopted measures to get grassroots trade unions "downsized and unloaded", that is, to define their main responsibilities clearly in accordance with the actual situation of the trade unions.

Specifically, Gucun Town Federation of Trade Unions stipulated four responsibilities of grassroots trade unions, and clarified the specific tasks under each responsibility (the assessment index, and the corresponding scores). First, lay a solid foundation at the grassroots level, including encourage employees to join the trade union (based on the payment of membership dues,15 points), timely handle membership cards and member service cards (10 points) and establish trade union audit organizations and women organizations (5 points). Second, coordinate labor relations, including implementing the workers' congress system (10 points), establishing a collective consultation mechanism (10 points) and timely coordinating labor disputes (5 points). Third, sincerely serve the workers, including organizing activities to develop staff skills and enrich workers' amateur cultural life (10 points), organizing employees in need to participate in activities of the higher-level trade unions (5 points), organizing talented employees to join the cultural and sports association of the town federation of trade unions (5 points) and supporting workers in difficulties, especially those who are trade union members (5 points). Fourth, communicate and report, including timely communicating with the higher-level trade union when met with difficulties and resistance (8 points), becoming the first insider, the first speaker, the first mediator ("three first") when mass labor conflicts emerged (8 points) and timely asking the superior trade union for help when mass labor conflicts may occur (4 points).

The duties of grassroots trade unions had been specified, thus changing the traditional duties that were "general at both high and low levels". It not only reduced the burden of grassroots trade union cadres, but also made them easy to fulfill their duties. This was because the above specific duties would not get them into the plight of standing on the opposite side of the administration of the enterprise. In the contrary, some duties were even welcomed by the enterprise. In this way, at least the problem that non-public enterprise union cadres "dare not" and "could not" do anything could be solved by reducing the number of duties and the difficulty of fulfill their responsibilities. Regarding the problem that they "did not want to" do anything, Gucun Federation of Trade Unions adopted a series of methods to assess the performance of non-public enterprise trade unions in terms of the four main responsibilities. On this basis, it also established the job allowance system for part-time trade union cadres in non-public enterprise trade unions. The job allowance would be based on the scores of the above assessment index, and numbers of members of the trade union. In this way, it could stimulate enterprise trade union cadres.

In short, Gucun Town Federation of Trade Unions solve the problem that enterprise trade unions "dare not" "could not" and "did not want to" do anything to a great extent by getting them "downsized and unloaded" through relevant institutional arrangements. This helped stimulate the vitality of grassroots trade unions.

## 2. Higher-level Trade Unions Take the Role of Lower-level Trade Unions

As lower-level trade unions had got "downsized and unloaded", high-level trade unions must assume the responsibilities of the lower-level trade unions, especially safeguarding the rights and interests of workers, and also needed to strive for more social resources for lower-level trade unions to serve their members as much as possible. This was called "higher-level trade unions taking the role of lower-level trade unions". As a matter of fact, when grassroots trade unions found it difficult to perform their duty of safeguarding certain rights and interests of workers, local trade unions should "take the role of them". This mode appeared decades ago, which was promoted by ACFTU. For example, *Decision of ACFTU on Strengthening the Coordination of Labor Relations, Effectively Safeguarding the Legitimate Rights and Interests of Workers and Promoting the Construction of a Harmonious Socialist Society* approved in 2005 stated that "it should explore and promote the practice of higher-level trade unions taking the role of lower-level trade unions in safeguarding rights and interests that were difficult for them to undertake at the moment". In *Several Opinions of ACFTU on Further Strengthening Labor Dispute Mediation* issued in 2007, it also advocated that higher-level trade unions should take the role of lower-level trade unions in safeguarding certain rights and interests. Also, in *Opinions of ACFTU on Strengthening the Construction of Lower-Level Trade Unions in a New Situation* issued in 2014, it reiterated that when lower-level trade unions could not fulfill their duty of safeguarding the rights and interests of workers, higher-level trade unions should enhance their guidance and help them, or take the role of them.

However, compared with the past definition of "higher-level trade unions taking the role of lower-level trade unions" which only emphasized on the duty of safeguarding the rights and interests of workers, the definition in this paper was general. It not only focused on the duty of safeguarding that lower-level trade unions could not fulfill, but also included a variety of services. These services were aimed at the various requirements of workers that the lower-level trade unions could not meet due to their limited resources or poor abilities. These services include supporting workers in difficulties, mutual insurance for serious diseases, employee training and re-employment, which required the higher-level trade unions to find, coordinate, integrate and allocate resources. In other words, in the past, higher-level trade unions often "took the role of lower-level trade unions" to perform duty of safeguarding the interests and rights of workers, but Gucun Town Federation of Trade Unions innovated and developed their work, which was extended to a variety of services.

Take supporting workers in difficulties as an example. As most enterprises and public institutions did not have many workers, it was difficult to meet the needs of supporting workers in difficulties only with the funds of grassroots trade unions, so Gucun Town Federation of Trade Unions solved this problem by establishing a "mutual assistance" system, requiring workers to help those in need. Specifically, on the one hand, Gucun Town Federation of Trade Unions adopted the *Trial Measures for the Establishment of Gucun Town Mutual Assistance Fund for Workers in Need*. According to it, workers participated in the "One-Day Donation" campaign once a year, and when meeting with emergencies, they would donate again to help those in need. In addition, the Federation established funds for workers in need in the town trade union and grassroots trade unions by finding resources from the government and the society, thus establishing town-level and grassroots-level union supporting funds. On the other hand, Gucun Town Federation of Trade Unions actively encouraged workers to join the mutual assistance insurance plan organized by Shanghai Federation of Trade Unions. In 2014, there were more than 7,000 on-duty and retired workers to join such plans, and more than 3,700 patients had their medical fees reimbursed, with the amount of about 3 million yuan.

Take the promotion of staff quality as an example. This was the responsibility of trade unions. Although enterprises would also train their employees in order to develop, usually only large and medium enterprises would do so. For those who worked in small and micro enterprises, especially those in unstable industries, they rarely got trained to improve technical skills. So it is necessary for lower-level trade unions to coordinate in this area. On the one hand, under the guidelines of "preferring first-line workers", Gucun Town Federation of Trade Unions promoted the worker quality project with the integration of five factors – training, practice, competition, promotion and selection. On the other hand, in the adherence to the principle of going to the grassroots and going to the first line, the Federation held the "May 1 Labor Award" appraisal annually. In order to advance these work steadily, the Federation established a joint conference system for the professional development of workers. The members were  the Federation, related governmental departments, related colleges and universities, private vocational training institutions and other entities. The joint conference formulated the annual plan to promote the career development of workers in Gucun Town according to the need of integrating the career development of workers, including professional ethics, culture, skills, legal protection and talents. Furthermore, according to the respective functions of each member entity, the Federation defined the division of labor responsibilities, such as training, competition, resources, venues and policy implementation, so as to promote the career development of workers.

## VI. Conclusion

Throughout the reform in more than 40 years, China's trade union reform or system changes show the following trends and characteristics. First of all, in terms of the role of trade unions, it has become more and more clear that they were representatives of workers and defenders of their rights and interests. Secondly, in terms of responsibilities of China's trade unions, it has gradually transformed from "a production-centered mode with the integration of production, life and education" to the mode of four responsibilities, which stressed safeguarding the rights and interests of workers, supplemented by construction, education and participation. As the differentiate of the structure and demands of workers, the unions began to focus on all kinds of social services for workers and pointed out that it was as important as safeguarding workers' rights and interests. Thirdly, in terms of performing duties, China's trade unions drew lessons from international experience, put more emphasis on returning to and developing domestic socialized safeguarding and service mode dominated by the Party and the government. Finally, in terms of defining the responsibilities, there was gradually a differentiation  between local trade unions and grassroots trade unions. Grassroots trade unions tended to get "downsized and unloaded", and launched incentives to solve the existing problem that grassroots trade unions "dare not", "could not" and "did not want to" do anything, thus to stimulate them. "Local trade unions took the role of lower-level trade unions" by undertaking some of their duties. By pooling resources, local trade unions performed the duties of safeguarding and service that were difficult for lower-level trade unions to fulfill. To a certain extent, it can be said that the division of duties and the cooperation of China's trade unions have been most effective, with the existing organization system and personnel management system remained.

In short, on the one hand, China's trade unions need to adapt to the economic reform and the complex changes in labor relations caused by economic globalization. On the other hand, they must adapt to the requirements of the existing system. As a result, China's trade unions must strive to integrate the traditional and modern, international and local, in-system and out-of-system factors, so as to explore a unique way of their own. However, in the process of the reform of China's trade unions, there would be full of hardships and contradictions. Thus, the reform needs continuous exploration and innovation, and only be carried out in a step-by-step way.

## References

[1] Ching Kwan Lee. From organized dependence to disorganized despotism: Changing labor regimes in Chinese factories[J]. The China Quarterly, 1999(157): 44-71.

[2] The Editorial Team. Survey data on the status of Chinese workers (1978-2018)[M]. Beijing: China Workers Publishing House, 2018.

[3] Chen Ji. Trade Unions in Reform and Reform of Trade Unions[M]. Beijing: China Workers Publishing House, 1999.

[4] Qiao Jian. Theoretical Reflections on Trade Union Reform and Innovation[J]. Contemporary World and Socialism, 2010(2): 151-155.

[5] Qiao Jian. Trade Union Reform: "Quality and Efficiency" of the Path of Socialist Trade Union with Chinese Characteristics[J]. Journal of China University of Labor Relations, 2017(2): 72-83.

[6] Qiao Jian, Qian Junyue. Reflections on the Establishment of Trade Union in Private Enterprises[J] Human Resource Development of China, 2010(10): 83-87.

[7] Legal Affairs Office of ACFTU. Analysis and Suggestions on Labor Dispute Mediation since the 15th Congress of ACFTU[J]. Chinese Workers' Movement, 2013(11): 39-41.

[8] News Center of ACFTU. Overview of Achievements on Trade Unions' Coordination of Labor Relations through Legal Thinking and Approaches in Recent Years[J]. Staff and Workers Education of China, 2015(1).

[9] Wu Jianping. The Process, Condition and Limitation of Local Trade Unions' "Borrowing Power"[J]. Sociological Studies, 2017(2): 103-127.

# From "State-led" to Multiple Drivers: New Trends and the Typology of the Collective Consultation in China[*]

*Wen Xiaoyi*[**]

**Abstract:** Collective consultation in China is generally considered to be state-led, however, through field studies in the Pearl River Delta, Yangtze River Delta, and Northeast China, it is found in this paper that there are different types of collective consultation, and it is entering an era with multiple drivers due to changes of the supply and demand of labor market, the enhanced bargaining position of workers, and the adjustment of the roles of local governments and employers. From the perspective of procedural rules and substantive rules, collective consultation is divided into four types: state-led, worker-led, employer-led, and trade union-led. It compared these four types from the perspective of benefits for the workers and the stability of the labor-capital management order. The formation mechanisms and practical effects of new types of collective consultation are also discussed in this paper. It is believed that the types of collective consultation are determined by the forms of worker organization. The possible future directions of collective consultation and the constraints it faces are also discussed in the last part of this paper.

**Keywords**: collective consultation; labor union; typology; procedural rules; substantive rules

## I. Origin of the Issue

The collective consultation system, as the core system of labor relations in market economy, is not only an important means to protect and adjust workers' wages and benefits, but also the main method for the state to regulate and stabilize

[*] This paper was published in *Sociological Studies*, Issue. 4, 2016.

[**] Wen Xiaoyi, professor, Dean of the School of Labor Relations and Human Resources of the China University of Labor Relations. Email: wenxiaoyi008@sina.com.

labor relations. As China became the largest exporter of the world's production, and the high level of labor relations risks, all parties have high expectations for the collective consultation system. They hope that this system, which is already very mature in developed economies, will also play an important role in China. However, it seems that this expectation is far from being fulfilled. Existing studies show that the collective consultation system, on the one hand, does not have much practical impact on workers' wages and labor conditions (Taylor and Li, 2007; Chang, 2009); on the other hand, the process of collective consultation fails to attract the independent forces from workers or employers, it merely facilitates the implementation and monitoring of existing legal regulations (Cheng, 2004). Scholars generally characterized the current collective consultation as a "state-led" model, in which neither managers nor trade unions are completely free to represent the interests of employers and workers – they are subject to the direct instructions of the state. The wages and labor conditions are decided based on the regulations of the local government (Wu, 2012).

However, there are challenges caused by the changes in reality. In recent years, due to the changes of supply and demand in the labor market various types of collective consultation are emerging. The most typical type is the "collective consultation driven by work stoppage" occurring in many places. In order to address the work stoppage, local governments encourage workers to elect representatives, propose bargaining terms and negotiate with employers on wage increases and improvements in labor conditions, and sign collective agreements to return to work (Ren and Xu, 2008; Xu and Chen, 2011). It seems that this type of collective consultation in which workers are the initiators cannot be regarded as the "state-led" model. Moreover, the industry-based collective consultation on wages in the Yangtze River Delta (Xu, 2008) and the collective consultation based on direct elections in trade unions in the Pearl River Delta (Yang and Li, 2012) have also diversified the types of collective consultation in China. Obviously, since there are few cases of specific interactive negotiations between employers and employees, the major issue in the existing collective consultation studies is "why there aren't". With the emergence of different types of collective consultation, the obvious interactions between employers and employees, and collective agreements reached with substantive outcomes, it needs to change the perspective of study. Therefore, this paper attempts to construct a theoretical typology of collective consultation based on field studies, compare the formation mechanisms and practical effects of various types of collective consultation, and on this basis, analyze the future development trend of collective consultation in order to provide references for labor relations governance.

## II. Typology of Collective Consultation: A Theoretical Framework

Based on the classical "input-output" theory, it is believed that employees and employers are interdependent but with different interests, and the existence of conflicts in industrial relations is inevitable. Therefore, a mechanism that can reconcile the contradictions is needed. According to this mechanism, the inputs are differences and conflicts of interest, while the outputs are rules that can constrain the behavior of all the parties. Besides, the rules can also link competing interest groups together (Albert, 1967; Flanders, 1968). Employees and employers can reach consensus through a compromise mechanism and then establish and maintain a system that includes procedures and systems, so that differences in their interests can be resolved and their behaviors can be regulated. Collective consultation is the primary manifestation of the compromise mechanism, and the key to whether rules can be formed (Salamon, 1992). From the perspective of the systems theory, if the rules are set only by employees and employers, the organizational function of the third party that reconciles the divergence of interests of employees and employers will be ignored. Therefore, the formulation of rules should be regarded as the result of the actions and interactions of employees and employees' organizations, employers and employers' organizations, and the government. Also, rules should be interpreted as a "web of rules" that include the rule-making process, substantive rules, and procedural rules. Substantive rules are the most important economic outcomes of collective consultation, including substantive outputs such as wages and benefits, and labor conditions, while procedural rules refer to the procedures for establishing and managing rules, it is the function of collective consultation to manage divergences and regulate the behavior of each party.

On this basis, substantive rules and procedural rules are selected as the dimensions for dividing the type of collective consultation in this paper. Substantive and procedural rules are internally consistent, but also relatively independent. On the one hand, procedural rules are the conditions, procedures and steps for the formation of substantive rules, and the means and methods for the realization of the materialized outcomes of collective consultation, presenting an instrumental value. On the other hand, due to the changes of power between employees and employers, the substantive rules are complicated and full of uncertainties. The final results of collective consultation can be either good or bad. It cannot be predicted in advance. However, procedural rules are fixed. They are not bound with a specific substance. The procedural steps of collective consultation and the means of regulation are highly technical and unnegotiable, which makes the procedural rules relatively independent from the substantive rules (Ji, 1999). The uncertainty of substantive rules largely comes from the complexity of the environment of the labor relations system, while procedural rules seek to be independent from the changes of the environment, making procedural activities relatively closed and isolated, so that the roles and functions of procedural participants can be simple and clear, thus the functional autonomy and independence of procedural rules can be achieved (Wan, 2003).

The ultimate function of both substantive rules and procedural rules is to resolve conflicts of interest, settle disputes between employees and employers. But their mechanisms are not the same. Substantive rules reconcile the conflicting interests through "satisfactory" results, while procedural rules settle disputes between employees and employers through the "correct" process. Even if the outcome of negotiations does not necessarily satisfy all the parties, employees and employers will tend to accept it, if the procedure itself is neutral, equal and open (Chen, 1997). That's why the procedural rule of "negotiation and consultation" has become the core element of the labor relations system (Dunlop, 1958). Thus, based on these two dimensions, collective consultation can be divided into four types: state-led collective consultation, worker-led collective consultation, employer-led collective consultation, and trade union-led collective consultation (see Figure 1).

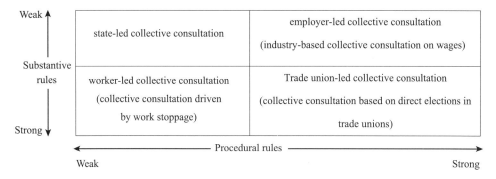

**Figure 1    Four types of collective consultation**

## III. Case Study and Comparative Analysis

The study is based on the field studies in Northeast China, Yangtze River Delta and Pearl River Delta during 2010-2015. A total of nine collective consultation cases are involved in this study. The materials collected consist of three main parts: first, interviews with staff of trade unions, worker representatives, employer representatives and major participants in various types of collective consultation; second, interviews with staff from regional trade unions and relevant government agencies; third, documents and relevant media reports about these types of collective consultation. Four typical cases are selected for comparative analysis.

## 1. Four Cases of Collective Consultation

### 1.1 State-led case: collective consultation in City S

City S is a provincial capital city in Northeast China. The municipal party committee and the municipal government hold a citywide meeting on the collective contract once a year. All the government departments are required to attend, and assigned tasks about the collective contract. In 2012, the municipal government set a series of assessment indicators including the coverage rate, the filing rate, the qualification rate and the compliance rate of collective contract, which were included in the assessment of the government at district and county level. It was stated clearly that the government at district and county level was the main body responsible for promoting collective contract work. Districts and counties with unsatisfactory collective contract progress would be regarded as unqualified in the assessment. As the promotion of the subordinate government officials is related to the assessment, officials at all levels pay attention to the collective consultation tasks and try their best to achieve the targets. Governments at all levels also established leading groups for collective consultations on wages. The deputy secretary would usually be in charge of it, with the participation of departments of industry and commerce, taxation, finance, human resources and social welfare, trade unions and others to collaborate in comprehensively advance collective consultation on wages within the district.

For local governments, there are many administrative means to pressure enterprises to sign collective contracts. When enterprises applied for registration and annual inspection, the industry and commerce department and other departments would check whether they have established a trade union and a collective consultation system on wages. For enterprises that have not established a collective consultation system and did not provide a collective contract, the human resources and social security department would not issue the wage handbook, and the taxation department would not implement a pre-tax deduction policy for employees' take-home pay. It means that the governmental departments have cooperated with each other to establish a set of collective contract supervision mechanism: enterprises that did not sign collective contracts would not be able to operate normally. Apart from that, the collective contract system has also become an important criterion of the honorary title for enterprises. If the system was not established, the enterprises and the persons in charge could not be awarded honorary titles at the municipal level or above, nor become candidates for the National People's Congress or the Chinese People's Political Consultative Conference (CPPCC). The collective consultation in City S has been promoted on a wide scale, with the number of enterprises that have signed collective contracts increasing greatly. It was claimed that "the collective contract system was established in basically all kinds of enterprises with trade unions, and the full coverage of collective contract system was basically achieved". Therefore, the collective consultation work in City S was chosen as a national exemplary case.

*1.2 Worker-led case: collective consultation after the work stoppage at Plant H*

In April 2015, there was a collective work stoppage in Plant H in Shenzhen. In March of that year, the minimum wage standard of Shenzhen was adjusted. Then the executives of the enterprise adjusted its wage structure by canceling employees' full attendance award, seniority award and job allowance, as well as incorporating them into the basic wage to meet the minimum wage standard. It triggered a work stoppage which involved nearly 1,000 workers. The district trade union and the labor department intervened. They let workers to elect 10 representatives in proportion to the number of workers in the workshop. With the support of the trade union, these worker representatives negotiated with the enterprise. The negotiation lasted until late at night, but no agreement was made. Both sides agreed to continue the negotiation the next day. However, the worker representatives did not show up the next day. Instead, they drafted a written opinion and asked the Chairman of the trade union to hand it to the negotiator of the enterprise. The executives of the enterprise also provided a written reply based on the workers' opinions, only agreeing to increase the performance bonus and part of the subsidies, and refusing to accept all the requirements proposed by the workers. The chairman of the trade union passed on the feedback to the workers, and listened to their opinions. On the morning of the third day, only a small percentage of workers returned to work. The chairman of the trade union said that most of the workers were dissatisfied with the enterprise's reply and demanded for more wage increases. The employer also expressed its dissatisfaction with the worker stoppage for several days, and threatened to terminate their labor contracts. This made the workers who had returned to work stopping working again.

In order to avoid further deterioration of the situation, the chairman of the district trade union led a team to the workers' dormitory to persuade workers to return to work. Then workers returned to the plant one after another. And the chairman of the trade union and the worker representatives continued to negotiate with the enterprise. However, the negotiation took a very long time, and workers started to worry that some worker representatives may have been bribed. Some of the workers began to gather, and the negotiation was once in a stalemate. Thanks to the efforts of all parties, the situation was finally brought under control. In the meantime, the district trade union continued to communicate with the executives of the enterprise, and put pressure on them, in order to urge the enterprise to try to meet the workers' requirements. In the evening of the same day, the workers and the employers finally reached an agreement, and the workers' night shift was resumed. The main contents of the agreement were as follows: the workers' basic wages rose by 716 yuan; the wages should be adjusted annually according to the relevant laws and regulations, the employees' work performance and the operation of the enterprise; the enterprise set a unified performance award which integrated the full attendance award, seniority award, job allowance, and so on; the enterprise agreed to provide employees holiday subsidies and high temperature allowance; the enterprise promised to improve the working environment as soon as possible; the enterprise promised not to revenge the workers who have participated in the work stoppage.

*1.3 Employer-led case: collective consultation on wages in the wool sweater industry in Town W*

There are hundreds of wool sweater enterprises in Town W which is in Zhejiang Province. Due to the serious shortage of workers, the enterprises were competing with each other to attract workers through high wages, and the competition was becoming increasingly fierce. In order to end the vicious competition, employers started to try to establish a self-regulatory mechanism. In 2002, Town W established a wool sweater industry association, with its immediate task was to establish a unified labor cost standard in the region. However, the industry self-regulatory mechanism was not successful, because the member companies were still rise the wage. Meanwhile, labor conflicts began to erupt due to the inability to meet the wage commitments. In order to maintain social stability, the local government assigned the town trade union to solve the problem. The union suggested the trade association and the worker representatives to negotiate collectively about the wage standard; the consensus about the wage standard reached would be implemented under the supervision of the government and the trade union. This proposal was accepted by the government and the association. Then based on the survey and research in different enterprises, the trade union decomposed the wool sweater production into several types of work and several processes, and determined the general labor cost standard together with the industry association. At the same time, the town trade union initiated the selection of worker representatives, which were chosen among the workers of several large member enterprises of the industry association, and reviewed by the town trade union.

The first "Earnest Talks about the Wage of Workers in the Wool Sweater Industry" was held in Town W on June 13th 2003. 8 enterprise owners, 13 worker representatives and several officials from the municipal labor department and the town trade union participated the meeting. The production of wool sweater involved 5 types of work and 59 processes, and the price of it was to be determined by the negotiators. For workers, their wages were calculated based on the daily income. If the total daily income for a certain type of work was 60 yuan, and the production quota was 6 pieces for 8 hours of work, the minimum labor cost for a piece of product should be 10 yuan. In contrast, enterprises calculated the labor cost based on many factors such as the size of the enterprise, the business environment, and the impact of exchange rates. In the end, the industry association and the town trade union signed the *Collective Consultation Agreement on Wage (Labor Cost) of Workers in the Wool Sweater Industry in the Second Half of 2003,* and publicized it in the whole town. With the support of the industry association, the first industrial trade union for non-public enterprises was established in Town W since the founding of the People's Republic of China. The industrial trade union committee consisted of nine people, with the vice chairman of the town trade union serving as chairman. The remaining eight people were front-line workers selected from the worker representatives who have participated in the wage negotiations. Since then, collective wage negotiations between the industry association and the industrial trade union have been held once a year. During 2003-2014, there were a total of twelve rounds of collective consultation in the wool sweater industry; and wages of workers have been increased more or less.

### 1.4 Trade union-led case: collective wage consultation in Company Y

Company Y is a wholly-owned subsidiary of a well-known Japanese company. Its main business is producing auto parts and computer components. It has about 600 employees. There were many work stoppages in this company. In 2012, leaders of the trade union of Company Y were re-elected. With the support of the district trade union,  new union members were elected in accordance with democratic procedures in the employee representatives conference. In 2013, the trade union of the company started to carry out collective consultations, formulate the method of electing employee representatives for collective negotiation on wages. There were 40 employee representatives elected. Then 7 representatives for the consultation were also elected. Subsequently, employees and employers started a two-month collective consultation, with a total of five rounds of meeting (each meeting lasts about four hours).

In the first round of meeting, employee representatives proposed a salary adjustment plan with clear objectives and complete distribution methods. In the second round of meeting, at the request of the employer, employee representatives released a survey of the monthly household expenses of 100 ordinary employees, which showed that the average monthly household expenses of an ordinary employee were 3,795 yuan. After the tough negotiation, two sides finally agreed on an approximate range of wage increase, which marked a breakthrough of the stage. In the third round of meeting, employees first proposed a wage increase plan that was 5% higher than that of employer's  proposal. The negotiating team of the employer could not accept it. After the break, the negotiating team of the employer proposed two adjusted plans. But there was still a large gap between the plan of employees and the plans proposed by the employer. So the two sides didn't reach an agreement. In the fourth round of meeting, the district trade union sent its staff to participate. But the two sides still insisted on their respective proposals, and the meeting came to a deadlock. At this point, the district trade union reiterated the purpose and significance of collective consultation on wages, and suggested that the two sides should agree on the balance point and further negotiate on the percentage of increase later. With the efforts of all parties, the tension in the negotiation was eased. Then the employer again adjusted the wage increase plan by adding a "special bonus" as an incentive. After that, employees asked for an adjournment to inform all employees and listen to their opinions. In the fifth round of meeting, in which the district trade union also participated, employees responded to the employer's proposal; and the two sides agreed on the percentage of wage increase, but there were still differences in the calculation of special bonuses. After the adjournment, the district trade union communicated with employees and the employer respectively, encouraging both sides to concede some of their demands. After the coordination of the trade union, each side took a step back and finally reached an agreement on the calculation of the bonus; and the two sides signed a collective agreement. Since then, the company's trade union implements collective consultation with the employer every year; and the wages of employees have been increased substantially.

## 2. Comparative Analysis of the Cases

The collective consultation in City S is a typical state-led case. For this type of collective consultation, there are usually "three many and three few" in the collective contracts eventually signed: there are many principle clauses and few specific provisions; many clauses which are copying of legal provisions and few clauses which are based on the actual situation of the enterprises; many general descriptions and few concrete actions (Cheng, 2004). This type of collective consultation rarely results in improved benefits for workers, nor does it restrain the behaviors of employees and employers through collective agreements. Although the number and the coverage rate of collective contracts are increasing, the number of conflicts between employees and employers remain high. During the field research, there was a major labor dispute in an enterprise in City S. It occurred exactly one month after the signing of the collective contract. In the collective contract, it was stipulated that the wage per working hour of front-line workers was 4.8 yuan. According to this, even if they work 12 hours a day, plus 4 hours' overtime, the total income of a day was 76.8 yuan. However, it was troubled by the shortage of workers, so that the actual wage of front-line workers was at least 150 yuan a day, which almost doubled the wage standard indicated in the collective contract.

The worker-led collective consultation represented by the case of Plant H has demonstrated strong substantive rules and weak procedural rules. The work stoppage in this case caused a real impact on both enterprise production and social stability. The impact was increasing as the work stoppage continued. Therefore, the enterprise must make greater concessions and provide substantive interests to address it as soon as possible. The purpose of the work stoppage was not consultation, but the consultation is conducted to solve the work stoppage issue. It led to an incentive mechanism for work stoppage, which made it impossible for collective consultation to be a binding system for conflict resolution, but caused greater instability due to the substantive rules. Also, it is the weak procedural rules that urge enterprises to identify and dismiss active participants after the incident is resolved (Leung, 2015). Even so, the work stoppage has created an enduring memory among workers, and also strengthened their confidence to raise demands through it, which foreshadow a new round of unrest. Just eight months later, another work stoppage occurred at Plant H.

Compared with the worker-led collective consultation, employer-led collective consultation shows the exact opposite characteristics. This is firstly reflected in the way that workers' collective action is affected. In the case of Town W, according to the information provided by the local labor department, after the collective consultation on wages in 2003, the number of petitions dropped to 17 for that year, involving a total of 120 people; in 2004, it further dropped to 3, involving 3 people; in 2005, there was only 1 petition, involving 3 people; and from 2006, there was no petition at all. Since 2003, the town's wool sweater industry association has implemented collective consultations with the industry trade union every year, which has been institutionalized and normalized. However, the substantive rules of collective consultation have not brought about any significant increase of benefits for workers. The collective consultation has only achieved slight wage increases; and later it became even lower than the local minimum wage increase. The main reason is that the labor relations conflicts faced by the industrial clusters represented by Town W are mainly due to the problem of "wage arrears" caused by vicious competition among employers. The workers asked employers to fulfill their wage promises, but the employers were unable to do so, which led to conflicts. Therefore, the procedural rules arising from collective consultation in the industry were mainly to effectively regulate the behavior of individual employers. Under the constraints of the agreement, there were no more "false promises" or wage arrears. On the basis of the industrial agreement on labor cost, each enterprise could set its own labor cost according to its actual situation. The result of industrial collective consultation was that it restored the mechanism of the labor market to determine the wages of workers of Town W by restraining the behavior of employers. In fact, in the industrial collective consultation, the worker representatives' demands were not based on the income of the positions in their enterprises, but on the daily income in their regions.

And this demand itself was a signal of the regional market wage.

The collective consultation on wages of Company Y is the closest to the prototype of collective consultation in market economy conditions. Because the trade union of the company conducted democratic elections and brought together the collective power of workers, the union-led collective consultation has generated substantial economic outcomes. In the case of Company Y, the annual wage increase of all employees after the collective consultation was more than 10%. In specific consultations, the trade union would propose a specific amount of wage increase instead of a proportional one. The final outcome would often that all employees could receive a specific amount of pay raise, which in practice would lead to a more substantial wage growth for frontline workers. Institutional wage increases not only satisfy workers, but also make trade unions an institutional mean to express workers' interests. So that, in the process of interaction between trade unions and workers, risks are effectively controlled and mitigated. More importantly, with its stronger presence, companies will come to consult the trade union on all systems and policies that involve workers' real interests, so that the trade union will have the power and ability to influence the company system.

The union-led collective consultation is characterized by the game between different organizations. In the case of Company Y, the trade union elected representatives for the consultation among workers, attracting a wide attention of workers. The high level of attention and extensive involvement of workers could strengthen the union's bargaining power and put a pressure during the negotiation process. The negotiation process was tough. When the employer put pressure on workers based on its management authority, the workers' representatives would also have their strategies: "I can't make a decision. I'll go back and ask everyone's opinion" was often their response. In one round of consultation, the company was so determined not to give in that the trade union had no choice but to post a notice on the bulletin board informing all workers that a "mobilization meeting for collective consultation" would be held on a certain working day. This "threatening" notice succeeded in forcing the company to make concessions. In this case, there would be many rounds of collective consultation before the collective contract is finally signed. It is the game of both sides in the rulemaking process and the full discussion it brings that leads to longer-term compliance of the rules (Clegg, 1970).

## IV. Workers' Organizational Patterns and the Practical Effects of New Types of Collective Consultation

From state-led to multiple drivers, the macro impetus for the transition of collective consultation comes from the changes in the labor market. Since 2004, the increasing difficulty in recruiting workers and the phenomenon of labor shortage have indicated the reversal of supply and demand in the labor market, which undermined the original structure of labor relations. Workers started to frequently express their demands for "increased benefits" through collective actions, which required local governments to maintain stability, grassroots trade unions to play a representative role, and made it more likely for employers to suffer from work stoppage losses. In the face of workers' increasingly radical activism, local governments, trade unions and employers are also making systematic changes. They are establishing rules and norms through the rule-based function of collective consultation to encourage workers' participation. On the one hand, they all have the willingness and ability to promote the collective consultation as an institutional arrangement that meets their interests and facilitate the formation of a collective consultation pattern of multiple drivers; on the other hand, the key to the function of the collective consultation lies in the collective organization of workers. Through the power of various parties, different forms of worker organizations have been formed in different regions. On this basis, specific types of collective consultation and the corresponding characteristics of rules have been established (see Table 1).

**Table 1    Structural conditions under different types of collective consultation**

| Type of collective consultation | Regions | Demands of Workers | Demands of Employers | Role of the Government | Worker organization |
|---|---|---|---|---|---|
| State-led | Nationwide | — | — | Intervention of public power | Local government or trade unions of higher level |
| Worker-led | Seaside area | Wage rises, improve working conditions | Resume production ASAP | Limited participation | Worker representatives |
| Employer-led | Yangtze River Delta | Prevent wage arrears | Unify wage standards | Construct a platform for the consultation | Industrial trade unions |
| Trade union-led | Pearl River Delta | Institutional increases in wages | Stabilize the relation between enterprises and workers | Encourage the institutional exploration | Trade unions in the enterprises (by direct election) |

## 1. Election of Worker Representatives and Worker-led Collective Consultation

Unlike other types of collective consultation, worker-led collective consultation is one in which workers force enterprises to negotiate by means of collective action. For this type of collective consultation, there was usually an accumulation of risks between employees and employers long before in the enterprise. Workers are dissatisfied with wages, labor conditions, and management systems. Once a work stoppage occurs, workers are likely to demand for a higher rise in wage, and various things, which would have the characteristics of compensation. In the case of Plant H, workers demanded for 12 things, such as the high temperature allowance, improving working environment, and vehicles for commuting. One of their demands was a 1,000-yuan increase of basic wage, nearly 50% more than the existing wage. Facing these demands, employers were angry and anxious. They felt angry because they believed that the demands of workers were unrealistic, and their management authority was challenged. They felt anxious because they wanted to resume the production as soon as possible. The longer the work stoppage lasted, the greater the loss would be. This also explains why there are "strong substantive rules and weak procedural rules" for worker-led collective consultation. In order to solve the problem, the enterprise must come up with a plan with high compensation to meet the demands of workers. In fact, this kind of angry attitude would stimulate new risks between employees and employers.

The withdrawal of local governments from direct intervention in work stoppage is a structural condition for the emergence of worker-led collective consultation. Most local governments in coastal areas are troubled by labor conflicts. On the one hand, unstable labor relations have a significant impact on the local economic and social environment; on the other hand, direct intervention in labor conflicts always puts the local governments in the front line, thus taking on many responsibilities that they should not be borne. Under such pressure, some local governments have started to reassess their roles in the process of dealing with labor relations matters, reduce direct intervention and encourage negotiations between employees and employers.

Driven by new model of labor relations management, new approaches are emerging in many regions. Employers respond directly to workers on matters of the plants. They solve problems through negotiating with each other about the demands of workers. In this process, the local government doesn't intervene directly, but creates spaces for collective consultation. Of course, the withdrawal of the local government does not mean that collective consultation can be formed naturally. The biggest obstacle is that workers involved in the work stoppage often appears to be unorganized. When employers are ready to negotiate, they do not know who could represent the workers. Instead of one "group of workers", employers are facing many "groups of workers", while nobody is willing to represent the whole group, summarize and express the demands of all workers. In the absence of a formal representative organization, workers are afraid to stick their neck out. That's when the trade union of higher-level or human resource and social security department of the government need to help workers elect their representatives.

In the election process, the first priority is to win the trust of workers. The trade union and government should be patient with workers, and more importantly, convince them that they are on the same side. In the case of Plant H, when the chairman of the district trade union, who was responsible for handling the work stoppage at Plant H, appeared in the plant, he was accused by workers of "colluding with the employer". He shouted to workers: "We are from the trade union. We are not officials. We are here to represent you. We are 100% on your side!" This kind of public announcement often has an immediate effect. After gaining the trust of workers, they should begin to mobilize workers to elect representatives to collect and summarize the main demands of workers. The biggest challenge in the election of worker representatives is the qualification of the worker representatives themselves. Workers are often not familiar with the elected representatives. And the election process is often full of arbitrariness – even some "mischievous" workers become representatives. As a result, there might be many rounds of election; the number of representatives would increase; and even the outcomes of the negotiation that were not easily reached might be repeatedly rejected by the workers, delaying the generation of a collective agreement. Last but not least, the trade union and government act as a "third party" in process of negotiating, trying to encourage the two parties of the negotiation to reach an agreement. It is worth noting that in order to reach a collective agreement as soon as possible, they not only need to put pressure on the employers, but also need to put pressure on the workers.

Although substantive benefits can usually be obtained in worker-led collective consultation, the election of worker representatives under the leadership of the trade union and government is a temporary measure which is unstable and unsystematic. So that it is the key reason for the weak procedural rules in the workers' collective consultation. The fact that the representatives can't represent every worker, and are not familiar with each other often result in the protest of workers or the demand of replacing representatives. This makes the negotiation process full of uncertainties. It is worse that the group of the representatives would be no longer exist when the negotiation ends. Driven by high turnover rate, workers will once again be unorganized. In this situation, there is still no normal channel for dealing with this kind of risks; workers still lack representative organizations. As a result, the same issue may repeatedly trigger work stoppages in the same enterprise.

## 2. Industrial Trade Union and Employer-led Collective Consultation

The emergence of employer-led collective consultation stems from the fierce competition in recruiting workers among labor-intensive enterprises in the industrial cluster areas in the Yangtze River Delta. In these regions with highly homogeneous production, affected by changes in the labor market, employers promised high wages in order to recruit workers, resulting in frequent job hopping. On the one hand, employers would delay paying wages or withhold the deposits to prevent the resignation of workers. Many enterprises pay wages once every six months, and do not pay workers if they leave. On the other hand, promises of high wages are often not kept. So that there are an increasing number of work stoppages and collective petitions that workers require the employers to keep their promises on wages.

It doesn't take too long for the employers to realize that coordination and regulation of recruiting practices are needed. Thus, they often ask the regional trade associations to actively intervene to address uncontrolled competition among employers over labor costs. However, the establishment of industrial self-regulatory mechanisms does not have the expected outcomes. In the case of Town W, 113 employers set up a wool sweater industry association, and unified the standard of labor cost to prevent the increase of wages. However, although all member enterprises of the association want others to follow the standard, they themselves are still adjusting wages depending on the actual situation. Once some enterprises believed that it would be beneficial if they didn't follow the standard, they would explicitly or implicitly violate the self-regulation agreement, which would trigger a "domino" effect and cause a new round of rising wages. The reason for the failure of the self-regulatory mechanism is the neglect of two core issues: the first is the absence of a disciplinary mechanism, the second is that they don't take the extent of acceptance of wages of workers into consideration. The above problems can be well solved if the industry association and worker representatives could negotiate with each other, reach a consensus about the standard of labor cost, and sign a collective agreement. The implementation of the agreement should be supervised by the government and the trade union of higher-level.

Unlike those in worker-led collective consultation, worker representatives in industrial collective consultation are scattered throughout the plants, and are basically selected by employers. Their role is not to claim benefits from employers, but to convey to employers the bottom line of workers, which is the level of wage that enable the workers to live and work in the region. Only if the level of wage negotiated is above this bottom line, workers would accept it ; thus it would be possible  to unify  the standard of labor cost among employers. The way that worker representatives are initiated determines that the outcome of industrial collective consultation will not bring substantive benefits to workers. It only reflects the local labor market wage level, and will be confirmed  periodically through collective agreements. Therefore, unlike other new types of collective consultation, the process of industrial collective consultation rarely involves rounds of negotiation. Collective agreements are generally reached through a single round.

At the same time, the trade union of higher level has established industrial unions, which is a stable organization  for worker representatives. The trade union system follows the principle of localized management, and is divided by region, not by industry. Industrial union is a new form that is widely adopted in the Yangtze River Delta. However, its nature is different from that of the industrial unions in Western countries. The industrial unions in these countries are generally membership-based. Members of its managing level are elected from the top. In the case of Town W, the chairman of the industrial union is the vice chairman of the trade union of Town W, and the members are selected representatives of workers. Most of these representatives are skilled workers or foremen who have influence among the workers. They are not only paid more than ordinary workers, but also take management responsibilities such as those of workshop supervisors. Intentionally or not, the trade union of higher level and employers will also enhance the role of these representatives as well as their reputation, making them the stars of the workers' group. Therefore, unlike those elected during work stoppages, the worker representatives of industrial unions are not only the elite members of workers, but also preferred by the employers and trade unions of higher level. It ensures the stability of industrial unions in the structure of collective consultation. Also, the willingness of employees and employers to cooperate with each other is the basis for the industrial collective consultation on wages, which contributes to strong procedural rules. During 2003-2014, the wool sweater industry in Town W held the collective consultation every year (12 rounds in total). The wage standards in the collective agreements, which were uniformly implemented, were in line with the changes of wages in the local labor market. Labor conflicts were rarely seen in the region.

Of course, there are uncertainties in employer-led collective consultation. The biggest challenge comes from small and medium-sized enterprises (SMEs). Large enterprises, which are deeply troubled by the frequent flow of workers and labor conflicts, believe that a collective consultation system can stabilize the labor environment, reduce losses due to the production fluctuation, and generate more benefits compared to the costs paid. However, for small enterprises with limited production scale and high labor cost ratios, the increase in wages brought by the collective consultation is unaffordable, and even threats the survival of them. Therefore, it is necessary to introduce disciplinary measures from the government to prevent SMEs from undermining the collective consultation. In the case of Town W, it took 2 hours before many small business owners were persuaded by the local government and signed the agreement. Besides, the local government also set up a hotline to listen to the complaints about wages from workers. Employers would be warned and punished if they were found not implementing the agreed standards. This also shows that employer-led collective consultation is in the interest of large enterprises. The unified labor cost agreed through the collective consultation becomes a means for major players in the industry to seize the market, eliminate rivals, and increase production concentration rate. In the collective consultation in Town W, the local government as well as the large business owners made certain compromises due to the continued opposition of the small business owners. In *2010 Wool Sweater Industry Wage (Labor Cost) Negotiation Agreement*, it is stipulated that "the enterprise must pay the wages during 25th-28th of the following month after the settlement; in case of difficulties, the payment can be postponed after consulting with the trade union, but the monthly payment must not be lower than the national minimum wage standard". Even so, small businesses were still struggling to survive; and the number of them was declining. By the time of the 12th round of collective consultation on wages in 2014, the number of wool sweater enterprises in Town W had been reduced to 64.

## 3. Direct Elections and Trade Union-led Collective Consultation

The trade union-led collective consultation is the most important institutional exploration in the field of collective consultation at present. The root of labor conflicts lies in the imbalance of power of employees and employers. Although legal documents such as the *Trade Union Law* stipulate that members of trade unions of enterprises should be democratically elected by workers, it is difficult to be followed in practice. In the background of continuous labor conflicts, some enterprises and local governments are reassessing the role of trade unions, encouraging workers to democratically elect members of trade unions that can represent them, promoting direct election, and exploring institutionalized ways to manage labor conflicts.

In reality, Japanese-funded companies have become the main type of companies actively promoting direct elections of trade unions, partly because such companies are often influenced by nationalism,  thus it is more likely to have labor conflicts; and also because the lean production model of these companies requires a high degree of stability in the production chain (Wen, 2014). The products of one plant are the raw materials for another plant in order to achieve fast transportation as well as zero inventory. Thus, plants are interdependent with each other. However, once there is a strike, the entire production of the whole company will be halted. The damages and losses are not limited to a certain plant, but also the entire system of the company. Therefore, Japanese-funded companies consider direct elections of trade unions as a form of autonomy of Chinese workers. Although the employer need to make a concession about corporate profits through collective consultation, but in exchange, the production can be ensured, and the business can be operated in a stable way. In addition to the promotion of employers, the direct elections of trade unions are supported by local governments. In Guangdong Province, the "Ricoh experience" shows that the direct election of Ricoh's trade union resulted in higher wages and benefits for workers, while the company was able to solve the problem of frequent flow of workers and labor disputes. The company's turnover rate is less than 4%, compared to 20% in the same industry, thus it achieved a long-term balance between employees and employers. This mechanism that can stabilize labor relations in enterprises has been praised and promoted by some local governments (Min, 2012). For example, in 2012, the Shenzhen Federation of Trade Unions announced that direct election would be adopted in 163 trade unions of enterprise (Wu, 2012). In 2014, the Guangdong Federation of Trade Unions announced that it planned to achieve democratic election of trade unions of enterprise in the whole province in five years (Yi, 2014).

It should be emphasized that, the direct election of trade union does not mean that the Party and the government are no longer lead the trade unions of enterprise anymore. The direct election of trade union of enterprise is not a mass election, in which there is no candidate. The trade union of higher level can still lead the trade unions of enterprise by choosing candidates beforehand. Of course, the way how the candidates are elected is very important. If the candidates are selected from top, the public opinion basis will hardly be solid. In the case of Company Y, the candidates were elected in three steps. First, the nomination of candidates was completely open to everyone. Various methods were adopted to nominate candidates, such as self-nomination, mutual nomination, recommendation by the trade union and the enterprise. Second, the candidates in the shortlist were elected through the votes of member representatives. Third, the list of candidates was finalized after reviewing by the trade union of higher level. Then the trade union congress elected the chairman and members of the trade union of enterprise. It can be seen that this is the way jointly approved by workers, employers and trade unions of higher level, thus it can ensure the stability of the structure of representatives.

Although the democratic election of trade union can solve the problem of the legitimacy of trade unions, the question of "why workers should join a trade union" still needs to be addressed. If trade unions do not bring benefits to workers, an effective organizational base can never be formed. Since the core interest of workers is their wages, increasing wages naturally becomes an important task for trade unions. If wage increase can be achieved, trade unions would gain the actual support of workers. Collective consultation is essentially an important tool for trade unions. Most of the enterprises that implement direct elections of trade union also welcome the collective consultation. In the process of collective consultation, the trade unions will elect representatives for negotiation before the collective consultation begins. In the case of Company Y, candidates for the workers' delegation for collective consultation on wages were first selected through the recommendation of the trade union. Then the details of the candidates were publicized to everyone. A workers' (trade union members') congress was held to elect 40 representatives through democratic vote. The trade union members and 40 elected representatives together formed the workers' delegation. Finally, 7 representatives were elected within the delegation. The election of representatives is common in union-led collective consultation. There are several important reasons why trade unions of enterprise would not participate directly on behalf of workers in the negotiation with employers . First, wage is the most important issue in labor relations; therefore, more public support from workers is needed. It is also related with the legitimacy of directly elected trade unions. The election of representatives is also a means for trade unions to demonstrate their democracy. Second, the election of representatives for negotiation is itself a collective consultation strategy of the trade union. In order to get employers to accept collective consultation and to make concessions in the process of negotiation, trade unions need to be able to restrain employers. The high level of concern among workers about the election of representatives and the process of consultation itself is a kind of pressure. Third, in the specific consultation process, the trade union can in fact be a balancing force between the employer and the representatives of workers by constantly adjusting the expectations of both parties, which could contribute to achieve  an outcome. Even if the consultation process is tough, members of the trade union of enterprise need to consider the affordability of the enterprise while helping the workers. This, of course, is also related to the administrative roles of some trade union members. Therefore, with the participation of workers, workers could obtain greater substantive benefits through this kind of collective consultation. The divergent interests of workers and employers can be managed through the trade union of enterprise and the intervention of trade unions of higher level, so that the outcomes of the collective consultation can be accepted by employers and satisfied by workers. The long-term institutionalization of trade union-led collective consultation can finally be ultimately achieved.

## V. Conclusion and Discussion

Since market-oriented reforms have caused the division and conflict of interests between workers and employers, the need of a mechanism to address it and to avoid the disruption of social order by labor conflicts requires the establishment of a collective consultation system. However, on the one hand, the top-down promotion approach makes the collective consultation process administrative; on the other hand, compared to the collective consultation, the government is more familiar with the direct intervention in labor conflicts and better at controlling the direction and intensity of intervention forces, so that the collective consultation would be easily marginalized. Recognizing the state intervention and direct regulation of grassroots labor relations is necessary to understand the state-led type of collective consultation. However, with the further development of the market economy, the state-led consultation is facing increasing challenges. The reversal of supply and demand in the labor market has increased the capacity of bargaining of workers and the ability to take actions collectively for better working conditions and higher wages. It has a continuous impact on the production order and social order. In this context, collective consultation as a means to stabilize the industrial order has gained the attention of some local governments, employers and trade unions. Different forms of worker organization have been emerged, while employees and employers have begun to interact autonomously, and rules set in collective consultation have been used to stabilize or restore the industrial order. Collective consultation in China has transformed from state-led model to a model with multiple drivers. New types of collective consultation with different contents and characteristics have emerged, and have brought out different outcomes.

From the perspective of institutional sustainability, the key to worker-led collective consultation lies in the concessions of employers. Employers must come up with conditions that meet the majority of the demands of workers in order to address the problems through the collective consultation. Because of the variety of demands of workers and the unorganized nature of workers, there is a structural tension between the demands of workers and the extent of meeting these demands. This means that negotiation would be an effective approach to settle disputes, thus to maintain the social stability. In other words, if employers could make more concessions, there would be more room for collective consultation; if not, the government would intervene to maintain social stability. The key to employer-led collective consultation is the need for sufficient authority of industrial organizations to regulate SMEs in order to prevent rule-breaking of small employers. This depends on the local government's determination to foster large enterprises, improve the market concentration, and enhance the competitiveness of local enterprises; and the authority of large enterprises and their ability to mobilize government resources. The key to trade union-led collective consultation is the institutional development of the trade unions of enterprises – they should be independent and could represent workers to the greatest extent. However, there is no consensus on this point. Concerns about its impact on economic development and the loss of control over grassroots trade unions still worry many of us (Wen, 2014). Therefore, it can be predicted that worker-led collective consultation will gain greater recognition as an effective means of settling labor disputes, employer-led collective consultation will be more widely used in specific industrial cluster areas, while the future of trade union-led collective consultation is unclear because it touches on deep-rooted problems of the trade union system.

Finally, despite the emergence of diverse types of collective consultation, state-led collective consultation is still the mainstream method, and state power remains the main driver of collective consultation. However, it no longer takes a dominating role. Consultation and negotiation has become an important principle in dealing with mass incidents. The role of local governments has shifted from "government-led" to "government-guided". The system of direct election of trade unions of enterprises has been partially recognized. Many employers have benefited a lot from institutionalized collective consultation. Based on the long-term observation, it can be found that the awareness of workers is enhancing; trade associations and trade unions of enterprises play an important role in labor relations; and rules for settling disputes and conflicts through negotiation are gradually being established, although the effect and the scope of application of these rules are still relatively limited at present.

## References

[1] Chang Kai. Report on Labor Relations in China: Characteristics and Tendencies of Labor Relations in Contemporary China[R]. Beijing: China Labor and Social Security Publishing House, 2009.

[2] Cheng Yanyuan. Study on Collective Consultation System[M]. Beijing: China Renmin University Press, 2004.

[3] Feng Gang. Institutional Weakness of Trade Union of Enterprises and its Background [J]. Society, 2006, 26 (3): 81-98.

[4] Min Jie., Ricoh's Experience of Trade Unions Elected by People [J]. China

Newsweek, 2012 (20): 27-30.

[5] Shen Yuan. Social Transformation and the Re-formation of the Working Class [J]. Academic Developments, 2006(23): 23-24.

[6] Wen Xiaoyi. The Internal State Mechanism in Collective Bargaining: Evidence from the Collective Bargaining by Wenling Sweater Industry [J]. Society, 2011(1):112-125.

[7] Wen Xiaoyi. Direct Election of Labor Unions: Experience and Lessons of Guangdong Province [J]. Open Times 2014(5): 54-65.

[8] Wu Qingjun. Collective Consultation and "State-led" Labor Relations Governance[J]. Sociological Studies, 2012(3): 66-89.

[9] Xu Xiaohong. Zhejiang Mode of Labor Relations: Self-coordination and All-win[J]. Zhejiang Social Sciences, 2008(11): 9-15.

[10] Yang Zhengxi, Li Min. Choice of the Type of Collective Wage Consultation under Different Labor Relationship Models: Study of the Case in Guangdong[J]. Human Resources Development of China, 2012(10): 84-89.

[11] Clarke, S., Chang-Hee Lee & Qi Li. Collective Consultation and Industrial Relations in China[J]. British Journal of Industrial Relations, 2004, 42(2).

[12] Chen, F. Between the State and labour: the conflict of Chinese trade unions double identity in market reform[J]. China Quarterly, 2003,176(3).

[13] Chen, F. Union power in China – source, operation and constraints[J]. Modern China, 2009, 35 (6).

[14] Howell, J. All-China Federation of Trade Unions Beyond Reform? The Slow March of Direct Elections[J]. China Quarterly, 2008,196(6).

[15] Lee, C.H, Brown, W&Wen X. Y. What Sort of Collective consultation Is Emerging in China[J]. British Journal of Industrial Relations, 2015, 53(4).

[16] Leung, P. Parry. Labor Activists and the New Working Class in China: Strike Leaders' Struggles[M]. Palgrave Macmillan, 2015.

[17] Taylor, B.&Li, Q. Is the ACFTU A Union and Does It Matter?[J]. Journal of Industrial Relations, 2007, 49 (5).

[18] Warner, M.&Ng Sek-Hong. Collective Contracts in Chinese Enterprises: A New Brand of Collective consultation under' Market Socialism?[J]. British Journal of Industrial Relations, 1999, 37(2).

# Labor Education

- Historical Evolution and Reflection on the Labor Education Since 1949

# Historical Evolution and Reflection on the Labor Education Since 1949[*]

*Li Ke, Qu Xia[**]*

**Abstract:** Since the founding of the People's Republic of China, the evolution of educational policy for labor education has gone through five periods: the transition from new democracy to socialism; the exploration of socialist construction; the reform and opening up; the 21st century; the new era of socialism with Chinese characteristics. The theoretical orientation and practical form of labor education in the five periods are different, but they all show obvious exogenous characteristics: the speeches of important leaders are the main driving factors; in order to meet the needs of social development, a long-term mechanism to ensure the sound operation of labor education is absent. To give full play to the value of labor education, the top priority of today's labor education is to build a labor education system of inherent vitality, with knowing truth goodness and beauty in labor as the root; the integration of education on morality, intelligence, physical fitness, aesthetics and labor as the soil; and the cultivation of correct labor values pointing the direction of growth.

**Keywords:** Labor education; Educational policy; The combination of educational and productive labor

The educational policy that combines education and productive labor is what the Communist Party of China (CPC) has always insisted on. On September 10th of 2018, at the National Education Conference, General Secretary Xi Jinping emphasized the need to adhere to the path of developing socialist education with Chinese characteristics, and to cultivate socialist builders and successors with all-round moral, intellectual, physical and aesthetical grounding with a hardworking

---

[*] This paper was published in *Journal of Educational Studies*, Issue. 5, 2018.

[**] Li Ke, PhD in Management, Researcher, Dean of Labor Education School, China University of Labor Relations. Qu Xia, PhD in Education, Associate researcher, Deputy Dean of Labor Education School, China University of Labor Relations.

spirit (Xi, 2018). The labor education was identified as an important part of education for all-round development. However, it is undeniable that, in practice, the phenomenon of "labor education being marginalized in schools, families and society" still exists (MOE et al., 2015). What is the reason for the gap between the concept of labor education and the practices? How to deal with it? Aimed at addressing these questions, this paper analyzes the conceptual orientation and practical form of labor education[1] in the Party's educational guidelines and policies since the founding of the People's Republic of China, in order to further explore the problems of labor education, and to propose new ideas of building a labor education system of inherent vitality.

## I. Labor Education in the Transitional Period from New Democratic Society to Socialist Society (1949-1956)

On the eve of the founding of the People's Republic of China, the *Common Program of the Chinese People's Political Consultative Conference* listed "love of labor" as one of the five social moralities. From Xu Teli's article *On National Ethics*, it can be found that "love of labor" was made a national ethics to cultivate an attitude in line with the production methods of the new democratic era and to establish harmonious labor relations (He, 1998a). In terms of the content of labor ethics education, Xu made two points in particular – the change of attitude towards labor ("those who do not work shall not eat") and the guarantee of labor rights ("give laborers the right of labor"). He combined the morality, power and duty of labor to consolidate labor discipline. In 1950, Qian Junrui, then Vice Minister of Education, clearly pointed out in *The Current Policy of Education Development* that "to serve the workers and farmers and to serve production construction are the major guideline for the currently implemented new democratic education" (He, 1998a). He also regraded labor education as an important part in the implementation of the policy that required "education to serve production construction". He believed that it was necessary to motivate people to join labor production through labor education, to praise and popularize inventions and creations in the process of laboring, and to organize all the people who were not engaged in labor production before to participate in it and transform themselves in the process of laboring (He, 1998a).

Therefore, during the period of the new democratic society, "combining education with productive labor" had not yet become the basic educational policy

---

[1] Labor education refers to the purposeful and planned educational activities for students in regular schools. The purpose is to cultivate their labor consciousness, labor emotions and labor habits, help them to understand knowledge about production and master life and labor skills. It does not include social labor education participated by intellectuals and leading cadres during 1949-1966, and the professional labor education organized by various vocational schools.

in China. In practice, based on a series of documents issued after 1950, including *Decision of the Ministry of Education on the Implementation of Curriculum Reform of Institutions of Higher Education*, *Order of the Ministry of Education on the Issuance of Provisional Teaching Plan for Secondary Schools (Draft) and Provisional School Calendar for Specialized Secondary Schools (Draft)*, *Provisional Regulations for Secondary Schools (Draft)*, *Provisional Regulations for Primary Schools (Draft)* and *Provisional Disciplines for Specialized Secondary Schools*, it could be concluded that in all kinds of higher education institutions and specialized secondary schools, labor education mainly took the form of professional internship, while in secondary schools, primary schools, industrial and agricultural crash courses and literacy cram schools, labor education was not included in the official teaching plan.

After four years of recovery and development, in 1953, China witnessed a marked increase in the number of primary and secondary school graduates, and in some areas even emerged marches carried out by graduates who could not continue their studies in schools of a higher grade as they wished. In response to this, the CPC Central Committee commented on *Report on Solving the Problems of Senior and Junior High School Graduates' Study and Engagement in Productive Labor* which was forwarded to the Ministry of Education, clearly pointing out that, "At present, it is difficult for the graduates of secondary and primary schools to enter into schools of a higher grade, which could be mainly attributed to the Central Ministry of Education tending to neglect labor education in the process of guiding secondary and primary schools in the past few years. In the reform of teaching and the reform of teachers' mindset, the Ministry has not focused on criticizing the erroneous educational guideline that despises manual labor and manual workers, nor has it clearly explained to the general public and students the nature and tasks of primary and secondary education, leading to the situation that the wrong educational guideline inherited from the past continued to dominate the teachers and students. The Central Ministry of Education should make an open self-criticism for this" (He, 1998a). After that, the Ministry of Education, the Ministry of Publicity, the Central Committee of the Communist Youth League and other departments issued a series of policies and organized various labor education activities to support the primary school and junior high school graduates who could not go on to schools of a higher grade to participate in productive labor.

Regarding the practical form of labor education at that time, the Ministry of Education issued *The Report on the Publicity and Education for Primary and Junior High School Graduates Engaged in Productive Labor* in 1955, pointing out that, "In the past year, many schools adopted such methods as visiting factories, farms and agricultural production cooperatives, meeting model workers, inviting labor models to make speeches, getting together with young workers, reading labor-related books for educational purpose, and participating in physical labor activities, which has yielded fruitful results. However, most schools failed to provide in-class labor education on a regular basis. In the future, apart from paying attention to extracurricular labor education, we should also enhance conduct labor education in the classroom and combine the two methods together. In addition, though most schools focused on improving the students' awareness through labor education, which is undoubtedly very important, the education on the basic knowledge of industrial and agricultural production was often ignored. In the future, apart from cultivating awareness and habits of labor, we should also pay attention to comprehensive technical education, so that students can understand the basic knowledge of industrial and agricultural production from both theoretical and practical points of view" (He, 1998a). Thereafter, production technique education began to become an important part of labor education, and was included in the *Notice on the Regulations of Extracurricular Activities in Primary Schools* alongside intellectual, moral, physical, and aesthetic education in 1955. In the *Teaching Hours for Secondary Schools (1956-1957)* and the *Instructions on the Implementation of Basic Production Technique Education in Regular Schools (Draft)* issued by the Ministry of Education in 1956, the weekly school hours and specific requirements for production technique education were clearly defined.

Hence, during the transition to socialism, labor education was highly valued by the CPC Central Committee as a means to relieve the pressure of primary and secondary school graduates to enter schools of a higher grade and to mobilize them for employment. During this period, labor education not only included the education on attitude and concepts, but also covered the production technique education according to the industrial and agricultural developments, so that a comprehensive production technique education system at a preliminary stage was built. However, these policies failed to deliver satisfactory results. On the one hand, since the students cannot continue their studies, they had no choice but to return to the countryside to work. As a result, many parents of students at primary and secondary school chose to take their children out of schools . According to reports from 12 provinces, including Hebei and Liaoning, in early 1956, about 10% of secondary school students dropped out of school, and in some schools the number of dropouts even accounted for more than 50% of the total enrollment (He, 1998a). It was evident that the social mindset of downplaying manual labor had not really changed at that time. When realizing that school education could not change the fate of engaging in manual labor, many people would choose to quit school. On the other hand, although an ideal system of production technique education was built at that time, it could not really be implemented considering the teaching conditions of most schools.

## II. Labor Education in the Period of Exploration of Socialist Construction (1957-1977)

In 1956, China entered a period of large-scale socialist construction across the board, with education developing at a highly rapid pace. According to statistics, in 1956, the number of primary school students reached 63,466,000, 2.6 times that of 1949; the number of junior high school students reached 4,381,000, 5.3 times that of 1949; the number of senior high school students reached 784,000, 3.8 times that of 1949; the number of secondary technical school students reached 539,000, 7 times that of 1949; the number of students in institutions of higher education reached 403,000, 3.5 times that of 1949 (Gu, 1994). At this time, the country's economic and financial resources could no longer support the continuous expansion of education. Consequently, a large number of primary and secondary school graduates were unable to progress to higher education and had to work. "The huge disparity between educational supply and demand becomes a highlighted manifestation of the contradictions among the people in the sector of education" (Li, 2017). Hence, in 1957, Chairman Mao Zedong explicitly proposed in *On the Correct Handling of Contradictions Among the People* that "our educational policy must enable everyone who receives an education to develop morally, intellectually and physically and become a worker with both socialist consciousness and culture" (He, 1998a), which established the goal of education for laborers.

It should be said that Mao Zedong's goal of cultivating "a worker with both socialist consciousness and culture" was in line with the development needs of China at that time. However, "since the main problem to be solved at that time was the political orientation of students and their participation in productive labor after graduation, politics was understood as class struggle, and productive labor was mainly interpreted as manual labor, a 'Left' deviation occurred when the educational policy was implemented in practice" (Li, 2002). From a series of documents on labor education issued by the Ministry of Education and the Ministry of Publicity from 1957 to 1966, and speeches on educational work by state leaders including Mao Zedong and Liu Shaoqi, it can be inferred that at that time, labor education was characterized by the following features at the conceptual level.

First, labor education was regarded as a way of conducting class struggle. In June 1958, Lu Dingyi, then Minister of Education, emphasized in his speech at the National Educational Work Conference that "the combination of education and labor is one of the main elements of the educational revolution" (He, 1998a). In August, Lu published another article, *Education Must Be Combined with Productive Labor*, which was reviewed by Chairman Mao. In this article, he regarded whether to insist on "combining education with productive labor" or not as manifestation of the struggle between capitalism and socialism at the battlefront of education. He believed that in a socialist country, the bourgeoisie would not dare to blatantly oppose the CPC's leadership, but they would hypocritically advocate concepts like "education for education's sake, separation of mental work from physical work, and education led by experts" while asserting that "education means reading, so the one who reads more will get more learned than and superior to others. In contrast, productive labor is the inferior, especially physical work and manual laborers". These statements could easily have negative influence on the mindset of young students. Therefore, the Party must stick to the stand with a clear-cut attitude that "education serves the politics of the working class and education should be combined with productive labor. In order to realize this target, education must be led by the CPC" (He, 1998a). In conclusion, labor education was highly valued at that time as it was mainly used as a political means of eliminating the division of physical work and mental work and carrying out socialist transformation.

Second, labor education was applied as a means to alleviate educational funding constraints. In the first half of 1957, Liu Shaoqi conducted a nationwide survey on the difficulties encountered by primary and secondary school students in furthering their studies and found that many families could not afford to send their children to school. Therefore, he came up with the idea of encouraging students to work while studying and to engage in after-school labor, which he viewed as "an important way to support the cash-strapped students and popularize education" (Li, 2017). In January 1958, the *People's Daily* published an editorial titled *Two Good Examples*, advocating that in order to save on national expenditure and meet students' basic needs, "the best way is to encourage students to work while studying, so that they can use their own income to cover all or a part of their own tuition fees and living expenses" (He, 1998a). Soon after that, the Central Committee of the Communist Youth League issued the *Decision on Promoting the Practice of Working While Studying Among Students*, and Dong Chuncai, then Vice Minister of Education, made a report on educational work titled *Strengthening Ideological Education and Labor Education, Proposing to Run Schools by the Masses and in a Thrifty Way*. In this way, labor education was identified as an important way to run schools and build up the country thriftily and to achieve greater, faster, better and more economical results in building socialism.

Third, labor education was seen as a fundamental way to solve the problem of theory being divorced from practice. At the opening ceremony of the Party School of the CPC Central Committee in 1942, Mao Zedong emphasized that "there are two kinds of incomplete knowledge in the world: one is the ready-made knowledge in books, while the other is partial and perceptual knowledge, both of which are one-sided. Only when the two are combined with each other can good and complete knowledge be produced." Moreover, he stressed that "there is only one kind of true theory in the world, the theory which is drawn from objective reality and proved in objective reality" (He, 1998a). In 1965, at a meeting in Hangzhou, Mao Zedong criticized the problem of theory being divorced from practice in school education. He said, "I am very skeptical of the current education system. From primary school to university, during a period of 16, 17 or even more than 20 years, the students don't see rice, sorghum, beans, wheat, millet or barley, nor do they learn how workers work, how farmers farm or how commodities are exchanged. Their health is also destroyed during this process. This is so harmful" (He, 1998a). Under the guidance of Mao Zedong's thoughts, labor education was regarded as the inevitable course to "closely integrate physical and mental work, study and labor, production and education, and theory and practice" (He, 1998a), and the only way to enable students to acquire complete knowledge, to be well-rounded, to be red and expert and to become intellectuals with the characteristics of workers as well as workers with the features of intellectuals.

Obviously, from 1957 to 1966, the political, economic and epistemological significance of labor education was elevated to an unprecedented level, and in practice, it was greatly promoted in an unprecedented manner. In terms of curriculum, "all schools have included productive labor as an official subject, and at different times, according to the actual situation, the weekly, monthly, and annual labor time for different types of schools and grades have been specified. Besides, a number of courses that combine education and productive labor are offered. For example, courses on the general knowledge of production, handcraft, and labor in primary schools; production knowledge classes and labor classes in secondary schools" (Cheng, 1998). Especially after 1958, schools set up factories, and factories set up schools. Students worked while studying, usually engaged in part-time jobs. Laborers and intellectuals learnt from each other. These phenomena became a fever sweeping the country. According to the national conditions of China at that time, it was very necessary to moderately promote the work-study practice, to organize students to participate in production work for education and training, and to establish a certain system. However, under the "ultra-leftism" trend of the Great Leap Forward, the labor education with work-study practice soon became a kind of fanaticism. "Working while studying" became "working without studying" and "working" was regarded as equal to "studying". Study was even replaced by labor in some cases.

During the Cultural Revolution, the political significance of labor education was excessively exalted. Furthermore, study was set against labor, mental labor against physical labor and intellectuals against workers and farmers. Consequently, labor education could not be carried out according to the normal internal rules.

## III. Labor Education from the Reform and Opening Up to the 21st Century (1978-1999)

After the Third Plenary Session of the 11th CPC Central Committee, along with the strategic shift of the Party's working focus, in-depth discussions were conducted about the relationship between mental and manual labor, the integration of education and productive labor, and the status of labor education in the education for all-round development.

First, the status of mental labor was re-identified by restoring the original meaning of education-labor combination in the context of modernization.

In the original sense of Marxist theory, the combination of education and labor refers to "combining modern school education with the productive labor of modern mechanical industry". "Through such combined education, it not only equips those who receive education with basic technical literacy necessary for modern society, but also nurtures their temperament and improves their knowledge and skills, thus promoting the harmonious development of human intelligence and physical strength." Therefore, "to combine modern education with modern production is a necessary way to increase social production and a fundamental method to cultivate a well-rounded person" (Liu, 1996). However, during the 20 to 30 years after the founding of the People's Republic of China, China's economic production was still dominated by physical and manual labor. Under such circumstances, if the policy of combining education and labor and integrating physical work and mental work was rigidly implemented, it would certainly affect or drag down the level of modern production knowledge and technical education. Therefore, after the reform and opening up, the CPC Central Committee was committed to reshaping the social atmosphere of "respecting knowledge and talents".

The Sixth Plenary Session of the 11th CPC Central Committee held in June 1981 adopted the *Resolution on Several Historical Issues of the Party Since the Founding of the People's Republic of China,* in which it is clearly stated that "we must resolutely eradicate the wrong concept of downplaying education, science and culture and discriminating against intellectuals) that existed for a long time and culminated in the 'Cultural Revolution'". "We must persistently carry out the educational policy which calls for an all-round development morally, intellectually and physically, for being both red and expert, for integration of the intellectuals with the workers and farmers and the combination of mental and physical labour" (He, 1998b). Therefore, as the basic line of "making economic development the central task" was established, the educational policy of the Party was adjusted accordingly. The expression "to serve the politics of the proletariat" was removed from the new policy, and the previous statement that "education must be combined with productive labor" was replaced by "we should integrate mental and physical labor, and enable intellectuals, workers and farmers to learn from each other".

Second, the question of whether and how to insist on the combination of education and labor was thoroughly discussed.

In April 1978, Deng Xiaoping made remarks at the National Educational Work Conference that "in order to cultivate qualified talents for socialist construction, we must seriously study how to better implement the policy of combining education and productive labor under the new conditions" and that "schools of all levels and types should make appropriate arrangements in terms of what kind of labor students should participate in, how to work in factories and villages, how much time should be spent, and how to closely integrate labor with teaching. What is more important is that education must keep step with the development of national economy." "As our national economy is developing in a planned and proportional manner, we should accordingly prepare a deliberate plan to train labor specialists and reserves" (He, 1998b). Obviously, from Deng Xiaoping's point of view, to persistently implement the policy of combining education and productive labor in the new era is not merely a matter of strengthening labor education within schools, but rather a macro-level demand for education to match with the development of national economy.

As the rectification task was completed and order was restored in the educational sector, the academic community also started to challenge the educational policy of "two musts" (i.e., education must serve proletarian politics and must be combined with productive labor – translator's note). Scholars such as Xiao Zongliu and Pan Yida argued that the "two musts" educational policy is "closely related with class struggle, basically a product of the class struggle" and "fails to reflect the inherent law of education, as well as the relationship between education and productivity and modernization". Therefore, it needs to be revised, improved or updated (Cao, 2006). This opinion was reflected in *Decision of the Central Committee of the Communist Party of China on the Reform of the Education System* published in 1985, in which "education must serve socialist construction" formally replaced the statement that "education must serve proletarian politics" and became the basic component of China's educational policy. Similarly, the expression "education must be combined with productive labor" was rarely seen in the central government documents and speeches of important leaders from 1983 to 1989, while the more commonly used wording was "we should combine mental and physical labor, and enable intellectuals, workers and farmers to learn from each other". In 1993, "education must be combined with productive labor" was reaffirmed in the *Outline for China's Educational Reform and Development* which clearly stated that "education must serve socialist modernization, must be integrated with productive labor, and must cultivate builders and successors who are well-rounded morally, intellectually and physically" (He, 1998c).

He Dongchang explained in *Profound Changes in China's Educational Thoughts Over the Past 20 Years* that, "Since 1978, the education community started to have different perceptions of the educational policy proposed in the CPC Central Committee's instructions on education in 1958, that is, education must serve proletarian politic and be combined with productive labor. There was a time when a concise and systematic statement of educational policy was missing. After the political turmoil in 1989, there was a greater need for such a statement to be  in place to provide a understanding basically recognized by all parties. To this end, the Education Society conducted a series of seminars, the views of which were incorporated into the *Outline for China's Educational Reform and Development* and later into the *Education Law of People's Republic of China*" (He, 2003).

Third, labor education was described as one of the components of education for all-round development.

In 1986, Li Peng, then Vice Premier of the State Council and Director of the State Education Commission, made a statement on the *Compulsory Education Law of the People's Republic of China (Draft)* at the 4th Session of the 6th National People's Congress (NPC). He proposed that "the policy of all-round development of morality, intelligence, physical fitness and aesthetics should be implemented, and appropriate labor education should be provided, so as to ensure children and teenagers can  receive a more comprehensive basic education" (He, 1998b). Labor education was mentioned here as part of a more comprehensive basic education. In October, Peng Peiyun, Deputy Director of the State Education Commission, made it clear in her speech at a seminar on the syllabus of moral education in secondary schools that "moral education should become an integral part of education for all-round development of morality, intelligence, physical fitness, aesthetics and labor so that they can interact with and complement each other" (He, 1998b) . In Peng's speech, the concept of "education for all-round development with five aspects" was officially proposed. After that, a series of documents were issued by the State Education Commission including *The Plan of State Education Commission and State Sports Commission on Developing After-school Physical Exercise and Improving the Technical Level of School Sports (1986-2000), Teaching Plan for Full-time Primary Schools for the Blind (Draft), Opinions of State Education Commission and Central Committee of the Communist Youth League on Strengthening the Work of Children's Palace*, in all of which the expression of "education for all-round development with five aspects " can be seen. However, after the *Outline for China's Educational*

*Reform and Development* was issued in 1993, this expression was changed into "cultivating socialist builders and successors of socialism who are well-developed morally, intellectually, and physically". In the *Education Law of the People's Republic of China* issued in 1995, the term was formally defined as "socialist builders and successors who are well-rounded morally, intellectually and physically".

Li Lanqing, then Vice Premier of the State Council, explained why the concept of "education with five aspects" was changed into "education with three aspect", saying that "when the Political Bureau discussed about this issue, it was considered that the policy of all-round development of morality, intelligence and physical fitness is a major policy which has been persistently implemented by our Party for many years. It has been proven to be correct and effective in practice and has been known and accepted by the education sector, the whole Party and the whole nation. Therefore, the policy should be kept. However, this does not mean that we can ignore aesthetic education and labor education. Moral education is a broad concept that should involve aesthetic education, and labor education should also be included in moral education and sports education" (He, 1998c). "This is because there are other forms of education in addition to moral, intellectual, physical, aesthetic and labor education, ... but they can be categorized into moral, intellectual and sports education, in a broad sense" (He, 1998c). Based on these considerations, after the 1990s, the central government tended to consider labor education as an element incorporated into moral, intellectual and sports education in a broad sense, denying the need for its independent presentation. And the previous statement of all-round development with morality, intelligence, physical fitness was adopted again.

In terms of labor education practices, the competency of labor skills has drawn great attention as one of the four elements of education for all-round development. In 1982, the Ministry of Education issued the *Opinions on Offering Labor Skills Classes in Regular Secondary Schools (Trial)*, which stipulated that: For labor skills classes in junior high schools, the arrangement should be 4 hours per day and 2 weeks per school year, totaling 144 hours in three years; and in senior high schools, there should be 6 hours of classes per week and 4 weeks per school year. It also put forward specific requirements for the performance assessment of labor skills education. Each student should write a labor summary, and the school should establish a labor file. At the end of each school year, students should be graded according to their performance in terms of attitude towards laboring, compliance with labor discipline and mastery of knowledge and skills. Students' performance will be graded as four levels, "excellent", "good", "pass", or "fail", and the grade will be recorded in the students' grade report. Students' attitude towards laboring and performance should form an important part of the evaluation on their conduct. Students with poor laboring attitude and performance cannot be selected as Merit Student (He, 1998b). This was the first time since the founding of the People's Republic of China that assessment standards and requirements of labor education were proposed in national education documents. After 1987, the former State Education Commission successively issued the *Syllabus of Labor Skills Courses in Full-time Secondary Schools (Draft)*, *Draft Syllabus of Labor Courses in Full-time Primary Schools* and *Several Opinions on Further Strengthening Moral Education in Primary and Secondary Schools*, all of which emphasized that the teaching plan should include the time for students to participate in labor and social practice, which should be incessantly institutionalized and standardized. In 1998, the General Office of the Ministry of Education issued *Several Opinions on Strengthening the Management of Labor Skills Education in Regular Secondary Schools*, specifying the leadership responsibilities of organizing labor skills education in secondary schools and the requirements for building up quality faculty. It explicitly stipulates that "when conducting education supervision and evaluation, education supervision authorities at all levels should include labor skills education in the index system of education supervision and evaluation", "should take whether labor skills courses are offered and whether enough importance is attached to labor skills education as one of the important criteria for selecting advanced units of education and advanced schools; and as one of the important standards for assessing education departments, schools and leaders" (He, 2003). In view of this, some researchers pointed out that "from the 1980s to the new round of basic education curriculum reform, labor education was 'elevated to a higher level' in terms of its status in the curriculum system and as an academic discipline. Labor courses were provided with adequate class hours to impart labor-related knowledge, skills, emotions, attitudes, and values in a systematic way. This embodies requirements of the educational policy proposed by the Party and the country" (Xu, 2015).

However, in terms of the actual results, comments were objectively made at the National Symposium on Labor Skills Education in Secondary Schools held in 1986 that, "The situation of offering this course is still very uneven across the country. At present, about a half or even more of the schools do not offer labor skills courses. Some educational administrative departments have not put this course on the agenda. The labor skills course is not given enough attention and leadership is not exercised effectively. Schools and the society have not fully understood the importance of this course and there is a lack of teaching equipment, venues, funding and teachers." The reasons for the above problems were also analyzed at the Symposium, "Whether in the education sector or in society, the phenomenon of merely pursuing the rate of admission to schools of a higher grade has so seriously affected basic education that the labor skills course cannot be offered as scheduled. Since labor skills education is a new subject and a very comprehensive one, new demands for venues, equipment, and teachers have emerged which are different from those of other subjects. And the society, parents, teachers, and students should better understand its importance" (He, 1998b). It can be concluded that after the 1980s, although the CPC Central Committee carefully adjusted the conceptual orientation of labor education policy, strengthened the systematic construction of labor education in practice, and stepped up to promote labor education, the practical effects of labor education were not satisfactory due to various internal and external factors.

## IV. Labor Education Since the Building of a Moderately Prosperous Society in All Respects (2000-2012)

Since the 21st century, China has entered a new development stage of building a moderately prosperous society in all and accelerating socialist modernization. The CPC Central Committee has reinterpreted the connotation of labor in the new period from a new historical height. On the one hand, the creative value of labor is highlighted, and the glory of labor and greatness of creation become the strong voice of the times. Facing the advent of knowledge-based economy and information age, then General Secretary Jiang Zemin made a remark with profound implication in the report of the 16th CPC National Congress, pointing out that innovation is the soul driving a nation's progress and the inexhaustible source of a country's prosperity. Moreover, he made "respect labor, knowledge, talent and creativity" (Four Respects) an important policy of the Party and the state. Since then, the "Four Respects" has been included in the reports of the 17th and 18th CPC National Congress, and written into the newly revised *Constitution of the Communist Party of China* after the 19th National Congress. The "Four Respects" is an extension and development of the Marxist view that "labor creates everything" and a further enrichment and expansion of Deng Xiaoping's thought of "respecting knowledge and talents" in the new era. Calling for respect for labor, it is important to respect creativity. Labor is about creativity – without creativity labor is mere simple repetition. Creativity cannot be achieved without labor – without labor, creativity is only empty talk. Respecting knowledge, talent and creativity is intrinsically consistent with respecting labor, and the three aspects are necessary requirements for respecting labor in modern society.

On the other hand, humanistic care for workers has become an important value orientation of the Party in the new era. In the report of the 16th CPC National Congress, then General Secretary Jiang Zemin creatively proposed the concept of "beneficial labor" and made it clear that "We need to respect and protect all work that is good for the people and society" and "All legitimate income, from work or not should be protected". Then General Secretary Hu Jintao reiterated the idea that "labor is the supreme honor and workers are the greatest people" in his speech at the National Commendation Conference for Model Workers and Advanced Workers held in 2010. He proposed the concept of "decent work" and made improving people's livelihood the focus of social development in the reports of the 17th and 18th CPC National Congress.

To be in line with the new connotation of labor in the new era, the Party's educational policy has been adjusted accordingly since the 21st century. In June 1999, Jiang Zemin pointed out at the Third National Educational Work Conference that "We must comprehensively implement the Party's educational policy and adhere to the principle that education should serve socialism and the people. We need to persistently combine education with social practice, take improving the quality of people as the primary purpose, focus on building students' innovative spirit and practical ability, and strive to cultivate socialist builders and successors who 'cherish lofty ideals and moral integrity, well-educated and disciplined' featuring all-round development in morality, intelligence, physical fitness and aesthetics" (He, 2003). Based on this speech delivered by Jiang Zemin and the *Talk on Education* in 2000, in the *Decision on the Reform and Development of Basic Education* issued by the State Council in 2001, it was regarded as the fundamental policy to guide the reform and development of basic education in the new century that "We must stick to the principle that education must serve socialist modernization and the people, and we must combine productive labor with social practice, to cultivate socialist builders and successors who were well-rounded in morality, intelligence, physical fitness and aesthetics" (He, 2003). This expression inherited the original statement of China's educational policy and incorporated the new ideas of the state leaders in the new period. As a new expression of China's educational policy in the period of building a moderately prosperous society in all respects, it was officially written into the report of the 16th CPC National Congress and the *Education Law of the People's Republic of China* revised and released on December 27th, 2015.

It is the first time to incorporate "serving the people" into the educational policy, which fully demonstrates the Party's human-centered commitment to "building the Party for the public good and exercising power for the people" in the new era. In addition, the new policy emphasizes that education should not only be combined with productive labor, but also with social practice. The concept of "combining education with productive labor and social practice" is the enrichment and expansion of the idea of "combining education with productive labor" in the new era. "Social practice focuses on the application and innovation of knowledge. Conducting social practice is a process of testing, applying and innovating ideas and knowledge". Social practice has a broader meaning and is  more relevant to the times and reality. In the information society it includes not only productive work and scientific activities, but also involves various social activities of the tertiary industry" (Luo, 2001). Therefore, it can better reflect the diversity of labor practices and the infinity of labor creation in the new era.

In terms of the practical form of labor education, along with the advent of information society and knowledge-based economy, the technological dimension of labor education has been more highlighted. In the eighth round of basic education curriculum reform launched in 2001, the comprehensive practice course, as a new form of labor education, became compulsory from primary school to high school, which mainly include information technology education, research-oriented study, community service, social practice, and labor and technology education. It "stresses students should enhance their consciousness of exploration and innovation through practice, learn how to conduct scientific research, and develop the ability of applying knowledge comprehensively. The curriculum is designed to promote close connection between school and society and to foster a sense of social responsibility among students. When the curriculum is applied, information technology education should be strengthened to develop students' awareness and ability to utilize information technology. Students should understand the necessary general technologies and division of labor and to develop primary technical skills". At the same time, secondary schools in the rural areas are required to "try out the practice of helping students to obtain 'two certificates' through 'green certificate' education and other technical training programs. Regular secondary schools in the urban areas should also offer vocational and technical courses" (He, 2003). From the relevant statements in the *Outline for Basic Education Curriculum Reform (Trial)*, it can be concluded that focusing on technology, emphasizing practice and pursuing innovation are the new practical orientations of labor education in the new era. This is consistent with the emphasis of the central leading bodies' that labor creates value in the new era.

After entering the new century, as the connotation of labor was continuously enriched and took on implications of the new era, the extension of labor education was also expanded, from "combining education with productive labor" to "combining education with productive labor and social practice", and from labor technique courses to comprehensive practice courses including information technology, general technology, production technology, vocational technology, social service and social practice, research-oriented study etc. However, the continuous expansion has also entailed a problem that the substantial connotation of labor education became increasingly ambiguous and divergent from the initial intention in practice. A number of studies show that replacing labor education with integrated practical activities has actually led to such problems as a decline in the status of labor education courses, unclear course objectives, difficulties in securing class hours, and the use of course facilities and venues for other purposes. In addition, comprehensive practical activities, as a brand new course, has not been studied thoroughly. What's the relationship between the four major learning areas within the course? How to produce a consistent twelve-year curriculum from primary school to senior high school? Many issues have not been carefully reviewed and delicate design is absent, which directly leads to the lack of legitimacy, standard, goal and basis for labor education when it is actually implemented (Xu, 2014; Du, 2014; Chen and Huang, 2015). The fact that it was 17 years after comprehensive practice activities were implemented that the *Guidance for Comprehensive Practice Classes in Primary and Secondary Schools* was issued can also justify scholars' criticisms to some extent.

Obviously, it has been increasingly highlighted that the Party upholds the governing concept of providing humanistic care for laborers, but the humanistic dimension seems to be neglected in the labor education in the new century while the technological dimension has been attached great significance. In fact, with the progress and development of society, physical workers can become more cultured, leading a more colorful and rich life, doing  more technology-driven work and witnessing an increase in their income and social status. But physical work will never disappear entirely (Du, 2016). Therefore, one of the most important purposes of contemporary labor education is to teach young people to form a correct view of labor, to better understand the development of the labor field and labor groups in society, to sincerely love and respect physical work and physical workers, and to strive for the building of a fair and just society in which all "workers are allowed to participate in development and share the fruits of development".

## V. New Development of Labor Education with Xi Jinping Thoughts on Socialism with Chinese Characteristics for a New Era as Guidance

Since the 18th CPC National Congress, General Secretary Xi Jinping has made "adhering to social fairness and justice, eradicating obstacles that prevent workers from participating in development and sharing the fruits of development, and striving to enable workers to get decent work and achieve well-rounded development" (Xi, 2013) one of the administrative goals, and regarded "the contradiction between unbalanced and inadequate development and the people's ever-growing needs for a better life" as the principal contradiction facing Chinese society in the new era of socialism with Chinese characteristics, stressing that "We must therefore continue commitment to our people-centered philosophy of development, and work to promote well-rounded human development and common prosperity for everyone" (Xi, 2017). Xi Jinping's thoughts on socialism with Chinese characteristics in the new era has inherited and further developed the Marxist concept of labor, with new grounds opened for thoughts on socialist labor with Chinese characteristics in the new era. Xi Jinping's thoughts on socialist labor with Chinese characteristics responds to the major concerns of the new era, containing the view on labor practice – "doing practical work will make a country thrive", the view on labor development – "national rejuvenation", the view on the value of labor – "respect for labor", and the view on labor education – "love for labor". It has become a powerful conceptual weapon and concrete action guide to promote the development of the Party and the people.

General Secretary Xi Jinping has high expectations for the young people to cultivate deep affection for labor, "through various measures and methods, we should educate and guide the young people to firmly establish the idea of loving labor and develop the habit of laboring, so as to cultivate generations of highly competent workers who are diligent and good at working"; "Children should be educated to love labor and creation from an early age. They can sow hope and reap fruits through labor and creation, and also strengthen their willpower and improve themselves through labor and creation" (Xi, 2015). These important statements emphasize the necessity of conducting labor education for children from an early age from the perspective of the creation function of labor. However, the current situation of labor education for young people is less than encouraging. In recent years, labor education for students at primary schools, secondary schools and institutions of higher learning has been greatly weakened. As for schools, labor and technical courses are often replaced by other courses, there are insufficient teachers, venues and funds, and the plan and assessment for labor education are not in place. Some schools even use labor as a means of punishment. focusing more on labor and less on education and neglecting the cultivation of laboring concepts and habits. As for families, physical and productive labor is overlooked in family education. Parents often only care about their children's academic performance. The children will be spared of physical work as long as they have good academic performance. As for society, the ideas of getting rich overnight and getting something for nothing have become more popular, and the role of physical and productive labor is downplayed.

It is a fundamental requirement of the Party and the State for education in the new era to effectively strengthen labor education and strive to cultivate young people to be high-quality workers who are diligent, good at working and love labor. In August 2015, the Ministry of Education, together with the Central Committee of the Communist Youth League and the National Permanent Standing Commission of the

Young Pioneers of China, issued the *Opinions on Strengthening Labor Education in Primary and Secondary Schools* (hereinafter referred to as "Opinions"). It aimed to improve the labor competence of students at primary and secondary schools through labor education, enable them to form good laboring habits and positive laboring attitude, get rid of bad laboring values, and cultivate the spirit to study diligently, work voluntarily and create bravely, and lay a good foundation for their lifelong development and happiness. On December 27th of 2015, in the 18th meeting of the 12th NPC Standing Committee, the decision on amending the *Education Law* and the *Higher Education Law* was approved by voting, which means that the *Education Law* and the *Higher Education Law* that had been in force for 21 years and 17 years respectively would be revised at the same time. Contents such as "serving the people" and "combining education with social practice" were added in Article 4 of the new *Higher Education Law*; a requirement for "a sense of social responsibility" was added to the statement on the mission of higher education in Article 5. This amendment is not only an institutional response to the contradictions and problems arising in the process of higher education development and reform, embodying the spirit of rule of law that legislation needs to keep pace with the times; but also an institutional guidance for the future reform and development of higher education, highlighting the value orientation of higher education reform and development in China. From the changes in the expressions of these legal provisions, we can see that higher education, as an important part of national education cause, should not only pursue instrumental rationality, but also value rationality. The value is to serve the people.

In Marx's view, the combination of productive labor with intellectual education and sports education is not only a way to increase social production, but also the only way to cultivate a well-rounded person. The famous educator Tao Xingzhi also stated that "The purpose of labor education is to balance the development of hand and brain, to enhance one's ability to be independent, to gain true knowledge of things and to understand the weal and woe of laborers" (Tao, 1988). It is because labor plays an important role in educating people by shaping a sound personality, strengthening one's willpower and building a noble character, Xi Jinping further emphasized at the National Conference on Ideological and Political Work in Colleges and Universities that it is necessary to strengthen education through practice. We should adhere to the policy of combining education with productive labor and social practice, and allow the young people to understand national situation and society through engaging in practice. They can enjoy the rewards and fun brought by labor while improving their capabilities and strengthening their willpower, so that they can really respect labor and love labor from the bottom of heart.

# VI. Conclusion: To Build a Labor Education System of Inherent Vitality

Looking back at the historical evolution of labor education since the founding of the People's Republic of China, it can be found that the promotion and implementation of labor education in China have shown obvious exogenous characteristics. It is the exogenous characteristics that make it difficult for Chinese labor education to deliver satisfactory results, despite all the hard work. The exogenous character of labor education in China is manifested both in the exogenous nature of the driving force and the purpose. A labor education system of inherent vitality should be built with knowing truth, goodness and beauty in labor as the root, the integration of education on morality, intelligence, physical fitness, aesthetics and labor as the soil, and the cultivation of correct labor values pointing the direction of growth.

## References

[1] Xi Jinping. "Adheres to the Path of Development of Socialist Education with Chinese Characteristics" [EB/OL]. http://xhpfmapi.zhongguowangshi.com/vh510/#/share/4509214?channel=weixin.

[2] Ministry of Education, Central Committee of the Communist Youth League and National Permanent Standing Commission of the Young Pioneers of China, Opinions on Strengthening Labor Education in Primary and Secondary Schools [EB/OL]. http://www.moe.edu.cn/srcsite/A06/s3325/201507/t20150731_197068.html.

[3] He Dongchang. Important Educational Documents of the People's Republic of China (1949-1975) [M]. Haikou: Hainan Publishing House, 1998.

——He Dongchang. Important Educational Documents of the People's Republic of China (1976-1990) [M]. Haikou: Hainan Publishing House, 1998b.

——He Dongchang. Important Educational Documents of the People's Republic of China (1991-1997) [M]. Haikou: Hainan Publishing House, 1998c.

——He Dongchang. Important Educational Documents of the People's Republic of China (1998-2002) [M]. Haikou: Hainan Publishing House, 2003.

[4] Gu Mingyuan. Chinese Education Series • Marxism and Chinese Education (Volume II) [M]. Wuhan: Hubei Education Press, 1994: 1638-1639.

[5] Li Qinggang. "Institutional Innovation in the Exploration of the Correct Handling of Contradictions Among the People" [J]. Beijing Dangshi, 2017(3): 5-10.

[6] Li Qinggang. "Study of the Education Revolution" During the "Great Leap Forward" [D]. Party School of the CPC Central Committee, 2002: 27.

[7] Cheng Youxin. New Exploration of the Issue of Integrating Education and Productive

Labor [M]. Changsha: Hunan Education Press, 1998: 307.

[8] Liu Shifeng. Study on the Combination of Education and Labor [M]. Beijing: Educational Science Publishing House, 1996: 10.

[9] Cao Xia. "Changes of the Guiding Principles of Education and the Analysis Since the Reform and Opening up" [D]. Hangzhou: Zhejiang Normal University, 2006: 18-19.

[10] Xu Changfa. "Labor Education is the First Education of Life" [J]. China Rural Education, 2015(10): 4-6.

[11] Luo Jianqin. "From 'Combining Education with Productive Labor' to 'Combining Education with Social Practice' [J]. Mao Zedong Thought Study, 2001(3): 103-105.

[12] Xu Changfa. "Development of Labor Skills Education in China" [J]. Educational Research, 2004(12): 11-16.

[13] Du Rui. "The Pain of 'Three Absences' in Labor Skills Education" [N]. China Education Daily, 2014-11-26.

[14] Chen Jing and Huang Zhongjing. "From 'Physical Education' to 'Competency Education' –The Development and Changes of China's Labor Education Policy" [J]. 2015(16):33-38.

[15] Du Zuorun. "Labor Education –An Issue Worth Thinking About" [J]. Modern University Education, 2016(3): 29-33.

[16] Xi Jinping. "Speech at the Seminar with Representatives of National Model Workers" [N]. People's Daily, 2013-04-29.

[17] Xi Jinping. "Secure a Decisive Victory in Building a Moderately Prosperous Society in All Respects, Strive for the Great Success of Socialism with Chinese Characteristics for a New Era" [EB/OL]. http://www.xinhuanet.com/2017-10/27/c_1121867529.htm.

[18] Xi Jinping. "Celebration of 'May 1st' International Labor Day and National Commendation Conference of National Model Workers and Advanced Workers" [N]. People's Daily, 2015-04-29.

[19] Tao Xingzhi. Selected Works on Life and Education [M]. Chengdu: Sichuan Education Press, 1988.

# Social Security

- "Combination of Social Pooling and Individual Account" Model in China's Basic Pension System: Historical Changes and Reform Suggestions

# "Combination of Social Pooling and Individual Account" Model in China's Basic Pension System: Historical Changes and Reform Suggestions[*]

*Guo Peng[**]*

**Abstract:** Since the Third Plenary Session of the 18th CPC Central Committee, there have been subtle changes in Chinese government documents regarding the "individual account" of the basic pension system, from "gradually turning the individual accounts of pension into real ones" to " improve the individual account system". These changes have a profound significance. It marks that the Chinese government recognized the change of the individual account in the public pension system, and the "combination of social pooling and individual account" system is now at the crossroad of reform. China should seize the opportunity of "transferring part of the state-owned capital" and lowering the contribution rate of the first pillar enterprises to compensate for the historical debts of pension, and on this basis, separate the function of social relief and the accumulation of individuals in the basic pension system, establish zero-pillar social pension; find ways to incorporate reduced contributions into enterprise annuities, and promote the development of the second and third pillars; establish a normalized actuarial mechanism and standardize the adjustment methods of benefits; gradually realize the nationwide basic pension planning based on the central adjustment fund.

**Keywords:** combination of social pooling and individual accounts; pay-as-you-go system, historical debt

The urban employee basic pension in China is based on the "combination of social pooling and individual account" model,[1] which originated in the 1990s. Under

[*] This paper was published in *Guizhou Social Sciences*, Issue 7, 2017.

[**] Guo Peng, Ph.D. in Economics, Associate Professor at the China University of Labor Relations. She specializes in pension insurance. Email: gracepguo@gmail.com.

[1] The "Basic Pension system of urban employees" is referred to as "basic pension", "pension insurance" or "public pension" for convenience, the meaning of them is the same.

the historical background, the pay-as-you-go (PAYG) public pension system was combined with the contribution-based individual account system, and thus a new system was established. At that time, workers who had already retired ("the elderly") and workers who started to work before the establishment of the system and had not yet retired ("middle-aged people") paid no contribution. Therefore, a large sum of debts was emerged. However, the government failed to realize the seriousness of this problem and did not provide sufficient funds outside the system to compensate. Instead, it chose to obfuscate debts and digest debts within the system, which led to the inherent inadequacy of China's pension system. The approach of dealing with historical debts within the system requires workers to bear not only the pension benefits of the "elderly", but also those of the contemporary retirees, which means that they were forced to take a "dual responsibility". That's why a policy of high contribution rates was formulated. Even so, the social pooling fund was still not enough to meet the demand. In order to solve this problem, the government adopted the "mixed account management" approach. When the social pooling fund cannot make ends meet, the individual account funds would be used to fill in the gap.

The system has been operated for more than 20 years, which proves that the system based on the "combination of social pooling and individual accounts" model with heavy historical debts would inevitably lead to "mixed accounts management" and empty individual accounts, thus making the original intention of the system a mere formality. In recent years, the issue of "empty individual accounts" attracted social attention, an increasing number of people are questioning the current pension insurance system. Therefore, it is necessary to discuss the reason of formation, process of development and existing problems of the pension system, and propose reform schemes in a targeted manner.

### I. "Combination of Social Pooling and Individual Account" Model in China's Basic  Pension System: Changes of the System

Before the reform and opening up, China adopted a planned economic system, and established a Soviet style pension system[1], which characterized by pay-as-you-go (PAYG) and corporate-planned system with single source of funding. With the deepening of economic structure reform, this kind of egalitarian practice of "everybody eating from the same big pot" had been unable to adapt to the requirements of the new structure. With the progress of the reform of state-

---

[1] At that time, experts from the USSR were invited to discuss the social insurance system. A labor insurance system was established based on the national conditions. Similar to the USSR, the system did not require workers to pay the contributions. But the social insurance fee was paid by the State Treasury in the USSR, while in China, the enterprises were responsible for that.

owned enterprises, the number of enterprise retirees had increased significantly. The old system was not able to cover the costs of pension during the peak period of retirement. It also exacerbated the conflict between the newly-built and old enterprises due to the inequality of the pension expenses. For some old enterprises in the textile, food, and salt industries, the pension expenses were even higher than half of their total payroll expenses. For example, five major salt factories in Zigong of Sichuan Province, had to pay the amount of pension equivalent to 69% of their total payroll expenses (Han and Jiao, 1997). At the same time, some newly-built enterprises in emerging industries, such as electronics, instrumentation and chemical engineering, did not even have a retiree.

In response to the inequality of pension expenses of different enterprises, relevant Chinese authorities have organized domestic and foreign experts to conduct extensive investigations and discussions. In the National Insurance and Welfare Work Conference held in 1983, it was proposed to establish a social pool of pension for the state-owned enterprises. In 1984, China started implementing the pilot projects of managing pension of state-owned enterprises by a social pool in Jiangmen and Dongguan of Guangdong Province, Zigong of Sichuan Province, Taizhou of Jiangsu Province and Heishan County of Liaoning Province (Han and Jiao, 1997), which marked the beginning of the reform of the pension system in China. In this paper, the development of China's pension system is divided into two phases:

## 1. Phase I: Introduction of Individual Contributions under the Influence of the International Labor Organization (Early 1980s-1986)

In 1982, the State Commission for Economic Restructuring (SCER) was established. SCER invited three experts from the International Labor Organization (ILO), the United States and Singapore to visit Beijing, Shanghai, Wuxi, Dalian and Shenyang in order to explore the reform of China's pension system (Hu, 2012). During this period, the social insurance system (the German Bismarck model) advocated by the ILO became the mainstream model for China's pension system to follow.

ILO advocated the establishment of social security systems in several countries after World War II. The ILO model involved four factors: coverage, access to the benefits, financing method and administration, among which the financing method was the core factor. According to ILO's suggestion, countries should establish a PAYG social insurance system, and workers should support the retirees of the same period of time. Based on the concept of ILO, the implementation of individual contribution system demonstrated the consistency of social insurance rights and obligations. It could not only change the concept of complete dependence on the state for labor security, alleviate the burden of the state and enterprises, ease the economic pressure brought by the aging population, but also directly linked pension with the number of contribution years of individuals, and reflected the relationship between rights and obligations. Besides, it realized the adoption of international standards, in line with the international practice (Hu, 2012).

The practice of individual contribution was introduced into China during this period. Back then, China's social security system existed as a complementary measure to the reform of state-owned enterprises, with its primary purpose of serving the reform of state-owned enterprises. It was specified in Article 26, Chapter 5 of the *Interim Provisions on the Implementation of the Labor Contract System in State-owned Enterprises*, (issued by the State Council) that "all newly recruited workers in state-owned enterprises shall be subject to the labor contract system. Workers under the labor contract system shall pay a certain percentage of their own pension". This provision marked the beginning of the change of model in China similar to that of the USSR, in which the state and the enterprises were responsible for paying the social insurance of workers; and reflected the introduction of the social insurance model advocated by ILO, which was based on the Bismarck social insurance model.

## 2. Phase II: Under the Influence of both the World Bank and the International Labor Organization, the "Combination of Social Pooling and Individual Account" Model was Established

### *2.1 Different opinions arose, pilot projects were implemented in various regions (1986-1997)*

After the oil crisis in the 1970s, Western countries suffered from economic crisis. In the economics circles, neoliberalism began to replace Keynesianism, and became the mainstream economic ideology in the West. With the U.S. President Reagan and British Prime Minister Thatcher taking office, Western countries started to cut the generous benefits provided by the welfare system which had been established since World War II. Under this macro background, the PAYG system advocated by ILO was widely questioned. The Latin American countries, especially Chile, started to conduct privatization reform of public pension systems, which also intensified the debate over the advantages and disadvantages of the PAYG system and the fully funded system. After the 1990s, with the publication of the World Bank's report *Averting the Old Age Crisis: Policies to Protect the Old and Promote Growth* (World Bank, 1995), the World Bank started to intervene in the field of public pension reform in various countries.

In China, there were two different voices regarding the reform of the pension system: one was led by experts from the State Commission for Economic Restructuring (SCER) and the World Bank, which advocated the establishment of a fully funded pension system in China. The other, which was represented by the Ministry of Labor and ILO, proposed the adherence to a PAYG system based on social pool. At that time, the pilot project of SCER was implemented in Fujian Province while the pilot project of the Ministry of Labor was implemented in Guangdong Province. In July 1989, Fujian Province launched the first pilot project on the implementation of the "combined system of social pool and individual account" model for urban collective enterprises. At the end of 1989, SCER organized domestic and international experts to research and analysis relevant issues. And it was concluded that China should adopt a new pension system which combined the social pool and individual account, entailing both the advantages of the PAYG system and the fully funded system. Later, pilot projects were implemented in Shenzhen, Hainan, Shanghai and other provinces and cities (Song, 1998).

In 1991, the State Council issued *Decision of the State Council on the Reform of the Pension System for Enterprise Employees*, which played an important role in promoting the finalization of the pension system. It confirmed that China's pension insurance should be implemented based on the social pooling; and clarified that the coverage should be expanded from district, county and city level to provincial level, and the national level in the end; the source of the pooling fund should be the state, enterprises and individuals. Also, the direction of the establishment of a multi-level pension system was proposed (Zhou and Zhang, 2015). In 1993, the reform towards the "combination of social pooling and individual account" model was specified in *Provisions of the CPC Central Committee on the Establishment of Socialist Market Economic System*. In 1995, the principle of the combined system was re-emphasized in *Notice on Deepening the Reform of the Enterprise Employees' Pension System*, but the detailed plan was not clarified. At that time, the scheme proposed by SCER placed more emphasis on the establishment of individual accounts, while the scheme proposed by the Ministry of Labor emphasized on the establishment of social pool. By allowing local governments to choose either reform scheme based on their actual conditions, these two schemes coexisted in China. In result, hundreds of pension reform plans emerged across the country in just two years, which caused many difficulties in practice.

*2.2 Agreements were gradually reached, the "combination of social pooling and individual account" model was established (1997-2001)*

The variation of regional systems greatly affected the management efficiency. In 1996, SCER and the World Bank published *Study on the Design of Supplementary Pension and Individual Saving-based Pension Programs in China* and *Old Age Security: Pension Reform in China* respectively, proposing the establishment of a three-tier pension system and recommending the establishment of a standardized three-pillar system by 2010. In 1997, after gathering opinions of all parties and considering the advantages and disadvantages of the two schemes, China issued the *Decision on Establishing a Unified Basic Pension System for Enterprise Employees*, which unified the contribution rate of basic pension insurance, and stipulated that the proportion of contributions paid by enterprises should not exceed 20% of their total payroll expenses, while those paid by individuals should be no less than 4% of their income. From 1998, the rate would be increased by 1 percent every two years, and finally reach 8% (State Council, 1997). At that time, considering the basic national conditions, the Chinese government believed that it was not the right time to separate the accumulations of individual accounts from the first pillar, so as a transitional measure, the framework of the "combination of social pooling and individual account" model was maintained, and a small-scale enterprise supplementary pension insurance was established first (Song, 1998).

### 2.3 A pilot phase of "real individual accounts of pension" (2001-2003)

In 2000, the *Notice on the Issuance of the Pilot Project for Improving the Urban Social Security System* marked the start of separating the management of "social pooling fund" and "individual account fund", and turning the individual accounts of pension into real accounts other than nominal accounts (so-called "empty accounts"), while reducing the contribution rate of individual accounts from 11% to 8%, and stated that the money in the individual accounts would no longer used for the employer contributions. Later, the pilot project of real individual accounts of pension was implemented in Liaoning Province in July 2001, and expanded to Heilongjiang Province and Jilin Province in 2004 and 2005, with the support of the World Bank. During 1999 and 2002, the World Bank provided loans of 5 million dollars in total to turn the individual accounts of pension into real accounts in Heilongjiang Province and Qingdao (World Bank,1995). In *Decision of the State Council on Improving the Basic Pension System for Enterprise Employees*, it was proposed that the practice of "turning individual accounts of pension into real ones" should be expanded to the whole nation. The State Council approved the expansion of the pilot of "real individual accounts" in eight provinces (Shanghai, Tianjin, Shandong, Henan, Shanxi, Hubei, Hunan and Xinjiang) in 2006, and in Jiangsu Province in 2008. So far, a total of 13 provinces in China have implemented the pilot project.

However, in 2009, there was a misappropriation of accumulated funds in individual accounts of pension in Liaoning Province, the first province that implemented the pilot project. The situation in other provinces was not optimistic either – most of the 13 provinces needed a huge amount of financial subsidies or loans to meet current expenditure needs, and the process of turning individual accounts of pension into real accounts came to a halt (Xiao, 2016). Since there were few successful experiences in these provinces and cities, the issue of whether individual accounts should be real accounts became a focus of debate among Chinese government and the academic community, and it has been pending for a long time. In the report of the 18th CPC National Congress in 2012, the government still insisted on using the expression of "gradually turning the individual accounts of pension into real ones".

### 2.4 Improving the individual account system (2013-now)

As the size of the empty individual accounts continued to expand, there was an increasing voice which opposing the change of individual accounts into real ones. In the Third Plenary Session of the 18th CPC Central Committee, *Decision of the Central Committee of the CPC on Several Major Issues Concerning Comprehensively Deepening the Reform* was approved, in which the concept of "improving the individual account system" was proposed for the first time. The change of terms used reflected that the Chinese government started to re-examine the "individual account" system, and marked a critical point of the reform of the "combination of social pooling and individual account" model in China's basic pension system. Especially, the financial situation of pension funds in the old industrial bases in Northeast China, such as Heilongjiang Province, continued to deteriorate, and the dependency ratio of the system declined, which made the practice of "turning individual accounts of pension into real accounts" even more unsustainable.

According to data published by the Ministry of Human Resources and Social Security (MHRSS), the dependency ratio in terms of Basic Pension Insurance for urban employees nationwide was 2.87:1 in 2015. During the same period, the dependency ratio in terms of enterprise pension insurance in Heilongjiang Province was the lowest (1.33:1)[1]. The pension fund in this province could cover the expense of only one month (MOHRSS, 2015). In 2015, Heilongjiang Province dissolved its relationship of entrusted investment management with the National Council for Social Security Fund[2]. By the end of 2015, the accumulated book amount of individual accounts reached 4,714.4 billion yuan, while the accumulated balance of the pension insurance fund was only 3,534.5 billion yuan over the same period. The accumulated book amount of enterprise was 4,544.3 billion yuan, and the accumulated balance in the area where the real individual accounts were set was 327.4 billion yuan. Obviously, even if all the capital accumulated in the pension insurance fund were used to fill the individual accounts, there would still be a deficit of more than one trillion yuan (Zheng, 2016). Under this circumstance, the Chinese

---

[1] Dependency ratio: ratio of number of insured employees to number of pensionary.

[2] http://www.ssf.gov.cn/cwsj/ndbg/201606/t20160602_7079.html.

government delegated a number of institutions to conduct a "top-level design" of the pension system, research the main problems of China's pension system, and explore ways to "improve" the individual accounts and the "combined system".

With the announcement of *the State Council's Decision on the Reform of the Pension System for Employees of Public Institutions* in 2015, the pension systems for employees of public institutions and those of enterprises have been unified in China. In the first half of 2017, MHRSS issued a Notice, which introduced *the Measures on Unifying and Standardizing the Interest Rate for Individual Accounts of Employee Pension Insurance.* It was proposed that "the interest rates for individual accounts of basic pension insurance for employees of public institutions and enterprises should be unified, and be announced annually by the state". Factors such as "the increase of the employees' salary, and the balance of the fund" should be taken into consideration when setting the interest rate which should "be adjusted based on a reasonable coefficient", and not be lower than the interest rate of fixed deposit in the bank. On June 8th 2017, MHRSS issued a Notice, in which the interest rate for individual accounts of basic pension insurance for urban employees (include those of the public institutions and enterprises) was 8.31%. During October 1st 2014 and December 31st 2015, the interest rate for individual accounts of basic pension insurance for employees of public institutions was 5%. Previously, the average interest rate for individual accounts was only 2% to 3%. This was an important step in implementing the "improvement of individual accounts" proposed in the Third Plenary Session of the 18th CPC Central Committee. Since then, the interest rate of individual accounts has been always kept at a high level. During 2017 to 2020, the interest rate of individual accounts was 7.12%, 8.29%, 7.61% and 6.04% respectively (MOHRSS, 2020).

## II. "Combination of Social Pooling and Individual Account" Model in China's Basic Pension System: Major Problems

Based on the above analysis, we can see that under international and domestic pressure, the combined pension system of China was a compromise between the individual cumulative account scheme advocated by SCER and the World Bank, and the PAYG scheme advocated by the Ministry of Labor and ILO. Most of the countries that have undertaken partially funded public pension reforms already separated a portion of their contributions from the original PAYG public pension system and established a separate second pillar. In contrast, in China's "combined account" system, the PAYG system and the funded system were all in one pillar to avoid the historical debt problem. For many years, China's pension system has been nominally a partially funded system, but in essence, it is still a PAYG system. After more than 20 years of practice, it showed that this combination of the first pillar (which is responsible for social relief) and the second pillar (which is responsible for individual accumulation and motivation) cannot help to clearly define individual rights and interests, nor can realize the original purpose of the reform of the partially funded system at that time. It failed to integrate the advantages of the two systems. Instead, it made the reform of the China's pension system difficult to be sustained with many problems.

## 1. Unclear Historical Debts Led to Potential Problems

During the period of planned economy, the profits of enterprises were turned over to the state; and all resources were distributed by the government according to the plan. With the deepening of reform and opening up, in order to correspond to the reform of state-owned enterprises, it was clarified that the responsibility of financing pension insurance was shared by the state, enterprises and individuals. Until the 16th CPC National Congress, China's social security system has been existed as a complementary measure to the reform of state-owned enterprises. In the report of the 16th CPC National Congress, it was proposed to "deepen the reform of the distribution system, and improve the social security system". Till then, the social security was independent from the framework of the state-owned enterprise reform. Since the "elderly people" and "middle-aged people" paid no contribution before, there was a large sum of debts (Guo, 2017). Besides, in some regions and industries, the practice of early retirement was adopted to alleviate the unemployment problem. It has helped to reduce temporary redundancies, but also brought a huge pressure on China's pension insurance funds in the long run. For example, around 1996 in Harbin, Heilongjiang Province, more than 10,000 people retired early, which resulted in a total of about 220 million yuan of both the reduction of revenue and the increase of expense of the pension insurance fund. This practice also blurred the boundaries between unemployment insurance and pension insurance. It treated the unemployed as the retired, putting enormous pressure on China's pension insurance fund (Song, 1998). Thus, China's pension system was born with a heavy burden.

## 2. Insufficient Attractiveness Made It Difficult to Expand the Coverage

The lack of effective solution to address the historical debt, and the hope to resolve the liabilities within the system, led to a series of problems. The primary problem is that China has to adopt a policy of high contribution rates to guarantee current benefit expenses, with the total pension contribution rates of enterprises and individuals  was once as high as 28%. As a direct consequence of high contribution rates, the evasion of contributions is common while the coverage is difficult to be expanded. By the end of 2019, the number of active workers in China joining the Basic Pension Insurance for urban employees was 312 million (MOHRSS, 2020), accounting for 70.42% of the total number of urban employee of that year. However, based on the data of recent years, it was estimated that the proportion of people who paid the contribution in 2019 was around 85%, so that the actual coverage rate was only around 60%. In addition, with the emergence of new industries and new forms of employment in recent years, there is a large number of informal workers. The high contribution rates, as well as the complicated transfer and succession policies have discouraged them from joining the pension insurance.

### 3. Lack of High-level Planning, Obstructing the Labor Mobility

At the beginning of the establishment of the system, the problem of unbalanced historical debts in different provinces was not effectively solved, which led to the "unfair starting point" of the pension system. For example, there are more laid-off retirees and heavy historical debts in the old industrial bases in Northeast China, while in the coastal provinces, such as Guangdong, there are more new industries and less historical debts. With the emergence of a large group of migrant workers in China, the regional gap was widened and the inequality was exacerbated.

Currently, China's pension insurance planning is at a low level. For many regions, they don't achieve the collection and expenditure of funds at provincial level, let alone the unified planning of personnel, capital and goods. As the level of economic development varies greatly across regions, local governments tend to formulate the pension system according to local conditions, resulting in different contribution rates and levels of planning. This seriously undermined the flexibility of the system, even became a major obstacle to labor mobility.

### 4. Actuarial Balance Cannot be Achieved, and the System is not Sustainable

The "combined system" of China's pension insurance has both social relief and personal saving functions. For the social relief part, the principle of equity should be followed, and the inter-generational redistribution will be achieved horizontally through the PAYG  scheme. For individual accounts, the one who contributes more will also get more benefits, and one's lifetime income redistribution will be achieved vertically through personal saving. Combination of these two systems makes it impossible to achieve actuarial balance. Coupled with the existence of historical debt, this practice has resulted in heavy dependence on financial subsidies. According to the data provided by MHRSS, the average annual growth rate of government financial subsidies granted to the pension system is around 17%. The financial subsidy was 2.4 billion yuan in 1998, and soared to 397 billion yuan in 2015 (MOHRSS, 2015). The total financial transfer payment from 1998 to 2015 amounted to 2561.8 billion yuan, among which the proportion of the central government subsidies was as high as 90% (Zheng, 2016). Although the data of financial subsidies was not published by MHRSS in the past two years, it is projected that the total amount of financial subsidies granted to pension funds would exceed 900 billion yuan in 2018 based on the data from previous years (Guo, 2020). However, even with such a high level of financial subsidies, the financial sustainability of China's pension system is still not optimistic. Since 2014, the contributions to China's pension fund have always been less than the amount of benefit expenses. Previously, with the central government's efforts to expand the coverage, payment of the overdue contribution and lump sum payment pushed up the current collection income in the short term, and concealed the real financial situation of China's pension funds. As the coverage expansion work reaching a bottleneck in recent years, the problem of financial sustainability of pension funds has gradually emerged.

## 5. Inappropriate Method of Pension Adjustment Undermines the Credibility of the System

China's existing pension benefit adjustment mechanism has a strong administrative overtone. Since 2005, China has been raising the pension benefits of enterprise employee every year through administrative order. Although this practice helped to stabilize society and avoid excessive benefits of enterprise employees and public institution employees, the annual increase in fund expenditures due to the adjustment was getting larger, which has put enormous pressure on the pension insurance. Also, this practice greatly reduced the predictability of policies related to pension adjustment. Under the premise of benefit rigidity, this practice also raised public expectations for higher pension rates, especially among retired workers, which undermined the financial sustainability of the fund. In 2016, against the backdrop of the economic downturn, the Chinese government reduced the pension adjustment ratio to 6.5%, which triggered widespread criticism. On April 13th 2017, MHRSS announced that the pension adjustment ratio was reduced to 5.5% (MOHRSS, 2017). In 2018, it was reduced to 5%, and maintained at that level. As the issue of pension adjustment has always been the focus of public debate, the adjustment by administrative order is detrimental not only to social stability, but also to the credibility of the system.

**The first pillar is in a dominant position, while the development of other pillars is lagging behind**

In the 1990s, China has clearly defined the goal of establishing a multi-pillar pension system. However, it has been difficult to make a breakthrough in the multi-pillar pension development over years. The main reason is that the rights and responsibilities among the pillars are not clear. Even to some extent, the high contribution rate of the first pillar in the long term has squeezed the development space of other pillars. By the end of 2019, the total number of participants of the second pillar of enterprise annuities in China was 25.48 million, accounting for only 6.7% of those of the first pillar (MOHRSS, 2020). The development of enterprise annuities is lagging behind and the third pillar is only in the nascent phase. The slow development of the other pillars has in turn increased the burden of the first pillar, forming a vicious circle.

## III. "Combination of Social Pooling and Individual Account" Model in China's Basic Pension System: Reform Suggestions

To sum up, China's combined system of pension insurance is the product of the controversies and compromises among different international and domestic sectors in the 1990s. The system itself is the key difficulty of reforming China's current pension system. On the premise of clarifying historical debts, China should separate the social pooling, which focuses on fairness and social relief, from the individual accounts, which undertake the task of personal motivation and saving.

### 1. Clearly Define and Effectively Solve Historical Debt Issues

The key to the success of the reform of the "combined system" is the reasonable resolution of historical debts. China should promptly clarify its historical debts and take effective measures, such as allocating state-owned assets and increasing financial subsidies, to pay off the debts. In 2015, Lou Jiwei, then Minister of Finance, stated repeatedly in public that only by transferring part of the state-owned capital to the social security fund, the historical debt of pension insurance could be effectively paid off. In 2017, Premier Li Keqiang stated again in the government work report that "transferring part of the state-owned capital to the social security fund" was a key task. The progress of this policy has been relatively slow in the past few years since its implementation. Therefore, the supporting policies should be formulated as soon as possible to speed up the transfer. Since the Chinese government pays high attention on this issue, and plans to pay off historical debts by transferring state-owned capital, it should calculate the accurate historical debts, and develop different transfer approaches, transfer ratios and transfer scales in phases and steps for different categories of state-owned enterprises (business enterprises, and the enterprise for public welfare, etc.), together with relevant departments such as the Ministry of Finance, the State-owned Assets Supervision and Administration Commission, and the Ministry of Human Resource and Social Security.

## 2. Take Rate Reduction as An Opportunity to Expand the Coverage

The Chinese government introduced a policy in 2016 which stipulated that provinces with an enterprise contribution rate of more than 20% may reduce the rate to 20%. For provinces with an enterprise contribution rate of 20% and a fund provision of more than nine months at the end of 2015, the enterprise contribution rate could be reduced by one percent point (State Council, 2016). In 2019, *Notice of the General Office of the State Council on the Issuance of a Comprehensive Plan for Reducing Social Insurance Premium Rates* stated that the enterprise contribution rate was reduced to 16% (State Council, 2019). This reflected the Chinese government's determination to reduce the social insurance costs of enterprises and lighten the burden on enterprises in the context of the "new normal". However, at present, there are no legal provisions for workers engaged in new forms of employment to have social insurance; the existing laws are not strict in punishing social security violations. Relevant laws and regulations should be revised and supplemented to regulate enterprises' contribution behavior and clarify legal responsibilities. A cross-departmental information sharing mechanism should also be established as soon as possible. Together with finance, taxation, auditing departments and local governments, the cross-departmental enforcement and supervision should be strengthened.

## 3. Gradually Improve the Level of Planning with the Central Government Fund as the Transition

In the Third Plenary Session of the 18th CPC Central Committee, it was proposed to "achieve nationwide basic pension planning". However, this goal could not be achieved due to the large disparity in pension fund balances across regions in China. On June 13th 2018, the State Council issued *Notice on the Establishment of the Central Adjustment System of the Basic Pension Fund for Enterprise Employees*, which stated that a central adjustment fund should be established. The central adjustment ratio of the basic pension fund for enterprise employees was 3% in 2018, 3.5% in 2019, and 4% in 2020. The support for financially strained regions was strengthened. Since the nationwide planning cannot be achieved for now, and there are some provinces that cannot make ends meet, this system can play a transitional role. However, to achieve the nationwide planning, it is necessary to split the social relief and personal saving functions of the first pillar, and separate basic pensions and individual account pensions.

## 4. Build a Regular Actuarial Mechanism and Standardize the Way of Benefit Adjustment

For the social pooling part that is separated from the social pension, the principle of actuarial balance should be adopted to build a regular actuarial mechanism and enhance the financial sustainability of the pension system. Based on international experiences, it should introduce an automatic adjustment mechanism that links benefits with demographic changes, commodity prices and wage increases, standardize the method of pension benefit adjustment, and strengthen the financial sustainability of the system.

## 5. Define the Boundary of Functions and Responsibilities of Each Pillar, and Build A Multi-pillar Pension System

Clearly define the responsibilities and obligations of the government, enterprises and individuals regarding the pension insurance, and realize the change from "combination of social pooling and individual account" to separating social pooling and individual accounts. On this basis, let each pillar play its due role.

**First, establish a social pension system.** China's social pension insurance for urban and rural residents runs parallel to the pension insurance for enterprise employees, with a large urban-rural gap and prominent conflicts. At the same time, the burden of subsidizing the pension system is very heavy. If social pensions were established on the basis of this amount of subsidy, the share of the adjustment payment in GDP would be below 0.5% before 2037. And after 2037, it would still be below 1.2% until 2090, despite the increase caused by the aging population (MOHRSS, 2020). For the no-income or low-income groups, they can join the social pension system by relying exclusively on financial subsidies. For other groups, explore a contribution mechanism similar to Japan's national pension system (Guo, 2017), and rely on the social pooling fund separated from the first pillar. On this basis, the Ministry of Civil Affairs, the Ministry of Human Resources and Social Security, the Ministry of Finance and other relevant departments will gradually integrate the urban and rural subsistence allowance system and the urban and rural residents' social pension insurance system into the social pension system, so as to achieve a "fair starting point" for employees and residents in the social pension system.

**Second, actively develop a multi-pillar pension system.** It should clarify the system boundary of the first pillar (i.e., public pensions) as soon as possible, as well as the rights and obligations among the various pension-providing entities. In the context of reducing the enterprise contribution rate in the first pillar, the reduced first pillar contributions should be gradually incorporated into the second pillar; and the development of enterprise annuities should be strongly supported in conjunction with tax incentives and other measures. It should explore the development of the third pillar that suits China's national conditions, change the status quo of the first pillar being dominant and build a multi-pillar pension system.

## References

[1] Han Liangcheng, Jiao Kaiping. Unification and Implementation of Enterprise Pension Insurance System[M]. Beijing: China Renshi Publishing House, 1997

[2] Aiqun Hu. The Global Spread of Neoliberalism and China's Pension Reform since 1978[J]. Journal of World History, 2012, 3(23): 609-638.

[3] World Bank. Averting the Old Age Crisis: Policies to Protect the Old and Promote Growth (Chinese version)[R]. Beijing: China Financial & Economic Publishing House, 1995.

[4] Song Xiaowu. 20 Years of the Construction of China's Social Security System[M]. Zhengzhou: Zhongzhou Ancient Books Publishing House,1998.

[5] Zhou Hong, Zhang Jun. Towards a Society with Social Protection for All: A Concise History of Social Security Transformation in Modern China[M]. Beijing: China Social Sciences Press, 2015.

[6] Guofa[1997] No. 26, [2017-01-16]. http://www.gov.cn/flfg/index.htm.

[7] Xiao Yanhua. Key Issues of China's Pension System Reform during the 13th Five-year Plan[J]. Shanghai Urban Management, 2016(4):11-17.

[8] Social Insurance Administration Center of the Ministry of Human Resources and Social Society. Annual Report on China's Social Insurance Development - 2015[R]. Beijing: China Human Resources & Social Security Publishing House, 2016.

[9] Zheng Bingwen. Assessment of the Operation of the Basic Pension Insurance in 2015[M]//Zheng Bingwen. China Pension Report 2016. Beijing: Economy & Management Publishing House, 2016

[10] MOHRSS. http://www.mohrss.gov.cn/SYrlzyhshbzb/shehuibaozhang/zcwj/ 2020-12-16.

[11] Guo Peng. Taking the "Transfer of State-Owned Capital" as an Opportunity to Improve the Pension System for Urban Workers[N]. China Labor and Social Security News. 2017-4-25(003).

[12] MOHRSS. http://www.mohrss.gov.cn/SYrlzyhshbzb/zwgk/szrs/tjgb/202006/

t20200608_375774.html 2020-12-16.

[13] Guo Peng. Report on the Status of Chinese Workers 2020[R]//Yan Xiaofei. Report on the Status of Chinese Workers 2020. Beijing: Social Sciences Academic Press, 2020.

[14] Renshefa[2017] No. 30. http://www.mohrss.gov.cn/gkml/xxgk/201704/t20170414_269473.html2017-04-16.

[15] "State Council executive meeting chaired by Premier Li Keqiang". http://www.gov.cn/guowuyuan/2016-04/13/content_5063747.htm2016-12-23.

[16] Guobanfa[2019] No. 13. http://www.gov.cn/zhengce/content/2019-04-04/content_5379629.htm2020-12-16.

[17] Guo Peng, The "Integration" of Japan's Pension Insurance for Enterprise Employees and Pension Insurance for Public Servants, and Its Implications for China[J]. Gansu Social Science, 2017(3):115.

# Digital Economy and Labor Rights Protection

- Development of New Forms of Employment and Workforce Building in the Context of Digital Economy

- Employment Status and Identification of Platform Workers and Protection of Their Rights and Interests

# Development of New Forms of Employment and Workforce Building in the Context of Digital Economy

*Ji Wenwen*[*]

**Abstract:** In recent years, the traditional driving forces of Chinese economy are shifting to new ones. On the one hand, the digital economy driven by big data, artificial intelligence (AI) and other new information technologies continues to develop fast; on the other hand, the traditional economy driven by labor and resources is slowly going downward. The development of China's digital economy has been remarkable: the related fields have gradually become fertile ground for new employment, with increasing new jobs created. In 2020, due to COVID-19, the downward pressure on economy increased dramatically, with many offline industries shutting down or recovering slowly; while the rise of new employment forms has undoubtedly alleviated the problem of underemployment in the traditional economy, and played the role of employment reservoir and stabilizer. This paper focuses on the current development of China's new employment forms in the context of the digital economy, and further analyzes the significance of this development in building China's workforce, as well as the possible future trends based on relevant theories.

**Keywords**: digital economy; new employment form; workforce; new trends

According to the data of previous years from the China Academy for Information and Communications Technology (CAICT), the total output of digital economy in China increased from 1.2 trillion yuan to 35.8 trillion yuan during 2002-2019. And the added value of the digital economy represented by new industries, new forms and new business models reached 28.8 trillion yuan in 2019, equivalent to 29% of GDP. The importance of the digital economy in the national economy has been further highlighted. During 2014-2019, the contribution of the digital economy to GDP

[*] Ji Wenwen, Ph.D. in Economics, Associate Professor of the China University of Labor Relations. She specializes in labor economics, education economics.

growth has always remained over 50%. In 2019, it reached 67.7%, which surpassed the level of some developed countries, and was significantly higher than the total contribution of the primary, secondary, and tertiary industries. The digital economy became the key driving force of the development of China's national economy.

In contrast to the surge of the digital economy, China's traditional economy has been going downward. As shown in Figure 1, since the global financial crisis, China's GDP growth rate has declined from 14.2% in 2007 to 7.3% in 2014. In 2015, the supply-side structural reform was officially launched. In 2019, China's annual GDP exceeded 99 trillion yuan, with a growth rate of 6.1% (0.9% lower than that of 2015). According to Okun's Law, the economic downturn is bound to bring huge pressure on employment. However, data shows that the number of new jobs created in urban areas has steadily increased from 12.04 million to 13.52 million in the same period. In 2020, affected by the COVID-19 pandemic, China's GDP in the first quarter showed negative growth, while the number of newly employed people remained over 10 million, according to the Ministry of Human Resources and Social Security (MOHRSS). The booming "new forms of employment" has undoubtedly become an important guarantee for stabilizing employment.

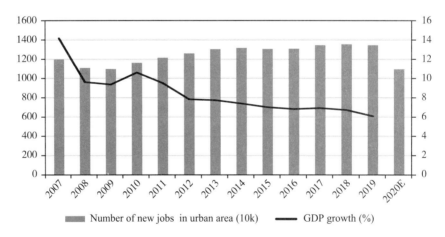

**Figure 1　GDP growth rate and new jobs in urban area of China, 2007-2020(E)**

Source: National Bureau of Statistics, *Statistical Communiqué on the National Economy and Social Development*, various years.

## I. Features of the New Forms of Employment in China

Employment is the cornerstone of wellbeing, and the wellspring of wealth. The term "new form of employment" first appeared in the *Communiqué of the 5th Plenary Session of the 18th CPC Central Committee* (approved on October

29th 2015). In 2019, in *Report on the Work of the Government* issued by the State Council, the employment-first policy was regarded as one of the macro policies for the first time, aiming to increase society-wide attention to employment and support for it. Developing the digital economy and strengthening support for new forms of employment can not only ensure employment for urban workforce, but also create non-agricultural employment opportunities of the surplus rural workforce. It will become an important option for China to optimize the employment structure, and achieve the goal of stabilizing employment. After several years of development, the new forms of employment show a series of features as follows.

## 1. New Forms of Employment in the Digital Economy Become An Important Driver of Job Growth in China

Data from CAICT shows that in 2007, China's digital economy accounted for 14.7% of GDP, and provided jobs for 44.11 million people (see Figure 2). The scale of digital economy has continued to expand rapidly over a decade. In 2018, the digital economy reached 31.3 trillion yuan, with a nominal growth of 20.9% on a comparable basis, accounting for 34.8% of GDP; 191 million jobs were created in the digital economy, accounting for 24.6% of total employment, with a year-on-year growth of 11.5% (significantly higher than the growth of total employment in the country during the same period). Boston Consulting Group (BCG) predicts that the digital economy of China will be close to $16 trillion in 2035, the digital economy penetration rate will be 48%, and the total employment in digital economy will be 415 million. New forms of employment can promote the upgrade of traditional employment patterns, and also create new jobs. Preliminary statistics show that for every 100 newly employed people, jobs of 72 of them are upgrading and 28 are newly created.

## 2. Employment in Digital Economy Shows a Structural Feature of "3-1-2"

With the development of digital industrialization, an increasing number of jobs are generated in digital economy. There were 191 million jobs in China's digital economy in 2018, accounting for 24.6% of the total employment in that year, with a year-on-year growth of 11.5% (significantly higher than the growth of the total employment of the country in the same period). In addition, the digital economy has a huge impact on the employment structure. In terms of industrial employment structure, the proportion of the tertiary industry will continue to rise. In the primary industry,  the scale, the degree of intensification and intelligence, as well as the agricultural labor productivity will be further improved, and more rural workforce will be replaced due to the agricultural automation. The employment in the secondary industry (traditional manufacturing industry) will continue to decrease.

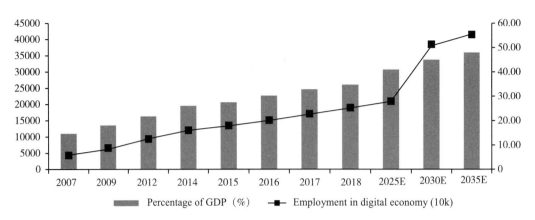

**Figure 2　Development of digital economy and employment, 2007-2035**

Sources: CAICT, *Information Economy Research Report of China 2015, Digital Economy Development in China* (2017), *Digital Economy Development and Employment in China* (2018, 2019); China Info100, *Information Economy Development Report of China 2016*; Boston Consulting Group International (BCG), *A Study of Employment and Talent in the Digital Economy, Towards 2035: 400 Million Jobs Opportunities in the Digital Age.*

In 2018, there were about 19.28 million digital transformation-related jobs in the primary industry, accounting for 9.6% of the total employment in the primary industry, with an increase of about 2%; while those in the secondary industry was 52.21 million, accounting for 23.7% of the total employment in the secondary industry, with an increase of about 1.4%, and those in the tertiary industry was about 134.26 million, accounting for 37.2% of the total employment in the tertiary industry, with an increase of about 4%. It can be concluded that the increase of the share of digital transformation-related jobs is the fastest in the tertiary industry and the slowest in the secondary industry. The digital economy shows the structural feature of "3-1-2" in terms of employment, because the digital transformation of the labor force in the tertiary industry is the least difficult while those in the secondary industry is the most difficult.

### 3. New Forms of Employment Continue to Optimize the Skill Structure in the Labor Market

With the advancement of technology, the high-income countries have experienced a significant job polarization, also known as "hollowing out"(World Bank, 2016), which is characterized by an increasing share of low-skilled jobs and high-skilled jobs, and a shrinking share of employment in middle-skill (Keller and Utar, 2019). This phenomenon was seen in Germany in the 1980s, and in the EU and the UK in the early 21st century (Dustmann and Schonberg, 2009; Goos and Manning, 2007; Goos, Manning and Salomons, 2009). During 2008-2018, the share of employment of high-skilled, in China increased from 6.8% to 20.2%, the share of employment of middle-skilled increased from 12.7% to 12.8%, and the share of employment of low-skilled decreased from 80.4% to 61.8% (Note: the share of employment of high-skilled refers to the proportion of employees with college degree and above; the share of employment of middle-skilled refers to the proportion of employees with high school diploma; and the share of employment of low-skilled refers to the proportion of employees with junior high school diploma and below). Under the background of digital economy, with the emergence of new forms of employment, there is no job polarization in China's labor market. Figure 3 shows the changes in the share of employment by levels of education during 2008-2018 in China. Generally speaking, the employment of high-skilled tends to increase as the level of skills of the workforce improves. However, it varies across workers with different levels of skill. For low-skilled workers, the decrease of the share of employment slows down as they have more education; for high-skilled workers, the share of employment increases with a marginal increase trend as they have higher skills; and for medium-skilled workers, the share of employment decreases with a slow linear trend as they have higher skills. In the future, with the progress of digital technology, the impact of China's new forms of employment on labor market structure will also be affected by the "race between education and technology" (Goldin, 2015).

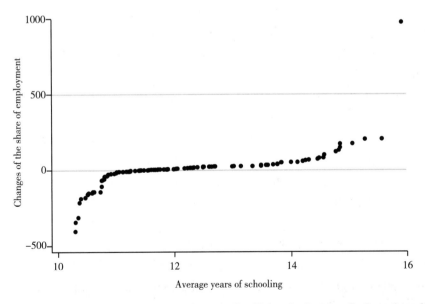

**Figure 3   Changes of the share of employment in China by levels of education, 2008-2018**

Source: *China Economic Census Yearbook; China Labor Statistical Yearbook,* various years.

## 4. The Education Level of People with New Forms of Employment Has Improved Significantly

In terms of education, 55.1% of full-time drivers on online platforms in China received high school education in 2016, and 20.7% received higher education; 43% of part-time drivers received high school education, and 44.8% received higher education. These numbers are significantly higher than the corresponding proportions of the total employment (Ji, 2019). The employee survey team of the China University of Labor Relations conducted a semi-structured interview on Tujia Online Information Technology (Beijing) Co. Ltd. from May to July 2019. The survey shows that the majority of employee of Tujia have bachelor's degree; the staff in internet technology positions, which account for 1/4 of the company's total headcount, have master's degree; almost all the staff engaged in customer service have college degree; and there are no employees with doctoral degree. Overall, the level of education is directly related to the requirements of the positions. International talents are mainly working in overseas business departments – more than 60% of them are domestic talents with overseas study experience, and have master's degree and above. Besides, employees in Tujia are from different countries and regions.

As shown in Figure 4, higher education graduates who entered the labor market increased from 848,000 in 2019 to 8.74 million in 2020, with an increase of 930.66%; high school graduates who entered the labor market directly without pursuing higher education rose from 4.585 million in 1999 to 8.192 million in 2009, and went down to 3.712 million in 2019; secondary vocational education graduates increased from 3.501 million to 6.749 million in 2012, and then dropped to 4.934 million; junior high school graduates decreased from 8.419 million to 1.253 million, with a decrease of 82.71%. Prior to 2001, the newly employed workforce was mainly junior high school graduates, and the proportion of this group continued to rise, reaching 61.8% in 2001, and then decreasing rapidly – in 2012, there was only 8.1% of new employed persons were junior school graduates. The proportion of newly employed persons with high school diploma reached 56.5% in 2009 and then gradually declined; most of them have received secondary vocational education. In stark contrast to this trend was the significant increase in the number of workers with higher education degree, from 13.8% and 17.1% in 2002 and 2003 respectively (it's the time when the first batch of graduates entered labor market after the expansion of enrollment in colleges and universities) to 67.8% in 2019. In China's urban labor market, the majority of newly employed people are now higher education graduates. According to the annual report on the employment quality of graduates published by Peking University in

2019, the proportion of flexible employment of both graduates with master's and doctoral degree at Peking University was increasing: the proportion of flexible employment of graduates with master's degree reached 42.44% in 2019, up by 4.01% compared with 2018; the proportion of flexible employment for graduates with doctorate degree was 25.67%, up by 3.11% compared with 2018 (Peking University, 2019).

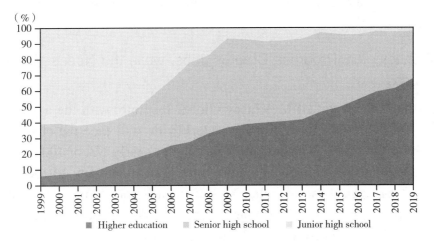

**Figure 4    Changes of the educational background of the newly employed people in China, 1999-2019**

Source: The author estimates the analysis results based on *China Labor Statistical Yearbook*, various years.

## 5. Various Features and Types of New Forms of Employment

The rapid development of new forms and new models of business such as platform economy, sharing economy, crowdsourcing and crowd innovation have triggered profound changes in employment, giving rise to new flexible forms of employment such as self-employment, freelance and part-time employment in addition to traditional form of employment. According to *Green Book of Population and Labor 2017* published by the Institute of Population and Labor Economics, Chinese Academy of Social Sciences, the share of "flexible employment" in China increased from 2.7% in 2013 to 9.1% in 2017, with a good trend of prospects (Zhang, 2017). Digital technology and online platforms have broken down the traditional organizational boundaries, providing individuals with market, R&D and production resources, lowering the entry barriers to the market for individuals, and allowing individuals to engage in economic activities without entering traditional enterprises. As a result, the form of employment gets more flexible and diverse, and becomes an important method to create jobs. There are mainly two forms of employment on the new platform of digital economy: crowdsourcing and gig work. For crowdsourcing, there are platforms for specific individual freelancers (e.g. TikTok) and microtask platforms for a group of people (e.g. ZBJ and Amazon M Turk). For gig work, there are also platforms specific individuals and microtask platforms for a group of people; however the former is more common, such as Airbnb in the accommodation and catering industry, Didi in the transportation industry, express delivery platforms in the delivery industry, and 58.com which is a classified platform.

### 6. Technological Progress Creates Jobs, while the Needs Varies Across Different Jobs

According to a report of McKinsey Global Institute, with the advancement of technology, roughly 375 million people worldwide will face the challenge of re-employment in the future, with China accounting for nearly 1/3, or 100 million. There are more jobs created in China than in the United States, Germany, Mexico and Japan; but they are less than those of India. As shown in Figure 5, in China, the demand for creative personnel (artists, designers, people working in entertainment industry and media workers) will grow by 85%; the demand for technical experts (computer engineers, specialists) will grow by 50%; the demand for teachers (school teachers, higher education teachers, professionals engaged in other areas of education) will grow by 119%; the demand for managers and administrative staff will grow by 40%; the demand for construction personnel (architecture engineers, construction workers, installation and maintenance workers) will grow by 9%; the demand for health care personnel (doctors, nurses, physician assistants, pharmacists, physical therapists, health-care assistants, caregivers and health technicians) will grow by 122%; the demand for professionals (account managers, engineers, business and financial experts, lawyers and judges, mathematics experts, scientists, and academics) will grow by 26%; the demand for jobs involving physical activities in a predictable environment (machine installers and repairers, security service providers, gaming operators, dishwashers, cleaners, food preparation workers) will decrease by 4%; the demand for jobs involving social interaction (include food service workers, retail and online sales workers, one-on-one therapists, attendants in entertainment industry, stylists, hotel and travel-related workers) will grow by 36%; the demand for jobs involving physical activities in unpredictable environments (mechanics of special area, emergency personnel, porters, machine installation and maintenance workers, workers engaged in agriculture, transportation maintenance workers, construction cleaners) will grow by 12%.

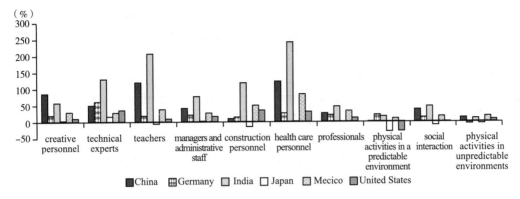

**Figure 5    Changes of the Needs of Jobs in Six Countries**

# II. Digital Economy, Employment and Workforce Building in China

The development of digital economy has complementary effect, substitution effect, scale effect and matching effect on employment (Ji, 2017), which also affects the building of China's workforce in the new era.

## The complementary or substitution effect of the digital economy on employment contributes to the efficiency improvement and structure adjustment of workforce

Two trends can be seen in the digital economy: first, replacing low-skilled and repetitive jobs based on previous technological advances; second, improving existing jobs for safety and efficiency purposes, for example, cooperative robots could help to improve the productivity of human, instead of replacing them, while reducing the risk of injury in the workplace.

In response to the needs of the digital economy, the new form of employment clarifies "what kind of people are needed" and "how many qualified people are needed" in the building of workforce in the digital economy. When the complementary effect is highlighted, it should focus on the career development of workers in the process of digital technology progress, and increase the number of talents in the innovation field and promote their capabilities. When the substitution effect is highlighted, it should promote the efficiency and adjust the structure of workforce. and with the help of upgraded digital technology, so as to achieve a win-win situation for workers and enterprises.

### 1. The Scale Effect of the Digital Economy on Employment Contributes to the Expansion of Workforce

As a new virtual factor of production, data accelerates the emergence of new businesses at a lower cost and creates new economic growth spaces. On the one hand, as the scale of the new economy continues to expand, new job demands are derived accordingly; on the other hand, many new jobs are created by enterprises based on data, such as big data platforms.

The scale effect of the digital economy on new employment contributes to the expansion of workforce. According to the data from All-China Federation of Trade Unions, there are about 4 million people working in the delivery industry in China, about 90% of which are in private delivery enterprises. In 2020, the Trade Union of Post and Telecommunications of China considered encouraging dispatched employees and outsourced employees to join the union as a major task, as well as the migrant couriers. As a result, there was a 20% increase of membership enrollment rate of couriers annually. On October 29th 2020, the Trade Union of National Defense and Post and Telecommunications of China held an online "ceremony of joining the trade union of 10,000 couriers" in Jiangsu Province. 10,000 couriers in 100 venues nationwide (such as Beijing and Wuhan) joined the ceremony simultaneously, and received the union membership card and badge.

### 2. The Matching Effect of the Digital Economy on Employment Contributes to the Mobility of Employees Internally and Externally

Thanks to the efficient algorithm, the information platform in digital economy avoids the mismatch of supply and demand in the traditional labor market. With the help of internet and big data, information can be shared at all times, supply and demand information can be dynamically matched, so that various job opportunities can be created with more flexible employment.

The matching effect of the digital economy on employment has built a platform to promote dual-channel development of workers. To strengthen the workforce building in the new era, it is necessary for talents to play their roles in industrial upgrading and industrial digitization, and the high-end creative talents should innovate and take the lead in digital industrialization. More flexible employment opportunities can improve the recognition of various vocational skill levels. Diversified employment can also contribute to the mobility of employees internally and externally. On the one hand, it encourages workers in fundamental areas to enter the special zone for talents in innovation; on the other hand, it improves the exit mechanism and matching and re-employment mechanisms to ensure a standardized and orderly work exit.

## III. Development Trend of Labor Market

In the past, jobs were closed linked to enterprises; and related labor market regulations were standardized principles in terms of wages, working hours, recruitment, dismissal procedures, employment security, etc. Although it lacked flexibility, it could ensure the formality. However, in the future labor market, new forms of employment will be more flexible.

## 1. Emergence of New Occupations, New Positions and New Talents

In December 2018, the Central Economic Work Conference included 5G, artificial intelligence, industrial internet and internet of things in the new infrastructure construction, namely "new infrastructure". On April 20th 2020, the National Development and Reform Commission (NDRC) clarified the scope of new infrastructure – it included three categories, which were information infrastructure, converged infrastructure and innovation infrastructure. New infrastructure can improve employment, stimulate consumption and production. The fast advancement of new technologies and new infrastructure will lead to new industries, new forms and new models of business, as well as more new occupations and new positions.

Since *Occupational Classification of the People's Republic of China (2015 version)* was published in 2015, three batches of new occupations have been added in February and November 2019, as well as in June 2020, with a total of 38 new occupations released. With further development of the digital economy, there will be more new occupations in the future; the government will enhance its support for flexible employment and start the top-level system design for new forms of employment. 13 departments (including NDRC) supported various new forms of employment by jointly announcing *Opinions on Supporting the Healthy Development of New Forms and New Models of Business, and Stimulating the Consumer Market to Expand Employment* in July 2020. As shown in Figure 6, in terms of industries, there are new employment opportunities emerged by the development of platform and virtualized industry clusters; in terms of sectors, there are a series of new employment opportunities generated by the further integration of digital technology with education, medical care, administration and public governance; in terms of enterprises, there are new employment opportunities in the process of digital transformation of traditional enterprises; in terms of new technology, there are new employment opportunities in the process of the advancement of intelligence, automation and unmanned technology; in terms of individuals, new occupations were recognized due to the market-based labor participation identification with the help of new technologies and new forms of business; new forms of employment include self-employed, flexible time-sharing employment, part-time employment and multi-site employment; in terms of sharing platforms, new employment opportunities based on service sharing are expanded to productivity and production sharing; in terms of factors of production, new employment opportunities are generated in the process of data construction and data circulation.

**Figure 6    New industries, new forms and new models of business promote new employment**

## 2. Penetration of Applied Technology, Coexistence of Substitution Effect and Complementary Effect

According to *China Artificial Intelligence Development Report 2018* released by Tsinghua University, as of June 2018, there were 1,011 AI companies in China, ranking second in the world; China accounted for 60% of global investment and financing in AI, making it the country with the largest amount of AI investment and financing. While improving the productivity of enterprises and the convenience of people's daily life, AI has reduced many repetitive and low-skilled jobs, changed the structure of the workforce, and had negative impact on labor demand. *World Development Report 2016* published by the World Bank showed that 55% to 77% of jobs which were low-skilled in China would be replaced by automation or AI.

Referring to the idea of Frey et al. (2017), Sun Wenkai et al. (2018) calculated the employment replacement rates of 19 major industries in China's urban area based on the national censuses in 1990, 2000 and 2010, and then estimated the total replacement of employment by adding the numbers up. The employment replacement rate is an important indicator to evaluate AI's impact on the labor market in China. The results of this study (see Figure 7) show that, in China, the employment replacement rate in the real estate industry is the highest (0.888), indicating that 88.8% of urban employees in this industry is at risk of being replaced. The employment replacement rates in the transportation industry, storage, postal and telecommunication industry, accommodation and catering industry, and electricity, gas and water production and supply industry are also above 0.6. Jobs in these industries are more routinized and repetitive, which are more likely to be replaced. In addition, the overall employment replacement rate in China's urban labor market is 0.45, which is close to the predicted rate of 0.47 by the United States.

The employment replacement rate is higher than 0.45 in five industries, including construction (0.59), wholesale and retail trade (0.5706), finance (0.5654), agriculture, forestry, animal husbandry and fishery (0.54), and water, environment and public facilities management (0.53). The employment replacement rate is lower in some service sectors – culture, sports and entertainment (0.2295), information transmission, computer services and software (0.2), scientific research, technical services and geological exploration (0.13), and education (0.088) – which require higher knowledge and skills and are less likely to be replaced. In 2017, the share of employment of the manufacturing sector and the service sector was 28.1% and 44.9% respectively in China (National Bureau of Statistics, 2018), which shows that the share of employment in industries with lower employment replacement rates is still low in China.

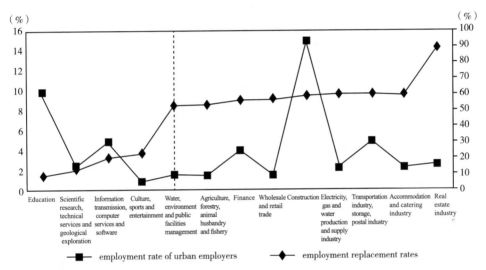

**Figure 7   Share of employment and employment replacement ratio across industries**

Sources: Sun Wenkai, Guo Jie, Zhao Zhong, Tang Cai. Research on employment structure changes and technological upgrade in China [J]. Economic Theory and Business Management, 2018 (6): 5-14; *China Labor Statistical Yearbook* (2017).

## 3. A Flexible, Stable and Inclusive Labor Market is Shaping Gradually

In China's labor market, the institutional segmentation, workplace segmentation (Kochan, Katz and Mckersie, 2008) and online/offline segmentation (Ji and Lai, 2016) existed. However, with the transition of economic system, industry structure upgrade and technological progress, it has gradually transformed to be inclusive. Since the concept of "new form of employment" was first proposed in the *Communiqué of the 5th Plenary Session of the 18th CPC Central Committee*, the government has strengthened its policy support through top-level planning, facilitating the development of new employment in the market, therefore an inclusive labor market has been shaped gradually.

The government has regulated the development of the new form of employment for five consecutive years. As shown in Table 1, in 2016, the new form of employment was considered as a labor pool in the process of industrial structural transition in 2016 when the employment guidance was followed this approach; in 2017, it was considered as an approach of promoting employment through self-employed, which was managed in an inclusive and prudent manner; in 2018, it was considered as a channel of promoting incremental employment, while the management was loosened. In 2019, "Internet+" promoted the transition and development of the industry, thus new forms of employment emerged. In 2020, in response to the COVID-19 pandemic, new forms of employment emerged and became a stabilizer of employment. Policy of identifying national leading talents was introduced to facilitate the promotion of talents in various industries and enable them to "give full play to their abilities in the proper position". In the future, it should address the legislative weaknesses in terms of new forms of employment, such as the legal protection of workers, and the protection of the legitimate rights and interests of consumers, so that the new forms of employment can be continuously improved (Zhang and Zou, 2020).

**Table 1     Policies and regulations of the Chinese government to support new forms of employment, 2016-2020**

| Year | Policies and regulations | Key points |
|------|--------------------------|------------|
| 2016 | March: *Report on the Work of the Government 2016.* | Strengthen the support for flexible employment and new forms of employment. |
| | July: *Interim Regulations on Online Taxi-hailing Business Operation* (issued by seven government ministries including the Ministry of Transport), *Guidance of the General Office of the State Council on Deepening Reform and Promoting the Healthy Development of the Taxi Industry.* | Qualifications of platform drivers such as household registration (*hukou*), vehicle license and vehicle requirements are regulated. Online car-hailing business is regarded as legitimate. |
| | November: *Notice on Employment Assistance in the Northeast and Other Regions with Difficulties* (jointly issued by several government ministries including MOHRSS). | Develop online car-hailing platform in pilot cities, and provide assistance to workers affected by excess capacity reduction. |

(continued)

| Year | Policies and regulations | Key points |
|---|---|---|
| 2017 | March: *Report on the Work of the Government 2017.* | Improve employment policies, enhance employment training, and strengthen support for flexible employment and new forms of employment. |
| | April: *Opinions of the State Council on the Work of Employment and Self-employment at present and for some time to come.* | Achieve the diversification of employment by supporting new forms of employment, improve the employment and social security system that adapts to the characteristics of new forms of employment. |
| | July: *Guidance on Promoting the Development of the Sharing Economy* (issued by eight government ministries including NDRC). | Regulation principle: "encourage innovation, be inclusive and prudent". |
| | October: *Action Plan for Human Resources Service Industry Development* (issued by MOHRSS). | Implement "Internet+" human resource service action, and promote the development of industries that can accelerate the growth of flexible employment. |
| 2018 | March: *Report on the Work of the Government 2018.* | Propose to utilize "internet+" to develop new forms of employment. |
| | August: *Electronic Commerce Law of the People's Republic of China.* | Clarify the qualification requirements for B2B e-commerce website operators. |
| | September: *Guidance on Developing Digital Economy to Stabilize and Expand Employment* (issued by several government ministries including NDRC). | It is emphasized that to develop digital economy, it should focus on increasing employment, improving the industrial structure, accelerating the learning of digital skills, and requiring the government to promote the improvement of labor laws and regulations, formulate labor policies related to new forms of employment, and effectively protect rights and interests of workers. |
| | October: *Report of the 17th National Congress of the All-China Federation of Trade Unions.* | Promote the establishment of a system of employment and social security adapted to the new forms of business, and establish a sound system of labor standards for new forms of employment such as employment on internet platforms. |

(continued)

| Year | Policies and regulations | Key points |
|------|--------------------------|------------|
| 2019 | February: *Notice on the Pilot Work of "Internet+ Nursing Services", and Work Plan of the Pilot of "Internet+ Nursing Services"* (issued by the National Health Commission). | Decide to implement "Internet+Nursing Service" pilot in Beijing, Tianjin, Shanghai, Jiangsu and Guangdong. |
| | March: *Report on the Work of the Government 2019.* | Accelerate the promotion of "Internet+" in various industries and areas. |
| | April: *Comprehensive Plan to Reduce Social Insurance Rates.* | Regulations about people with flexible employment to join the pension insurance. |
| | August: *Guiding Opinions of the General Office of the State Council on Promoting the Standardized and Healthy Development of the Platform Economy.* | Encourage the development of new forms of platform economy, create new occupations, new professions and new positions. |
| | December: *Opinions of the State Council on Further Stabilizing Employment.* | Support flexible employment and new forms of employment, implement pilot projects of occupational injury insurance for people with flexible employment. |
| 2020 | March: *Opinion of the General Office of the State Council on the Implementation of Measures to Stabilize Employment In Response to the Impact of COVID-19.* | Eliminate the restrictions of urban and rural household registration (*hukou*) within provinces for flexibly employed persons to join the basic pension insurance for enterprise employees; people who find it difficult to find a job and the college graduates who are not employed two years after graduation could receive a certain amount of social insurance subsidy, if they pay the social insurance fee when flexibly employed. |
| | April: *Plan of Promoting "Digitalization, Data Usage and Intelligence" and Developing New Forms of Economy* (issued by NDRC and Office of the Central Cyberspace Affairs Commission). | Implement flexible employment incentive plan. |
| | April: *Developing New Forms of Economy and Encouraging Flexible Employment* (issued by NDRC). | Provide various employment services and multi-tier labor securities for the flexibly employed people. |

(continued)

| Year | Policies and regulations | Key points |
|------|--------------------------|------------|
| 2020 | May: *Notice on the Pilot Projects of Skill Improvement for New Forms of Employment and Employment Promotion.* | 7 provinces and 15 regions including Zhejiang, Guangdong, Hubei and Shandong are the first to implement pilot projects of skill improvement for new forms of employment and employment promotion. |
| | May: *Report on the Work of the Government 2020.* | There are hundreds of millions of flexibly employment in China including gig works. For the low-income workers, they can choose to delay the payment of social insurance's contributions this year, while all administrative fees on employment are canceled. |
| | July (14th): *Opinions on Supporting the Healthy Development of New Forms and New Models of Business and Activating the Consumer Market to Expand Employment.* | 19 innovative supporting policies are proposed to accelerate the development of 15 new forms and models of digital economy. |

Source: Summarization based on relevant policies by author.

## IV. Build Harmonious Labor Relations in the New Era

During the First Industrial Revolution, there was a rise in labor conflicts and deterioration of labor relations in the UK. Statistics show that there were 57 labor conflicts in UK during 1741-1760, and then jumped to 113 by 1780, and 153 during 1781-1800 (Liu, 2020). As the industrial production capacity reached its peak and national trade union or federations in various industries were founded in the UK, workers' bargaining power improved, creating a favorable environment to ease labor relations. The skilled workers began to ask for shorter working hours and a reduction of workload. As a result, the working hours reduced to 9 hours a day, and the total working hours of a week reduced from 59 to 54; in the meantime, salaries of workers raised. In 1929, during the global economic crisis, there were more than 17 million unemployed people. The primary measure of the New Deal of the administration of Roosevelt was to stabilize employment. On the one hand,  it launched many work-relief infrastructure projects, and tried to get the support of small and medium-sized enterprise owners to create new jobs. On the other hand, it ensured the interests of the employed through *Fair Labor Standards Act* (*FLSA*), which stated that the working hours per week would be 40, and the minimum wage per hour would be 40 cents. With the effective implementation of a series of measures, the economy of the US began to recover slowly, and people's lives were improved.

In the new era, it is emphasized in the report of the 17th National Congress of the All-China Federation of Trade Unions that "we should promote the establishment of a system of employment and social security that adapts to the new forms of business and establish a sound labor standards system for new forms of employment such as employment of online platforms". On May 23rd 2020, during the panel discussion with members from the economic sector at the National Committee of the Chinese People's Political Consultative Conference (CPPCC), General Secretary Xi Jinping pointed out that new forms of employment emerged during the unexpected COVID-19 pandemic; and we should seize this momentum. Of course, the laws and regulations in this field are still inadequate for now. The major problems are the legal protection of workers and the protection of the legitimate rights and interests of consumers. Facing the challenges, we need to explore relevant issues, and address the legislative weaknesses as soon as possible, and continue to improve.

Labor standards in China are changing from survival-oriented to quality-oriented. Work-life balance, employment development, and elimination of employment discrimination have become the target. By analyzing the correlation between digital development and employment, as well as labor relations, we can shed light on the future construction of harmonious labor relations in the new era. In this paper, with the help of the indicators adopted by the World Bank to measure the digital divide, we selected the number of computers per million people at the industry level to demonstrate the degree of digitalization; the share of employment in industries and the share of women's employment as the employment indicators; the working hours per week and the monthly salary per capita to demonstrate the labor relations (Ji et al., 2019). Pearson Correlation Coefficient (PC) was used to analyze the correlation between the degree of digitization and employment, as well as labor relations. This method does not lead to causal conclusions, but helps us to show the correlation trend. The results are shown in Figure 8, which indicate that as the degree of digitization per capita in each industry increases, employment is not destroyed, instead, the working hours will be shortened and income will rise. This proves form another perspective that technology is beneficial, and the digital economy will bring more diverse forms of employment and higher quality of employment in the future. The paper then replaces the indicator of "computers per million people" with "the proportion of information-based enterprises that adopt information management in human resource" and "the proportion of internet companies that provide training to employees" to demonstrate the degree of digitalization. The results are consistent: informatization of human resource management is negatively correlated with weekly working hours, the proportion of employee training is negatively correlated with weekly working hours, and is significant at 10%. This means that human resource management informatization and training can contribute to the reduction of working hours.

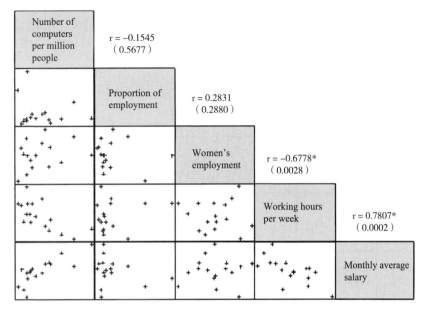

**Figure 8　Scatterplot of the correlation between industry digitization and employment based on Pearson correlation coefficient**

Note: * means t is significant at 10%.

Source: *China Labor Statistical Yearbook*; *China Economic Census Yearbook*.

We selected the volume of e-commerce transaction at the regional level was selected to demonstrate the degree of digital economy development; the regional employment and the share of women's employment as the employment indicator; the number of grassroots trade union organizations and the number of labor disputes settled annually by the labor dispute mediation committee of trade unions as the indicators of the trade union services and labor relations. The results of Pearson correlation coefficient analysis are shown in Figure 9, which indicate a significant positive correlation between digital economy development, regional economic development and employment. It is also consistent with the economic logic. In terms of trade union services and labor relations, digital economy development is positively correlated with trade union services, which also proves the effectiveness of "internet+" trade union services promoted by the All-China Federation of Trade Unions. At the same time, the results also show that digital economic development is negatively correlated with women's employment, and significantly negatively correlated with the number of labor disputes, which are undoubtedly the key directions for future work in building harmonious labor relations in the new era.

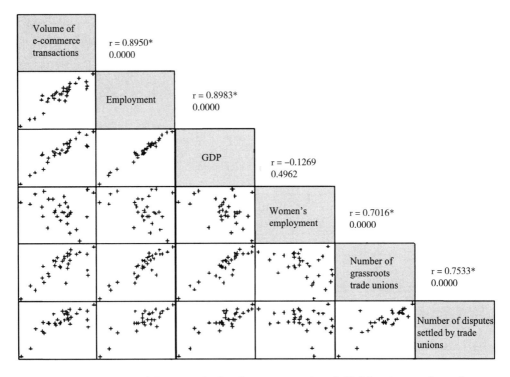

**Figure 9    Scatterplot of the correlation between regional digitization and employment based on Pearson correlation coefficient**

Note: * means t is significant at 10%.

Source: *China Labor Statistical Yearbook*; *China Economic Census Yearbook*.

## References

[1] World Bank. World Development Report 2016: Digital Dividends [R].Washington DC: World Bank, 2016.

[2] Wolfgang Keller, Hale Utar. International Trade and Job Polarization: Evidence at the Worker-Level[R]. NBER Working Paper No. 22315, 2016.

[3] C. Dustmann, U. Schonberg. Training and Union Wage[R]. IZA working paper No.1435, 2009.

[4] Goos M., Manning A. Lousy and Lovely Jobs: The Rising Polarization of Work in Britain [J]. Review of Economics and Statistics, 2007(89): 118-133.

[5] Goos M., Manning. A., Salomons A. Job Polarization in Europe [J]. The American Economic Review, 2009(2): 58-63.

[6] Claudia Goldin, Lawrence Katz. The Race Between Education and Technology (Chinese version)[M]. Beijing: The Commercial Press, 2015.

[7] Ji Wenwen. New Employment and Changing Labor Relations in the Digital Economy

[M]. Beijing: Social Sciences Academic Press, 2019.

[8] Peking University. Annual Report on the Employment Quality of Graduates of Peking University in 2019 [R]. Peking University Admission Office, 2019.

[9] Zhang Chewei. Green Book of Population and Labor 2017 [M]. Beijing: Social Sciences Academic Press, 2017.

[10] Ji Wenwen. The Digital Economy and the Future of Work [J]. Journal of the China University of Labor Relations, 2017(6): 37-47.

[11] Sun Wenkai, Guo Jie, Zhao Zhong, Tang Can. Research on Employment Structure Changes and Technological Upgrade in China [J]. Economic Theory and Business Management, 2018(6):5-14.

[12] Thomas A. Kochan, Harry C. Katz, Robert B. Mckersie. The Transformation of American Industrial Relations (Chinese version)[M].Beijing: China Labor and Social Security Publishing House, 2008.

[13] Ji Wenwen, Lai Desheng. Mechanisms and Practical Analysis of the Impact of Online Platform Employment on Labor Relations [J]. Journal of the China University of Labor Relations, 2016(4):6-16.

[14] Zhang Xiaosong, Zou Wei. Xi Jinping on "New Forms of Employment": Following the Trend and Address the Weaknesses [EB/OL]. (2020-05-23). http://www.xinhuanet.com/politics/2020lh/2020-05/23/c_1126023919.htm.

[15] Liu Jinyuan, The Anti-Association Act and Industrial Relations in Industrialized Britain [J]. World History, 2009 (4): 52-61, 160.

[16] Ji Wenwen, Lai Desheng. Can Trade Unions Safeguard the Labor Rights of Migrants Workers [J]. Management World, 2019(2): 88-101.

# Employment Status and Identification of Platform Workers and Protection of Their Rights and Interests[*]

*Xiao Zhu*[**]

**Abstract:** New technological innovations such as the Internet and artificial intelligence, as well as the development of the sharing economy, are changing the traditional way of employment based on industrialization, while the role of the sharing economy as a "reservoir" and "stabilizer" in employment is becoming more and more prominent. Online platform employment provides relatively fair employment opportunities and income for different groups, increases flexible employment, and increasingly presents obvious characteristics of gig economy. The platform employment has impacts on many aspects of labor relations, arousing disputes which focus on two employment modes of "offline gig work" and "online crowdsourcing work". The employment of platform workers is characterized by instability and lack of protection of rights and interests. Recently, the identification of platform workers and protection of their rights and interests have gained much attention. Recent judicial decisions show that the judge will no longer directly deny or avoid the identification of labor relations between platform enterprises and the employees. In the lack of evidence for the revision of law, based on the judicial activism, the existing norms will be interpreted according to specific cases, so as to make a judgment on whether the labor relationship exists. China should no longer bind the identification of workers to their work and the protection of their social rights and interests, but should build a multi-level system that fits all workers to protect their rights and interests. In particular, it is necessary to address the issues including social security rights with occupational injury insurance at its priority, rights to join the trade union and participate in its affairs democratically, and the assurance of appropriate and fair wages and working hours.

---

[*] This paper was published as a part of the book edited by Yan Xiaofei, *Research Report on the Status of Chinese Workers* (2019), Beijing: Social Sciences Academic Press, 2019.

[**] Xiao Zhu, professor, Executive Dean of the Law School, China University of Labor Relations. She specializes in labor law.

**Keywords:** platform workers; employment; identification; protection of rights and interests

Since 2003, platform enterprises have experienced a period of rapid development in China. In 2020, the transaction amount of sharing economy in China has reached 3,377.3 billion yuan, with a year-on-year growth of about 2.9%; the number of participants in the sharing economy in China was about 830 million, including 84 million service providers, with a year-on-year increase of 7.7%. The number of employees of platform enterprises was 6.31 million, up about 1.3 percent (SERC-SIC, 2021). In the sharing economy, while the prosperity of platform enterprises has positive influence on employment, the employment trend and patterns are increasingly controversial. The negative effects of platform economy on labor relations should not be ignored, especially in light of the employment status and identification of platform workers' and the protection of their rights and interests, which have become the hotspots for theorists, practitioners and decision makers.

## I. Employment Status of Platform Workers

### 1. How the Development of Platform Enterprises Promote Employment

New technological innovations such as the Internet and artificial intelligence (AI), as well as the development of the sharing economy, are changing the traditional employment mode on the basis of industrialization, while the role of platform economy as a "reservoir" and "stabilizer" in employment is prominent. The rapid development of information technology industry has greatly promoted the capacity to create and match jobs, and has increased flexible jobs. It has especially provided access to labor market for unspecialized talent at the margins of the market. It also provides employment buffer in the industrial adjustment, alleviates structural unemployment, provides a new way to get a job and start a business, and changes the employment ecology.

In 2020, China's overall employment faces unprecedented challenges due to the impact of COVID-19 pandemic combined with the persistent aggregate pressure and structural contradictions in the employment market. A total of 10.99 million new urban jobs were created in the first 11 months of 2020, or 122.1 percent of the annual target, according to the National Bureau of Statistics. The overall employment is stable and better than expected due to the implementation of a series of policies. It has also benefited from the development of the sharing economy, which has provided a large number of flexible jobs, and played an important role in expanding the access to employment, enhancing employment flexibility and increasing workers' incomes (SERC-SIC, 2021). A total of more than 1.1 million online car-hailing drivers from 824 state-level poverty-stricken counties achieve flexible employment through Didi in 2020, according to the Didi Development Research Institute (DDRI, 2021). In the first half of 2020, the number of riders who have received orders on Meituan reached 2.952 million, with a year-on-year growth of 16.4 percent; nearly 80,000 new riders on Meituan came from poor households registered by the state (MRI, 2021). By the end of 2020, more than 9.5 million riders, including 2.3 million riders from poverty-eliminated areas, had increased their income by working on Meituan (MRI, 2021).

## 2. The Employment Mode of Platform Economy and its Influence on Labor Relations

Platform employment shows the characteristics of the gig economy. Workers are no longer confined to one enterprise or one organization, but project-oriented. They work for multiple employers at the same time, and improve their working ability according to job demands, so as to enhance their adaptability (Mulcahy, 2017). The employment trends and characteristics presented in the gig economy are particularly evident in the platform employment, and have a significant impact on labor relations.

### 2.1 Employment mode of platform economy

Online car-hailing platforms, express delivery platforms and labor platforms, which are mainly based on the C2C model, are typical employment methods of the gig economy. It can be further divided into two categories: "offline gig work" and "online crowdsourcing work". The former is also known as work on-demand via apps, and the latter is generally known as crowd work (DeStefano, 2016). These two forms of platform employment are the most controversial ones. Their proportions vary in China and other countries. "Offline gig work" is the main form in China, while "online crowdsourcing work" is the main form in other countries such as the United States. In China, by 2020, more than 28 million drivers have earned income through Didi (DDRI, 2021); by the end of 2019, about 7.2 million deliverymen have earned more through Meituan (MHRSS, 2021); in the whole year of 2019 and the first half of 2020, the total number of riders who earned income through Meituan reached 3.987 million and 2.952 million respectively (MRI, 2021). Although there are some crowdsourcing platforms such as ZBJ.com, EPWK and Taskcn in China, their influence cannot be compared with that of well-known crowdsourcing platforms abroad, such as Upwork (Elance), Innoventive, especially Amazon's Mechanical Turk platform in the United States. Therefore, the current discussion in theory, practice and system design in China mainly focus on gig work.

There are various legal relationships between platform workers and platforms. The ride-hailing industry mainly adopts the way of signing civil agreements; some platforms based on the B2C model use contract labor; takeout delivery platforms mostly use crowdsourcing labor, while some of them adopt the form of agent and franchise. In the development of platform economy, employment mode is no longer limited to workers and platforms. More and more third-party outsourcing enterprises, agents or enterprises dedicated to human resources and labor dispatch participate in it. In accordance with the current laws and regulations, and in order to reduce the risk of labor disputes, many platform operators choose to cooperate with other enterprises and sign labor contracts with workers. For instance, delivery platforms are gradually decreasing their direct relationships with deliverymen by introducing the pattern of "platform-outsourcing enterprises-deliverymen". Under such a context, although workers with new form of employment provide services through the platform, labor relations only exist between workers and the third-party outsourcing enterprises, while labor dispatch relations between some workers and the third-party enterprises (Qiu, 2020). Many platform operators consider themselves as intermediaries which offer intermediary services and earn commissions by providing information services and matching services with users (Zhang, 2020).

### 2.2 The influence of platform economy development on labor relations

The development of platform economy has exacerbated employment "informality" and worker "atomization", further increasing the demand of organizations for flexible employment such as part-time labor. Thus, its labor relation is becoming increasingly flexible, which is in sharp contrast with the traditional labor relations in enterprises, adding to the doubts and disputes among different social groups about the platform employment. Some scholars suppose that the gig economy with platform employment as a typical example is essentially "fragmentizing and getting rid of labor relations" (Wang and Li, 2017). Such flexible employment actually deprive the labor rights and job security of some workers, while "overemphasizing flexible employment also puts gig workers, especially the 'full-time' workers, in severe instability of employment and income" (Wang and Zhang, 2019).

The development of platform economy also brings multiple challenges to the legal adjustment of labor relations. First of all, the platform employment fundamentally challenges the logical starting point of the labor law, that is, the worker's identification, namely the judgment of whether they are "subordinated" or "controlled" by the platforms. This ambiguity leads to institutional obstacles in the application of labor rights and social security rights based on this judgment. "Sharing platforms deliberately avoiding labor disputes brought about by the establishment of employment relations, and the violation of regulations of third-party outsourcing enterprises by not signing labor contracts. This has become one of the prominent new problems affecting the harmony of labor relations" (Wang and Zhang, 2019). Due to the lack of effective guidelines for the new employment mode, the legal consciousness of employers and employees is relatively weak. Therefore, in practice, some enterprises and platforms have infringed upon the legitimate rights of employees through "contract agreements" and "cooperation agreements", reflecting that the standardization of the project management of new forms of employment needs to be enhanced (Zhang and Tang, 2021). In addition, the new problems arising from the new employment model, such as flexible working hours, the uncertainty of working place and the performance of services in different places, bring new challenges to the working hour system, the identification of work-related injuries and the labor dispute settlement system based on the labor law, and put forward urgent needs for practices and system update.

## 3. Major Problems About the Employment Rights and Interests of Platform Workers

### 3.1 Platform work has increasingly become the main source of income for some workers, which is generally low and unstable

According to *the 8th Survey on the Status of Chinese workers*, new working groups, both full-time and part-time, who are engaged in online shops, online car hailing, online express delivery and food delivery, online self-media and Wechat public accounts, online life services and other online businesses, gained 3,449 yuan last month (total monetary income) – 3,473 yuan for full-time workers and 3,361 yuan for part-time workers – slightly higher than the national average level of their peers. The questionnaire survey of gig workers by Beijing Federation of Trade Unions shows that 65.8% of the full-time gig workers have an average monthly income of 3,000-6,000 yuan; the monthly income varies in terms of part-time gig workers: below 1890 yuan (35.32%), 1,891-3,000 yuan (34.5%), 3,001-4,000 yuan (17.4%), more than 4,000 yuan (10%); in the meantime, 70.78% of gig workers reported that their income was "increased" (Li, 2017). The average monthly income of drivers on Didi platform is 1,979 yuan. Those drivers include a large number of part-time drivers who work shorter hours and mostly just have a try. Calculated by standard working hours, the national average monthly salary on Didi platform is 6,438 yuan, higher than the 5,600.5 yuan for "car drivers" in Beijing, and 5,220 yuan for "car drivers" in Guangzhou (CEFERC et al., 2019).

Meanwhile, due to the high flexibility of emerging Internet-related jobs and high dependence on network customers, as well as the wage structure of "base salary +

variable part" generally implemented by platforms, the income of platform workers is highly uncertain, resulting in relatively high wage dispersion and low income of some employees. In terms of income, most workers reported that their income had increased after working on the platforms. However, the data from multi-platform surveys in Beijing shows that 56.95% of the workers are concerned about the unstable income, while those who worry about unstable customers account for 51.64 percent (Zhang and Feng, 2019).

### 3.2 Lack of rights at work, social security and democratic participation for platform workers

In China, the establishment of labor relations is the premise for workers to enjoy legal labor rights. Platform workers mainly establish legal relations with the platform as equal civil subjects. However, under the current adjusted framework of the labor law, it is lack of protection of their rights at work, social security and democratic participation, which are mainly reflected in the following aspects:

*Excessive working hours and hidden dangers in the working environment*

*The 8th Survey on Status of Chinese Workers* shows that the working hours of platform workers is 5.58 days per week and 45.69 hours per week, slightly higher than the national average level of employees (Li, 2017). 86.81% of platform workers work more than 6 days a week on average, and 31.6% of them work 7 days a week. Among all kinds of new forms of employment, housekeeping personnel have the least self-arranged rest time (Zhang and Feng, 2019). The survey conducted by the All-China Federation of Trade Unions (ACFTU) shows that the workers of the "three new", namely "new technology, new business form and new model" bear almost spontaneous outdoor labor protection and enterprise labor protection outside the enterprise, facing longer working hours, higher labor intensity, more occupational health risks and other problems. The absence of labor safety protection measures increases workers' outdoor work safety risks. In the case of high labor safety risk, only 27% of workers in the Internet industry enjoy commercial medical insurance, and only 25.6% enjoy the medical mutual assistance (Luo, 2018).

*Low social security participation rate or no participation*

The survey by the Beijing Federation of Trade Unions shows that 41.7% of the Internet platform workers paid social insurance contributions by themselves, 13.2% by individuals and their former employers, only 10.9% by individuals and platforms, and 34.2% did not pay social insurance contributions (Li, 2017). At present, platform workers cannot pay and enjoy industrial injury insurance. Only a few platforms, such as Didi and Meituan, prevent such risks by means of personal accident injury insurance. Most platform workers still do not enjoy such protection. The survey shows that 36.02% of the platform workers believe that "the problem they worried the most is not paying social insurance contributions, making them worry about their future" (Zhang and Feng, 2019).

*Insufficient democratic participation*

The survey of Beijing Federation of Trade Unions shows that the overall membership rate of gig workers of the "three new" is not high. Only 26.5% of the gig workers are trade union members, and the number of full-time gig worker members is even lower, accounting for 20.8%. The way for workers to join the trade union is not standardized. The most common way to join the trade union is through the unified arrangement of enterprises, which accounting for 66.6%. Only 0.2% applies online, which shows that there is still a long way to go for online affiliation and online union building (Li, 2017). In addition, at present, the platforms generally do not establish a communication and consultation mechanism with workers, and only a few enterprises have an "Internet-based" complaint channel, but its actual role is limited. The relevant work rules are often determined unilaterally by platforms, so that there is no effective negotiation mechanism to protect the rights and interests of workers. If there was a dispute between the platform and workers, either the worker leaves, or the conflict intensifies.

## II. Identification of Platform Workers

The identification of platform workers and the related rights protection are the issues that the theorists and practitioners in labor law field around the world continue to focus and strive to solve. Internet powers also explore different approaches according to their national conditions. In China, the existence of labor relations is the premise of the application of the labor laws, but neither the *Labor Law* nor the *Labor Contract Law* has a clear definition of "labor relations". The main basis in practice is still the *Notice on Matters Related to the Establishment of Labor Relations*. The existing labor law system is characterized by a "dual structure", similar to the western dual adjustment pattern of "employment" and "self-employed". Besides, the labor costs of enterprises engaged in "labor relations" are different from those not engaged in it, which further leads to the tension of the identification of labor relations, especially in light of the current binding relationship between labor relations and social insurance. Thus, the identification of labor relations is enforced strictly on the whole. However, this "one-size-fits-all" mode of labor law protection sees increasing problems to deal with in the face of the more flexible employment under the "three new". Therefore, "getting rid of labor relations" has become the basic practice of all kinds of platform enterprises, and the dead zone in labor protection continues to expand.

## 1. The Status Quo of Judicial Practice in the Identification of Platform Workers in China

### 1.1 Overview of judicial practice of identification of platform workers in China

In the judicial judgments released on the China Judgements Online, a total of 379 judicial documents of the year 2020 can be found with "Beijing Sankuai Technology Co., Ltd. " (Meituan), "Shanghai Lazhasi Information Science Technology Co., Ltd. " (Ele.me), "Beijing Xiaoju Technology Co., Ltd." (Didi), "Beijing Yixin Yixing Automotive Technical Development Service Co., Ltd. " (eDaijia), "labor dispute" and "tort liability dispute" as the key words for search engine. Excluding the jurisdiction, execution, mediation, ruling and other documents, a total of 277 substantive judgment documents can be found. These documents involve four platforms, namely Meituan, Ele.me, Didi and eDaijia. Among these cases, 51 labor disputes were related to gig workers, 33 of which were related to the confirmation of labor relationship. Among them, 11 cases saw the confirmation of labor relations by the court, while other 22 did not. In all these 11 cases, the confirmed labor relationship was between gig workers and franchisees of the platform, not between gig workers and the platforms. The number of tort liability disputes related to gig workers was 194, among which 132 cases required platform operators and partners to bear compensation liability.

According to a notice issued by the Beijing Third Intermediate People's Court in April 2021, over the past seven years, the court has adjudicated 143 labor dispute cases caused by new forms of employment. In 2020, the number of cases increased dramatically, more than doubling, due to the pandemic. Labor dispute cases related to the employment of new forms of business mainly focused on the industries such as online car-hailing, express delivery and logistics, food delivery, webcast, home services and internet finance. Among them, labor disputes occurred most frequently in online car-hailing, express delivery and logistics industries. The number of cases involved was 68 and 27 respectively, accounting for 47.55% and 18.89%. The second was the home services industry, which involved 21 cases, accounting for 14.69%; 16 cases in food delivery industry, accounting for 11.19%. Compared with the traditional employment mode, although the new mode is more flexible and diversified, employees are still in a relatively weak position and vulnerable when disputes occurred. Specifically, there were only 24 cases in which platforms or enterprises directly signed labor contracts with employees, accounting for 16.78%, while 28 cases in which no written contract was ever signed, accounting for 19.58%. Among related labor dispute cases, most of them (84 cases, accounting for 58.74%) are the cases in which workers required the confirmation of labor relationship, which was significantly more than traditional labor dispute cases. Even if workers did not explicitly request the confirmation of the labor relationship, but had other claims such as labor remuneration or economic compensation for the termination of the labor relationship, the nature of the legal relationship between the two parties often became the core content of the case review. According to data from the court, in 118 cases, or 82.52%, the court confirmed the existence of labor relations between workers and the related employers (Zhu, 2021).

### 1.2 Typical cases of identification of platform workers in China

Since a series of cases of "eDaijia" during 2014-2015, typical cases involving the identification of platform workers have come to the stage. In the three "eDaijia" labor disputes adjudicated by the Beijing First Intermediate People's Court,[1] the court, in accordance with the *Notice on Matters Related to the Establishment of Labor Relations*, pointed out that the drivers had no fixed working place and time, nor labor remuneration from the company by month, so only the evidence submitted by the drivers, such as work card and uniforms, was insufficient for the court to confirm the existence of labor relationship between the two parties. Therefore, the judgment was that there was no labor relationship between the two parties. However, in the traffic accident cases involving "eDaijia", local courts have different understandings. Some of the courts of Beijing argued that as the drivers of "eDaijia" were appointed by the company, if an accident occurred during the period of designated driving, it should be a duty behavior, so the company should bear the relevant compensation liability.[2] The others believed that there was no labor relationship between "eDaijia" company and the drivers, but the drivers were managed by the company, so the compensation liability should be jointly undertaken by the company and the driver.[3] The courts of Shanghai held that the "eDaijia" drivers and the company were in line with the general characteristics of the employment relationship, so the two parties should be identified as the employment relationship. When the accidents occurred, the drivers were performing their duty, which was a duty behavior.[4]

The cases of "365 Paotui" and "Great Chef" in 2017, as well as the "FlashEx" case in 2018, are very typical cases. In the case of "365 Paotui", the court affirmed that the labor relationship existed between the deliveryman and the platform, because the company believed that if the goods delivered were damaged, it would bear the

---

[1] (2014) Jing Yi Zhong Min Zhong Zi No. 6355[(2014) 京一中民终字第 6355 号 ], (2015) Jing Yi Zhong Min Zhong Zi No. 176 [(2015) 京一中民终字第 176 号 ], (2015) Jing Yi Zhong Min Zhong Zi No. 01359[(2015) 京一中民终字第 01359 号 ].

[2] (2014) Er Zhong Min Zhong Zi No. 07157 [(2014) 二中民终字第 07157 号 ].

[3] (2015) San Zhong Min Zhong Zi No. 04810 [(2015) 三中民终字第 04810 号 ].

[4] (2014) Pu Min Yi (Min) Chu Zi No. 37776 [(2014) 浦民一 ( 民 ) 初字第 37776 号 ], (2015) Hu Yi Zhong Min Yi (Min) Zhong Zi No. 1778[(2015) 沪一中民一 ( 民 ) 终字第 1778 号 ].

compensation for the original price; vehicles were provided by the company to deliverymen; the management of deliverymen was an integral part of the company's main business; deliverymen must abide by the company's delivery rules when working; the company payed deliverymen remuneration for their labor. [1] In the series of cases of "Great Chef", the court pointed out that in a labor relationship, the autonomy of the parties should be restricted by laws and regulations such as labor laws, labor contract laws, and normative documents issued by labor administrative departments. Labor relationship shall be identified by peremptory norms, and shall be determined in view of the cooperation mode of both parties and the specific work of the workers, but shall not be excluded only by the written agreement of the parties. Good Chef Limited had the rights to assign, dispatch, reward and punish *Zhang Qi* and *Guan Xiaomin*, and pay them fixed remuneration by month. Under the labor management of Good Chef, *Zhang Qi* and *Guan Xiaomin* were engaged in remunerated work arranged by Good Chef, working on behalf of it, and working at the place arranged by it. Both parties shall comply with the subject qualifications of employers and employees as stipulated by relevant laws and regulations. Good Chef only operated a business platform of cooks, while *Zhang Qi* mainly provided services based on his culinary skills. Considering the above factors, it should be recognized that there was a strong subordinate relationship between the two parties, and such relationship was the essential characteristic of labor relations.[2]

In the "FlashEx" case in 2018, the court also held that the nature of the legal relationship should be determined according to the fact review, and the parties could not exclude the application of the labor law through any agreement. The court held that the operator of "FlashEx", Tongcheng Biying Tech. Co., Ltd., was not an information service company, but a company engaged in the business of goods transportation. When Mr. Li performed delivery tasks, he needed to wear a name tag and abide by the specific requirements in the service process. As a deliveryman of "FlashEx", Mr. Li did not engage in other jobs, and working for "FlashEx" was his main source of income. Therefore, there was a subordinate relationship between Tongcheng Biying Tech. Co., Ltd. and Mr. Li, and a labor relationship between these two parties. The court proposed that Tongcheng Biying Tech. Co., Ltd. benefited from the services provided by *Li*, so it should bear the corresponding legal responsibility and corporate social responsibility. If it was allowed to employ workers at low cost, employers would be lack of initiatives to prevent employment risks, and to implement labor safety protection measures, which would increase social problems. In this case,

---

[1] (2017) Liao 01 Min Zhong No. 7210 [(2017) 辽 01 民终 7210 号 ].

[2] (2017) Jing 03 Min Zhong No. 11768 [(2017) 京 03 民终 11768 号 ], (2017) Jing 03 Min Zhong No. 11769 [(2017) 京 03 民终 11769 号 ].

the court specifically pointed out that internet companies should not be exempt from their legal and social responsibilities in spite of their adoption of new technological means and new mode of operation. Companies based on new technology can fully use the advantages of information technology to achieve legal operation and management. The court should not deny the basic rights of workers, namely judicial remedy on the pretext of the imperfection of relevant supporting system. In the end, the court ruled that there was a labor relationship between Tongcheng Biying Tech. Co., Ltd. and Mr. Li.[1]

According to the latest case communique released by the Supreme Court, in the case of labor contract dispute between *Li Linxia* and Chongqing Main Cast Studios Co., Ltd., the court analyzed whether there was a labor relationship between the two parties from three aspects: management mode, income distribution and task. First, although the cooperation agreement between the two parties stipulated the days and hours of *Li Linxia*'s webcasts per month. It also stated that the company might punish *Li* for issues related the sanitation of the broadcast room, the location of meals during breaks, and the loss and damage of her work badge, etc. These should be understood as contractual obligations that *Li Linxia* shall perform the task based on the cooperation relationship between the two parties, and in line with the related management regulations of the industry, rather than the company's management behavior in the sense of labor law.  Second, although *Li Linxia*'s income was paid by Main Cast Studio, it was mainly gained by attracting fans and getting rewards from them through webcasts. The company only distributed the income according to the agreed proportion, but could not control and determine the amount of income of *Li Linxia*. The guaranteed minimum income agreed by both parties in the cooperation agreement shall be the guarantee and incentive expenses provided by Main Cast Studio to its live-streaming partners, rather than the main source of income of *Li Linxia*. Therefore, the live-streaming income paid by the company to *Li Linxia* based on the cooperation agreement could not be considered as the labor remuneration paid by employers to employees. Third, the platform that *Li Linxia* worked on was provided and owned by the third party. The webcast was not a business of Main Cast Studio. The company's business included only planning of webcast, but did not include the dissemination of audio-visual programs through information networks. Although the bilateral cooperation agreement stipulated that Main Cast Studio enjoyed the copyright of *Li Linxia*'s webcasts, it cannot be inferred that *Li*'s live-streaming activities were the performance of duties. Accordingly, both sides did

[1] Beijing Haidian People's Court: "Claiming that there was an accident on the way of delivery, the deliveryman's suing the platform operator to confirm labor relationship was supported"[EB/OL].(2018-06-06).http://bjhdfy. chinacourt.org/public/detail.php?id=5470.

not conform to the legal characteristics of labor relations. In other words, labor relationship was not established in this case.[1]

In the case of the confirmation of a labor relationship between Suzhou Nuo Ark Distribution Service Co., Ltd. and *Lu De*, the court pointed out that a labor relationship between the worker and the employer mainly depended on factors such as whether the worker accepted the daily management of the employer, whether the worker received the labor remuneration, and whether the task belonged to the main business of the employer. For new occupations such as food delivery riders, who emerged in the era of internet and big data, they should also be identified in line with the principle of regulating the legal employment of enterprises and protecting the legitimate rights and interests of workers. Through Meituan app, *Lu De* became a rider of Nuo Ark, and engaged in food delivery service. First of all, the food delivery service was the main business of the company. Second, Nuo Ark assigned tasks to riders including *Lu De* through the system authorized by Shanghai Sankuai Technology Co., Ltd. This kind of work assignment was not one-to-one in the traditional sense, but many-to-many. However, in essence, it was the same as the mode in the traditional industries that operators selected workers from the production line. Third, the labor remuneration was paid by the company by task on a monthly basis. It was also in line with the characteristics of general labor relations. Therefore, the relationship between *Lu De* and Nuo Ark conformed to the general characteristics of labor relations, so the existence of labor relations should be recognized. The confirmation of the existence of labor relations was also conducive to the standardization of industrial employment and the protection of the rights and interests of riders.[2]

As can be seen from the recent judicial decisions, judges no longer directly deny or avoid the identification of the labor relationship between platforms and workers. When there is no basis for adjustment of the law, they will interpret the existing norms out of judicial initiative and based on specific cases, so as to make a judgment on the existence of labor relationship. In practice, some of the platforms change the actual labor relationship into contract relationship or service relationship between workers and contractors through contract, in order to avoid the labor relationship with its employees. Either, they agree through agreement that the enterprise only serves as an intermediary trading platform to provide information, and the two parties do not have a labor relationship dominated by management. As a result, when disputes occur, it is often difficult for workers to determine the nature of the legal

---

[1] The case of *Li Linxia* (plaintiff) v. *Chongqing Main Cast Studios Co., Ltd.* (defendant) for Labor Contract Dispute, Communique of the Supreme People's Court, 2020,10 (288): 34-37.

[2] (2020) Su 05 Min Zhong No. 6812[(2020) 苏 05 民终 6812 号 ].

relationship between the two parties. When judging whether an enterprise of new business and its employees have a labor relationship, the court resorts to substantive reviews, and holds the traditional judgment view flexibly. The reasons for the court's affirmation of the existence of labor relationship between the two parties mainly are: the cooperation agreement, contract agreement or service agreement signed by the two parties has the nature of labor contract in essence; there is a strong personal and property subordination between the worker and the employer; the employer has issued the work certificate or the employee certificate when the worker engages in traffic accidents or other litigation; etc. The worker has reached retirement age;  he or she fails to provide evidence to prove that he or she is under the management of the employer; the employer only provides customers or clients and job opportunities, rather than manage workers; the income of workers comes from platform customers or clients, not the platform; the employer only collects the intermediary fee from the worker according to the actual situation of orders, and does not manage workers. These are common reasons for courts to hold that there is no labor relationship (Zhu, 2021).

In short, based on the traditional identification standard of labor relationship, the court pays attention to correctly identifying the nature of the legal relationship between the two parties through the substantive reviews of the existence of subordination, so as to prevent the generalization of labor relationship, and to prevent employers from covering up the actual employment of labor in order to avoid the operational risk. At the same time, as the current employment models of new forms of business are diversified, sometimes standard labor relationship, non-standard labor relationship and other civil legal relationship coexist. Therefore, in the specific identification, the court should distinguish correctly according to different boundaries of legal employment relations and the specific situation of each case.[1]

## III. Protection of Rights and Interests of Platform Workers

### 1. Path Choices for the Protection of Rights and Interests of Platform Workers

Within the framework of traditional labor law, the protection of workers worldwide mainly focuses on the concept of an employment (labor) relationship, which is also the key to the division of rights and responsibilities between employer and employee in labor law, thus drawing a line between subordinate and independent work. From the perspective of legislation, under the legal framework of "dichotomy

[1] The era of new forms of employment has come! Here's a job tip[N/OL]. The Paper (2021-04-28). https://www.thepaper.cn/newsDetail_forward_12444666.

of employment and self-employment", if platform workers are included or excluded from the legal application of employment (labor) relationship, the clip-like difference between "applied" and "not-applied" in the rights protection will occur. From the perspective of employment, there are differences between the platform's control over its workers and the standard employment (labor) relationship. In many cases, the platform only control the online labor process of workers, excluding other time, so worker autonomy and platform control exist at the same time, and worker's freedom and employment cannot be clearly divided by the standards of the traditional labor law (Wu and Yang, 2018). From the perspective of regulation, the protection of rights and interests of platform workers is an urgent issue to be dealt with. At the same time, it is necessary to take into account and adapt to the trend of the progress in technology, economy and society. To protect the rights and interests of platform workers, there are roughly several approaches.

The first approach is to introduce new criteria and factors for platform employment under the elementary framework based on traditional rules of judging employment (labor) relationship, or under the guidance of the basic norms and principles of judging "controlling" or "subordination" relationship. The judicial initiative should be useful to explain and identify the facts of the case, so as to solve disputes when the existing judgment rules are not very clear. The basic idea of this approach is still under the "dichotomy". According to the actual working condition of worker in the specific case, the identity of worker is determined, and whether labor law can be applied or not in terms of the rights and interests of worker can also be judged. This approach depends on the judicial case settlement, which has strong uncertainty and unpredictability, while individual case can cause a large controversy from all walks of life, but it also keeps the problem-solving open.

The second approach is to create a third category of workers to address issues such as the identity of platform workers and the protection of their rights and interests, so as to break the existing "dichotomy of employment and self-employment". Some Chinese scholars hold similar views and suggest abstracting the types of "instrumentalized autonomous labor" (Su and Wang, 2016), "quasi-subordinate independent labor with atypical labor relations" (Wang and Wang, 2018) and "employee-like workers" (Wang, 2020) and applying separate and specific labor laws and regulations. In this regard, the author has written an article pointing out that there are many difficulties and controversies in designing the system and developing the theory of a third category of workers, including the ambiguity of developing rules and the unpredictability of the system effectiveness and practical results. In addition, the special institutional background and relatively weak theoretical basis make the system less applicable and feasible in China (Xiao, 2018).

The third approach is to reform the completely binding relationship between identification of workers and their labor and social security rights and interests, and build a protection system of rights and interests at different levels which covers all workers, in order to avoid the problem of identification of employment (labor) relationship. At present, the theoretical, practical and policy circles have basically reached a consensus that it is necessary to protect the basic rights and interests of platform workers, so as to provide basic rights allocation and protection for workers in such social relations. These fundamental rights and interests can be concentrated on the basic rights such as wages, working hours, safety at work and social security.

Among these three approaches, the first is a realistic one that can be understood as a conservative compromise, or as self-effacing; the second has strong institutional risk, and requires complete scientific basis and excellent legislative know-how; the third can temporarily suspend the dispute and solve the current outstanding problems. In fact, how to improve the employment and social security system under the "new technology, new form of business, new model" is included in the agenda of the Ministry of Human Resources and Social Security (MHRSS) in 2018 (Luo, 2018), and has become a major consideration of the decision makers for institutional reform. It is also embodied in *Opinions on Safeguarding the Rights and Interests of Platform Gig Workers* drafted by MHRSS.

## 2. Protection of Platform Workers' Basic Working and Social Security Rights

What basic rights at work and social security rights and interests should platform workers be endowed with is not only an issue just related to platform workers, but also requires comprehensive considerations of the positive effects of platform economy on employment growth, negative influences of platform employment on traditional industries such as manufacturing industry, and the affordability of platform enterprises and the sustainability of the whole social insurance system in the institutional arrangement. In China, the protection of the rights and interests of platform workers in the future will take into account the basic rights at work, right to health and safety, right to collective consultation and democratic participation, and right to social security in terms of category. Considering the specific content of rights and the extent of protection, among the basic labor rights, basic and universal rights such as non-discrimination, access to employment services and vocational training should be considered, as well as special occupational rights such as minimum wages and maximum continuous working hours. In the right to health and safety, it emphasizes the safety obligations and responsibilities that the platform should provide; requires the promoting of the rights of platform workers to join trade unions and participate in social collaborative governance under collective consultation and democratic participation; and stresses occupational injury insurance in social security rights. The following part will discuss hot issues related the rights and interests, which are widely concerned in theory and practice at present.

### 2.1 Social security rights of platform workers

Since the end of the 19th century, employment relationship has been the basis of social insurance system. According to the regulations of China's *Social Insurance Law*, for workers involving in labor relations, their basic pension insurance are paid jointly by employers and individuals; self-employed people who are not involving in labor relations and do not employ any workers, part-time workers who are not engaged in basic pension insurance paid by employers, and other workers with flexible employment can also enjoy basic pension insurance by paying contributions by themselves. As early as in 2015, the State Council proposed in the *Opinions on Vigorously Developing E-commerce and Accelerating the Cultivation of New Economic Driving Force* that the labor rights and interests of workers should be protected; Internet workers should be involved in various social insurance schemes according to the regulations; and for online merchants who have not been registered to do business, their employees should be engaged in social insurance in accordance with the payment method of workers with flexible employment. In March 2021, *The State Council's Opinions on the Implementation of the Division of the Work in the Government Work Report* proposed to support and standardize the development of new forms of employment, and accelerate the pilot projects of occupational injury insurance; keep providing social security subsidies to workers with flexible employment; ease restrictions in household registration (*hukou*) of social security in locality where workers are working and living.

The dilemma in social security system faced by platform employment is that, for pension and medical insurance, it is difficult to define the responsibility and basis of payment, and also hard to determine what kind of insurance treatment workers should enjoy. As for unemployment insurance, platform work challenges the definition of traditional unemployment standards. The original unemployment assistance policy cannot play its role, and fee payment also becomes a tough problem. For work-related injury insurance, the current identification of industrial injury and the employer's responsibility take the existence of labor relationship as a prerequisite, so the system breakthrough or other protection approaches should be come up with.

In terms of social security rights, the most prominent and urgent problem is work-related injury. In August 2019, *the Guidance of the General Office of the State Council on Promoting the Standardized and Healthy Development of Platform Economy* stated that the rights and interests of platforms, operators and platform workers should be protected. It also proposed to promptly study and improve social security policies for platform employment and workers with flexible employment, carry out pilot projects of work-related injury insurance, actively promote the plan for universal insurance coverage, and encourage more platform workers to be insured. At present, local governments begin to explore approaches to address it. There are mainly two models of operation. One is the adoption of work-related injury insurance fund represented by Weifang, Shandong Province. The other is represented by Wujiang in Jiangsu Province, which is operated by commercial insurance companies under the guidance of the government to establish an independent model of work-related injury insurance. The Ministry of Human Resources and Social Security plans to take this as a breakthrough point to explore the protection against work-related injury for platform workers, and basically form the idea of prioritizing "the overall social security framework", with "commercial insurance" as the supplement.

At the local level, in July 2019, Chengdu (in Sichuan Province) issued *the Opinions on Promoting the Subscription of Workers in the New Economy and New Forms of Business in Social Insurance*, which has taken into account the nature and characteristics of employment in entities of new economy to regulate the labor relations; established a mechanism to promote the subscription of workers in social insurance based on their categories, according to different forms of employment, in order to provide diversified and specialized social security public services for new economy entities; established a mechanism for departments to coordinate the subscription of workers in social insurance. [1] Article 57 of *the Digital Economy Promotion Regulations of Zhejiang Province*, which was put into force on March 1 2021, stipulated that for workers of new forms of business in digital economy, who register and take orders through the internet platforms and provide services such as online car-hailing, food delivery and express delivery, platform operators could provide them work-related injury insurance through monoline insurance. If platform operators apply for such insurance, social insurance agencies shall handle it.

*2.2 The right of platform workers to join trade unions and participate in its affairs democratically*

The International Labor Organization (ILO) proposed in *Recommendation No. 204 Concerning the Transition from the Informal to the Formal Economy* issued in 2015 that, member states should ensure that those in the informal economy enjoy freedom of association and the right to collective bargaining, including the right to establish and, subject to the rules of the organization concerned, to join organizations,

---

[1] General Office of the People's Government of Chengdu. Opinions on Promoting Workers in the New Economy and New Forms of Business to join the Social Insurance Program [EB/OL]. (2019-07-22).http://gk.chengdu.gov. cn/govInfoPub/detail.action?id=109659&tn=6.

federations and confederations of their own choosing; employers' and workers' organizations should, where appropriate, extend membership and services to workers and economic units in the informal economy. However, the collective labor laws of different countries have no general stipulation on whether the identity of employees and the establishment of employment (labor) relationship is the prerequisite for workers to enjoy the collective labor rights. The collective labor laws themselves are not consistent in the principles of identifying employees and employment (labor) relationship in the legal relationship in terms of collective labor.

In Article 3 of China's *Labor Law*, all "manual workers and mental workers in enterprises, institutions and agencies who considered their wages as the main source of income" are endowed with the right to join and organize trade unions. The "worker" in the *Trade Union Law* is not limited to those with a labor relationship. In China, this group of people can be covered by the protection of the collective labor law, and are endowed with the right to organize and join trade unions and the right to collective bargaining, without breaking the standard of identification of labor relationship. On October 29, 2018, during a discussion with the new leadership of the All-China Federation of Trade Unions (ACFTU), General Secretary Xi Jinping stressed that "trade unions should attract, organize and stabilize workers with flexible employment, such as express deliverymen, food deliverymen and truck drivers, as well as all kinds of platform workers, through a variety of effective ways to make the union  an organization that they are willing to rely on". For this kind of group, first of all, in terms of elements of membership identification, ACFTU should pay attention to economic subordination rather than organizational subordination, and focus on workers with weak capacity of anti-risk in the new form of employment, in order to avoid functional duplication with industry associations. ACFTU should explain the concept of "worker" from the perspective of legislative know-how, that is, it includes not only workers with labor relations, but also workers with economic dependence on employer (economic dependency). ACFTU may consider amending *Trade Union Law* and *Trade Union Constitution*, making arrangements by means of documents or responses to individual cases, and studying and drafting opinions on the enrollment of workers with new forms of employment. In terms of enrollment, it can adopt online application, and improve offline regional trade union federations. For example, it may select some key regions to explore the establishment of trade union federations at various levels, and promote the establishment of trade union federations in the freight and express delivery industry in advance. For those workers with new forms of employment who do not work in a certain enterprise, they can join the union through the direct enrollment of regional and industrial federations. ACFTU should first focus on the top key enterprises to set an example for other enterprises,  and promote the associated enterprises to establish unions. It should also prepare a list and promote the establishment of trade unions in main enterprises of the three key industries of freight, express delivery and food delivery. Meanwhile, it is recommended that, MHRSS, Cyberspace Administration, Ministry of Industry and Information Technology and ACFTU should, in accordance with *Suggestions on Supporting Flexible Employment through Multiple Channels* issued by the General office of the State Council on July 28 2020, fulfill their duties of safeguarding the rights and interests of labor, study and make policies on labor security for platform workers, and clarify the duties of internet platforms in protecting the rights and interests of workers. They should also guide internet platforms and affiliated enterprises to negotiate with workers to determine certain issues, such as remuneration, paid leave and occupational safety, and guide industrial (local) trade unions to negotiate with representatives of industry associations or enterprises to formulate industry norms, such as labor quota standards, working hour standards, incentives and disincentives.

In practice, ACFTU issued *the Work Plan for Promoting the Enrollment of Truck Drivers and Other Groups* (hereinafter referred to as the Plan) in March 2018. It requires that trade unions at all levels should cover truck drivers, express deliverymen, nursing workers, housekeepers, shopping mall information managers, food deliverymen, real estate agents and security guards in the greatest extent, with the "united action for the enrollment of truck drivers" as the lead. To deal with difficulties in establishing and joining trade unions in such industries as express delivery outsourcing and its franchisees, the Trade Union of National Defense and Posts and Telecommunications of China explored approaches first in companies such as SF Express and STO, and held a collective enrollment ceremony for outsourcing workers and migrant workers of franchisees of SF Express in Tianjin and those of STO in Beijing respectively. It enhanced the awareness of the front-line express delivery workers, especially migrant workers, about trade unions, and stimulated their internal motivation to join the unions voluntarily. [1] Since 2018, 8.743 million workers of this group have joined the unions. At the beginning of 2018, Shanghai set up the first trade union of online food delivery industry – Shanghai Putuo District Federation of Trade Unions in online food delivery industry. Putuo District of Shanghai has set up 5 unions for online food deliverymen, having a total of more than 400 workers. [2] Shanghai Federation of Trade Unions has set up a special basic guarantee for trade union members with new forms of employment, and implemented a "five-benefit" service(" 五送 " 服务 ) list, including insurance, physical examination, assistances in summer and winter, and security, with 205,100 participants. In 2021, ACFTU

---

[1] http://www.acftu.org/template/10041/file.jsp?aid=96841.

[2] https://www.chinanews.com/sh/2018/01-04/8416637.shtml.

will cooperate with the Ministry of Transport to carry out the Special Action of "Organization and Care" for Truck Drivers (2021-2023), and jointly hold on-site promotion meetings; strive for the support of the State Post Bureau and the express industry associations to launch the "Special Action on the Establishment and Service of Trade Unions in Non-public Express Enterprises"; implement the special action of "caring for the deliverymen", together withele.me platform. It will also concentrate on promoting the construction of trade unions, vigorously promote the enrollment mode of "covering all industries and ensuring the basic needs of each region", and strive to establish trade union federations in more than 60% of cities and counties (districts) in China within five years.

However, we should also realize that organizing platform workers to join the unions, and enabling them to enjoy and exercise the rights of collective bargaining are two different issues. Although there is no legal obstacle for relevant organizations to promote platform workers to subscribe in trade unions, there are still institutional barriers, such as the unclear negotiating parties and procedures of the collective bargaining, ambiguous scope of application and the unknown effect of collective contracts, which would affect workers' substantive rights of collective bargaining and other rights of democratic participation. Therefore, it is hard to follow the existing system of collective consultation to protect the rights of collective bargaining of workers in face of the employment mode of the sharing economy (Wu, Zhang and Zhou, 2019).

### 2.3 Guarantee of working hours and wages

In terms of wages, the mode that platforms pay/charge by task brings fundamental challenges to the remuneration mode based on working hours in many aspects, such as the projects, level, form, object and time of remuneration payment. The most prominent is the core of the wage protection system, namely whether the minimum wage system can be applied. Technically, the minimum wage for platform workers cannot be determined due to the change in the remuneration basis of the minimum wage system. In terms of actual effect, even if the minimum wage for platform workers can be determined in some ways by the measurement of various parties, whether it is a destruction of the market price mechanism, and whether it will substantially reduce the bargaining space for platform workers need to think.

In terms of working hours, China's Labor Law defined the standard working hour system, flexible working hour system and combined working hour system. However, in these three working hour systems, working hours are determined by employers. In contrary, the most prominent characteristic of platform employment is the determination of working hours by workers themselves, namely a strong flexibility. Even though the platform can influence the working hours of workers through effective incentives and rating mechanism, the final decision is still made by workers themselves. Thus, the current principles of the identification of working hours, extra work and paid leave defined in the Labor Law are difficult to follow. But the sustainability of labor and the safety of labor during the process of providing services (such as the driving safety of online car-hailing drivers) can be taken into consideration. The maximum working hours of workers in related industries should be restricted. However, the regulation mechanism is obviously different from the traditional working hour system defined in the labor law.

## IV. Conclusions and Recommendations

The development of platform economy has changed the traditional employment mode based on industrialization. The rapid development of information technology has greatly enhanced the capability of job creation and job matching, making the sharing economy as a "reservoir" and "stabilizer" of employment. Nowadays, there is a new trend of the platform employment: the fields it involves continue to expand, its capacity of creating jobs continues to strengthen, and it has more features of gig economy. In terms of the impact on labor relations, the development of platform economy has intensified the "informal" employment and the "atomization" of labor. It has also strengthened the demand for flexible employment and reduced the stability of labor relations, which brings multiple challenges to the legal adjustment of labor relations.

Among the platform employment modes, the two most controversial ones are "offline gig work" and "online crowdsourcing work". In China, the former is used more widely. However, at present, platform workers in China increasingly rely on income from the platform, which is generally low and unstable, and consider the platform work as their main source of income. The problem related to the protection of the rights and interests of platform workers, such as the rights at work, the rights to social security and to democratic participation, needs to be solved urgently.

Under the current global system of labor and employment law, the protection of the rights and interests of platform workers is still closely related to their identification, which is also a common difficult issue in judicial trials at home and abroad. In practice, judges in China and abroad deal with this issue according to the elements of determining the labor (employment) relation defined by laws and legal precedents, and based on the different circumstances of each case. However, it also reflects the inclination in adjudication and the formulation of rules. However, providing platform workers with legal basis for rights protection by changing the principles of identification of workers and judicial practice is not the only option.

One alternative option could be the creation of a third category of workers under the dichotomy of "employment and self-employed", or breaking down the complete binding relationship between identity of workers and their rights and interests, so as to provide workers with basic rights and interests of labor and social security. We need to consider carefully the institutional difficulties and the unintended practical consequences of establishing a third category of workers. Therefore, the promising approach should be the one to break down the relationship between workers' identity and their rights and interests, and gradually build the basic rights and interests protection system for platform workers, starting from handling the prominent contradictions in current rights protection system.

## References

[1] Sharing Economy Research Center of the State Information Center (SERC-SIC). Annual Report of China's Sharing Economy Development (2021). http://www.sic.gov.cn/archiver/SIC/UpFile/Files/Default/20210219091740015763.pdf.

[2] Didi Development Research Institute (DDRI). Understanding the Poverty Alleviation through Employment and the Portrait of the People on Didi Platform [EB/OL]. (2021-03-31). https://mp.weixin.qq.com/s/6lifVINdPmm2O0XjfffX5g.

[3] Meituan Research Institute (MRI). Rider Employment Report for the First Half of 2020 [EB/OL]. (2021-03-26). https://mp.weixin.qq.com/s/cMEfsTfLfvSxF88dLN8LIw.

[4] Ministry of Human Resources and Social Security (MHRSS). New Occupation: Analysis Report on the Employment of Online Deliverymen [EB/OL]. (2021-03-31). http://www.mohrss.gov.cn/SYrlzyhshbzb/dongtaixinwen/buneiyaowen/202008/t20200825_383722.html.

[5] China New Forms of Employment Research Center, Research Group of School of Labor Economics, Capital University of Economics and Business. New Economy, New Employment: Research Report on Employment Quality of China's New Forms of Employment – A Case Study of Didi Platform (2018) [R], 2018.

[6] Li Yufu. ed. The 8th Survey on the Status of Chinese Workers[M]. Beijing: China Workers Publishing House, 2017.

[7] Qiu Jie. Flexible Employment: Individuals and Society in the Digital Economy [M]. Beijing: China Workers Publishing House, 2020.

[8] Zhang Chenggang. Changes in Employment: Digital Commerce and New Forms of Employment in China [M]. Beijing: China Workers Publishing House, 2020.

[9] Wang Wenzhen, Li Wenjing. The Influence of Platform Economy Development on Labor Relations in China [J]. China Labour, 2017(1): 7.

[10] Zhang Mo, Tang Siyuan. Frequent Labor Disputes in On-line Car Hailing,

Express Delivery! Court Suggestions [EB/OL]. (2021-04-28). https://baijiahao.baidu.com/s?id=1698273045264429861&wfr=spider&for=pc.

[11] Zhang Chenggang, Feng Lijun. On Problems of Labor Relations and Its Countermeasures of the New Forms of Employment from the Perspective of Trade Unions [J]. Journal of China Institute of Industrial Relations, 2019, 33(6): 106-114.

[12] Wu Qingjun, Yang Weiguo. Sharing Economy and Human Capital Management on the Internet Platform: Re-Evaluating Labor Resources and Work [J]. Human Resource Development of China, 2018(6).

[13] Wu Qingjun, Zhang Yiyuan, Zhou Guangsu. Workers on Internet Platform and the Future of Labor Policies: A Research Based on Labor Identity Criteria[J]. Chinese Public Administration, 2019(4).

[14] Su Yu, Wang Quanxing. Legal protection of Autonomous Labor in Flexible Employment in China [J]. Southeast Academic Research, 2016(3).

[15] Wang Quanxing, Wang Qian. The Identification of Labor Relations and Protection of Rights and Interests of "Gig Workers" in China [J]. Legal Science Monthly, 2018(4).

[16] Xiao Zhu. Theoretical Reflection and Alternative Path of the Third Category of Workers [J]. Global Law Review, 2018(6).

[17] Wang Tianyu. The Interpretation Path and Its Normative System for "Employee-Like Workers" of Internet Platform Employment [J]. Global Law Review, 2020(3).

[18] Wang Yan, Zhang Lihua. A Study on the New Employment Pattern of Sharing Economy in China [J]. Journal of China Institute of Industrial Relations, 2019, 33(2).

[19] Luo Jing. Improving the Rights and Interests of "Three New" Workers is on the Agenda [N]. Labor Journal, 2018-03-14.

[20] Zhu Jianyong. What is the relationship between food deliverymen and platforms? Beijing Third Intermediate People's Court: More than 80 percent have identified labor relations [EB/OL]. (2021-04-29). https://baijiahao.baidu.com/s?id=1698344654444730169&wfr=spider&for=pc.

[21] Diane Mulcahy. The Gig Economy (Chinese version) [M]. Beijing: CITIC Press, 2017.

[22] Mark Freedland Fba & Nicola Kountouris. The legal Construction of Personal Work Relations [M]. Oxford University Press, 2011.

[23] Valerio DeStefano, The Rise of the "Just-In-Time Workforce": On-Demand Work, Crowd Work, And Labor Protection in The "Gig economy" [J]. Comparative Labor Law and Policy Journal, Vol.37, Iss.3, 2016.

[24] Miriam Cherry. Beyond Misclassification: The Digital Transformation of Work [J]. Comparative Labor Law and Policy Journal, Vol.37, Iss.3, 2016.

[25] Seth D. Harris & Alan B. Krueger, A proposal for modernizing labor laws for twenty-first-century work: the "Independent Worker". The Hamilton Project, Discussion

Paper 2015-10 (Washington, DC, Brookings Institution).

[26] Committee on contract, Report V (2B) Addendum, labour 86th Session, Geneva, June 1998.

[27] International Labour Office. Geneva. http://www.ilo.org/public/english/standards/relm/ilc/ilc86/rep-vadd.htm.

[28] McKinsey Global Institute. Independent Work Choice necessity and the gig economy [EB/OL]. (2016-10).https://www.mckinsey.com/featured-insights/employment-and-growth/independent-work-choice-necessity-and-the-gig-economy.

# Overseas Labor Relations

■ Constructing a "Trinity" Cross-cultural Harmonious Labor Relations Management System for Overseas Chinese Enterprises in BRI Countries

# Constructing a "Trinity" Cross-cultural Harmonious Labor Relations Management System for Overseas Chinese Enterprises in BRI Countries[*]

## *Ye Ying*[**]

**Abstract:** Labor issue is a major issue in risk-prevention for overseas Chinese enterprises in the Belt and Road Initiative (BRI) countries. Some Chinese enterprises do not know, care, nor adapt to labor standards, laws and regulations of their host countries in overseas investment projects, which weakens their international competitiveness. On the basis of empirical research, this paper summarizes the multidimensional risk cognition and prevention, and control measures of Chinese enterprises; proposes the construction of a cross-cultural harmonious labor relations management system that is in accordance with laws, guided by the concept of "cultural advance and manual retreat" and supported by professional talents. Many contributors may come into play for overseas labor relations risks of Chinese enterprises. Only by a multi-pronged and comprehensive approach can these risks be prevented. We should promote cultural exchange, contribute Chinese solutions and wisdom in cross-cultural management, and provide talent support for Chinese enterprises' internationalization strategy, so as to inherit the enterprises' cultural genes in the process of the development of overseas Chinese enterprises in BRI countries.

**Keywords:** overseas Chinese enterprises; legitimacy and compliance; talent support; harmonious labor relations

---

[*] This paper is based on *Trans-ocean Expedition: Management and Practice of Overseas Labor Relations of State-owned Enterprises under the Belt and Road Initiative*, China Electric Power Press, April 2020.

[**] Ye Ying, associate professor at the School of Labor Relations and Human Resources, China University of Industrial Relations. She specializes in labor economics and human resource management.

# I. Overview: Chinese Literature on Labor Issue in Overseas Chinese Enterprises in BRI Countries

## 1. Labor Issue is A Major Issue in Risk-prevention for Overseas Chinese Enterprises in BRI Countries

In related literatures on overseas Chinese enterprises in the Belt and Road Initiative (BRI) countries, some scholars believe that labor issue has become one of the most serious issues in the foreign investment of Chinese enterprises (Pan and Chen, 2018). Some others even believe that the biggest problem for Chinese enterprises in going global is in trade unions, which is manifested in the continuous friction between employer and employee caused by trade union culture (Ma, 2014; Xiao, 2018).

In overseas mergers and acquisitions (M&A), Chinese enterprises mainly face four major legal risks: inconsistent labor protection standards, labor disputes caused by M&A methods, high cost of dismissal, and trade unions hindering M&A (Li, 2011). Some scholars believe that there are also legal risks in labor contracts, labor disputes and government labor control, as well as the integration of human resource management of enterprises (Zhao and Xia, 2012). About 1/3 of investment projects terminated or failed due to the neglect or unfamiliarity with local labor laws (Liu, 2016). From the perspective of the quality of human resources, employees in some BRI countries generally are less educated and have limited labor skills, leading to the fact that many local workers can only engage in low-skilled jobs (Zhuang, 2017). Since 2013, 27 BRI countries have experienced a mass of protests and strikes, most of which aimed to raising wages and improving working conditions, or due to reasons such as unpaid wages, SOE privatization and layoffs, government policies, political and partisan divisions, environmental protection, etc. (Shi, Zhang and Zhu, 2020).

From the perspective of regions, in Asia, Chinese enterprises in Vietnam are tend to have misunderstandings in labor cost, labor efficiency and labor supply, because there are huge differences in standards and rules of labor relations mediation, trade unions, collective bargaining rights and basic labor rights between these two countries (Huang and Wu, 2019). In Africa, the legal risks of labor law faced by Chinese enterprises are increasingly evident, especially in employment, wage payment, overtime work, anti-employment discrimination, strong trade unions and unfair dismissal, etc. These occurrences are mainly due to Chinese enterprises' neglect in understanding or strictly complying with local labor laws (Hong and Huang, 2019). In Latin America, Chinese enterprises face lots of problems constantly in Brazil, such as labor dispute risks, difficulties in implementing the human resource management, as well as difficulties in controlling labor costs (Chen, 2016).

In summary, Chinese enterprises investing and operating in BRI countries face increasingly complex challenges in due diligence and compliance management, which require them to abide by local management principles, and embrace global standards and international norms. However, some Chinese enterprises do not know, care, nor adapt to labor standards, laws and regulations of their host countries in overseas business, which not only causes a large number of labor disputes, but also hinders them from using international norms and standards to develop their own international competitiveness. At the same time, some Chinese enterprises lack inter-disciplinary talents with international visions and operation capabilities. Generally, labor disputes, frequent strikes and the interference of trade unions are the biggest challenges for Chinese enterprises (Dai, 2018).

## 2. Characteristics and Analytical Framework of Labor Relations and Regulations in BRI Countries

How to summarize the characteristics of labor relations and regulations in BRI countries? Here, we will analyze it based on two framework paradigms of international employment relationship comparison and cross-cultural management.

International comparative studies of employment relations usually adopt the conceptual framework of "Varieties of Capitalism" (VoC), which focuses on five levels of collaboration that enterprises must address: industrial relations, vocational training and education, corporate governance, inter-firm relations, and relations with employees, thus summarizing two types of economies with different characteristics and their employment relations, namely, countries with coordinated market economies (CMEs) and countries with liberal market economies (LMEs) (Hall and Soskice, 2001). Regarding the question of whether the development trend of labor relations in all countries should be "convergence" or "divergence", authoritative scholars analyzed the characteristics and development trend of labor relations in 12 countries, and concluded that all countries are increasingly tend to adopt liberal employment relations policy, which includes the growth of non-standard employment, the emergence of dual models of employer coordination, and the increase of outsourcing, etc. (Lansbury, Wells and Bamber, 2016). Moreover, some international institutions and framework agreements are becoming increasingly important in the process, so they need to be recognized in international employment relations (Lansbury, Wells and Bamber, 2016). In this regard, the International Labor Organization (ILO) argues that there are evidences of a decline in binding social dialogues, such as tripartite social contracts and collective bargaining agreements, due to wide income disparities, changes of the nature of work and the more flexible labor market (ILO, 2018). Generally, there is an obvious trend of diversity and decentralization of labor relations within a country. However, in government-dominated countries, the mode of employment relations integrates different features such as liberalism, market coordination and state intervention at the same time (Chang, 2016).

As for comparison of employment relations in BRI countries, some scholars believe that due to historical changes, cultural traditions and different religions and political systems, there are obvious heterogeneity and dispersion across these countries, which are in different development stages (from pre-industrialization to post-industrialization) and pursue different economic development models. Therefore, it is difficult to summarize their employment relations mode with a single theoretical framework (Qiao and Li, 2018). Some foreign scholars analyzed 249 collective agreements in 11 countries. The results show that 98% of these agreements include clauses of wages, but only a few of them define the level of wages; up to 71% include provisions of social security, 89% include provisions of working hours, and 84% include work-family arrangements (Besamusca and Tijdens, 2015). After analyzing the legal adjustment of collective labor relations in 57 developing countries, scholars classified the adjustment modes into three categories: enterprise adjustment, social adjustment and national adjustment. The common risk of legal adjustment of collective labor relations in Chinese enterprises "going global" comes from the differences between collective bargaining in China and the host countries, and the misunderstanding of functions of trade unions and dealing with strikes in an incorrect way (Wang, 2018). Some scholars analyzed 5 different labor relations coordination modes in BRI countries, and compared the similarities and differences vertically (Han and Zhang, 2018).

After discussing various analytical frameworks for the comparison of international employment relations, some scholars suggested to expand the frameworks by including stakeholders beyond the three parties (labor, management and government), so as to adapt to the comparative study of developing countries. They believe that the academic circle of labor relations has always treated workers in the supply chain as the major stakeholders, but failed to include more stakeholders such as international organizations, governments of other countries, supply chain enterprises and non-governmental organizations, etc. In the future, the research boundary of international employment relations comparison should be expanded (Yang and Zhou, 2019; Zhang, 2019).

Another analytical framework is the cross-cultural management. Since the 1980s, Asia's economic boom was mainly attributed to the Confucian culture's virtues: order, discipline, responsibility, diligence, collectivism, thrift, while the West's decline was mainly attributed to self-indulgence, laziness, individualism, crime, poor education, disrespect for authority, and "being close-minded" (Huntington, 2010). Therefore, multinational corporations now pay more attention to the integration and mutual learning of different cultures in investment.

Facing challenges brought by globalization, organizations are more concerned with designing and implementing human resource management (HRM) practices to fit the global and local environment. Aycan (2005) presented a systematic review of literature. Cultural and institutional/structural contingencies would influence HRM practices in six key areas: human resource planning and career management, job analysis and design, recruitment and selection, performance appraisal, compensation and reward management, and training and development, which influence the operation and management of corporations. After years of empirical tests, cross-cultural management research finally rests on the creation and innovation of cultural integration and organizational culture, and is therefore applied to micro-management practice.

In China, with Chinese enterprises playing an increasingly important role in international arena, cross-cultural management has attracted the attention of domestic enterprises. Zhao Shuming (2001) believes that there is a basic convergence of the organizational structure, technological approaches, decision-making methods and control procedures in multinational enterprises, but employees' different cultural backgrounds make cultural differences an important factor which affects the outcome of management. Cross-cultural HRM is the interactive combination among the three dimensions of HRM practice, types of employees and types of host countries (Zhao, 2001). Multinational corporations will face six kinds of cultural risks in transnational operations, including risks of racial superiority, management, communication, business practice, taboo, as well as organizational risk (Peng, 2000). The HRM of multinational corporations in China is confronted with operation and management issues caused by the cultural differences between China and the West. Ultimately, these corporations adopted localization strategies (Chen and Wei, 2003). Employees with different cultural backgrounds would have different cultural values and social habits, thus different psychological contracts. Managers should carefully learn the local culture, and accept and respect the new culture (Yao, 2006).

So far, all enterprises face a dilemma in cross-cultural management: how to ensure cultural diversity and corporate unity (Lin, 2012)? The survey shows that about 82% of the failures of multinational corporations are caused by the failure of cross-cultural management. Cross-cultural management must be adjusted to adapt to the specific requirements of different societies. However, there have not been any successful cases of cross-cultural management in China's overseas investment enterprises for now.

### 3. Strategies and Suggestions for Overseas Chinese Enterprises in BRI Countries on Building Harmonious Labor Relations

In terms of labor relations coordination and corporate compliance, the government should fulfill its service functions to reduce legal risks by drafting multilateral contracts and improving judicial cooperation for Chinese enterprises "going out", and achieve the connectivity between macro legal environment at the national level and micro risk prevention at the enterprise level (Dai, 2018; Wang and Jiang, 2018; Wang, 2018). Enterprises should improve due diligence in labor and employment, find the appropriate cooperation mode with the host country's trade unions, strengthen collective bargaining capability, and develop a common management mechanism of labor disputes. They should also strictly abide by the laws and regulations of the host countries, and promote management compliance (Wang and Jiang, 2018; Wu and Huang, 2019; Shi, Zhang and Zhu, 2020).

Regarding human resources development and management, we should utilize the demographic dividend and aggregate advantages of countries to promote international cooperation on production capacity, give full play to the distinctive educational resources and advantages of these countries to carry out comprehensive cooperation in personnel training, build various human resource platforms for exchange and communication to facilitate international cooperation channels on human resources, as well as improve talent immigration incentives and policies (Zhang and Liu, 2017; Tian, 2019).

In terms of cross-cultural management, many scholars suggest to improve the training of local workers, facilitate training plans of elites in enterprises, and improve risk prevention capabilities by "localization" in overseas operations (Liu, 2016; Wang, 2018; Pan and Chen, 2018; Huang and Wu, 2019). Others propose to set up employers associations of Chinese enterprises to achieve the protection of collective rights (Hong and Huang, 2019). Some others suggest that it should integrate the concepts and practices of harmonious labor relations with Chinese characteristics, and establish a new model of cross-cultural labor relations management (Qiao and Li, 2018).

In conclusion, the existing literatures mainly stress the necessity and urgency of building harmonious labor relations and preventing labor relations risks from the perspective of labor issues as developing countries investment risks. Some literatures conducted empirical studies on labor relations legislation, law enforcement supervision and various labor standards in some developing BRI countries, and put forward useful policy and management suggestions.

The existing researches on this topic, from the perspective of theory and practice, macro to micro level, have obvious defects, especially the systematic research which combines certain enterprises' management practice and the labor laws and regulations of their host countries Meanwhile, both theoretical and case study lack convincing evidence, in which the subject is changing from traditional labors to overseas Chinese enterprises, especially the study of the policy of building harmonious labor relations from the perspective of HRM and cross-cultural management.

Due to the shortcomings of previous academic works and existing researches, and based on case studies of typical SOEs, this paper aims to conduct systematic research on Chinese enterprises' construction of harmonious labor relations, and explore the way of building systematically harmonious labor relations in overseas Chinese enterprises based on enterprise management compliance, cultural integration facilitation management and international talent management.

The **overall framework and objectives** of this paper are shown in Figure 1. It establishes the analysis framework of the risk factors affecting the labor relations of BRI countries, analyzes labor relations of SOEs in host countries, and clarifies the status quo and potential risks. It specifically selects cases of Chinese enterprise's "going global" in Brazil to study the establishment of a "trinity" new model of cross-cultural harmonious labor relations form the perspective of legitimacy, cultural advance, and talent support.

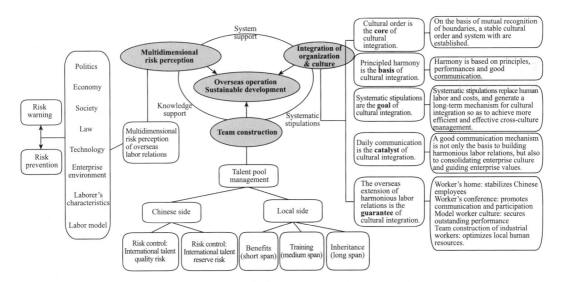

**Figure 1    Research framework of building harmonious labor relations of overseas Chinese enterprises in BRI countries**

## Methodology:

(1) Literature research: collect literatures (both in Portuguese and English) on

labor relations and labor laws of relevant countries to conduct a comparative review.

(2) In-depth interview: learn about the labor relations management system of SOE-invested enterprises, the recognition and comments of Brazilian employees and scholars  through field researches, video conferences, teleconferences and emails.

(3) Questionnaire survey: there are two types of questionnaire. One is the questionnaire on comprehensive labor relations for management level and employees, which is used to explore Brazilian employees' views and judgements on the status quo of labor relations; another is the questionnaire for all Chinese employees of sample enterprises.

## II. Perceptions of Multidimensional Risks on Labor Relations of Chinese Overseas Enterprises in BRI countries: A Case Study of Company K (a Wholly-owned Subsidiary of Company G in Brazil)

### 1. Overview of Company G's Overseas Investment

Since 2009, Company G has successfully acquired the full ownership of over ten companies in the Philippines, Portugal, Australia, Italy, Brazil, etc., and the partial ownership of companies in Brazil and Greece. At present, the overseas operating assets of Company G are expanding. There is a total staff of nearly 20,000 working in Company K, a wholly-owned subsidiary of Company G, and Company L, a holding company of Company G. Company G not only sent its directors and senior executives to engage in the management of these two companies, but also a group of professionals to participate in the daily operating work, and cooperate with local employees.

Overseas operation faces a complex and diversified employment environment, which is significantly different from that of China. Brazil attaches great importance to labor relations, and has corresponding labor laws, regulations and standards. In daily management, it is necessary for Chinese staff to recognize the factors that may impose risks on labor relations, be familiar with local laws and regulations on labor relations and trade unions, build a good relationship with local staff, properly deal with overseas trade unions, implement compliance management, and regularly review and prevent risks in labor relations.

In order to effectively prevent and control these risks, the Chinese enterprises also need to do a good job in cross-cultural human resources integration and dispatch management. For example, retain the key employees in overseas companies while improving the mechanism of dispatch, withdrawal, incentives and restriction so as to ensure that they could be successfully selected, dispatched, utilized and withdrew. This is crucial to the sustainable development of  overseas operations of these enterprises.

Therefore, for Company G's further progress in the overseas operation and management, dealing with issues of labor relations according to the law and regulations, the reduction of operational risks, the improvement of organizational efficiency, the promotion of brand building, it is necessary to study the labor relation management of its overseas projects and the risk prevention strategies. It can also provide reference for the company's potential investment projects and other overseas follow-up projects, as well as other SOE's international business.

According to the study, it concluded that Company G has taken the first step in establishing the system of harmonious labor relations, and played an important role in ensuring the expansion of the enterprise's core business. This is mainly reflected in the following aspects:

First of all, Company K has become a corporate entity with huge investment capacity and the capacity of long-standing operation in Brazil. It has developed extensively in Brazil against the trend of severe economic recession since 2014, promoted the steady growth of employees and stabilized employment. By July 2019, the total staff of Company K reached 749. During the crisis, Brazil's unemployment rate rose sharply, reaching 13.7% in March 2017, leaving more than 14 million Brazilians out of work. 3.7 million jobs were lost during 2015-2016. In March 2021, Company K was certified as "Great Place to Work" by an authoritative global human resources research and consulting company.

Second, Company K established a new organizational structure which strictly abided by the law, and introduced KPI performance measurement. The company's collective bargaining and communication mechanism between the management level and employees functioned perfectly. While a sharp rise of labor disputes appeared during the economic crisis, the number of labor disputes in Company K was at a relatively low level. On the one hand, the company improved the organizational and top-level management by setting up eight departments, namely project management department, legal department, financial assets department, development planning department, operation and maintenance management department, and comprehensive management department, all of which served for the coordination in strategy and planning. By focusing on the main business, and adhering to the principle of "Consultation, Contribution and Shared Benefits" and the market-oriented operation strategy, the company gives full play to its comprehensive advantages in technology, talent, management, capital, credit and brand; actively expands the market share; and innovates in operation and control model for overseas business. On the other hand, the company strictly abided by the Brazilian labor laws, and based on the actual situation of the company to steadily improve the labor rules and regulations of the company, establish KPI and PAP management systems for all staff, which directly linked with bonuses of employee. The performance assessment has been constantly improved, from no compulsory distribution in the earliest stage to 1-5 levels of indicators (each level represents 20% compulsory normal distribution) in 2018. This reform has promoted the staff's work performance. Also, the company holds collective bargaining meetings on raises of wages and other benefits every year, and on non-economic terms every two years. Chinese managing level also get involved in these talks, gaining valuable experience. The human resources department engages in the annual talk on behalf of the company, and tries to keep good relationship with all trade unions. The company has also taken a very strategic initiative to build channels of communication with employees throughout the year to increase their involvement. Therefore, the number of labor disputes in Company K remains at a relatively low level. The most typical labor disputes include outsourcing employees' demands for equal pay, overtime pay and claims of harassment at work.

Third, Company K recognizes the cultural differences between China and Brazil, and is willing to invest in training. By organizing personnel trainings in China, it facilitates cultural integration, and initially establishes the concept of cross-cultural management. Chinese managing level can consciously recognize the differences between Chinese and Brazilian employees. For example, Chinese employees would carry out the instructions from their supervisors unconditionally, while Brazilian employees need to be explained patiently the instructions and be persuaded. In collective bargaining, the Chinese enterprises mainly appointed Brazilian managers who accept Chinese management concepts and leadership, from the standpoint of the company. Brazilians are gentle and mild, fond of parties and get-togethers. The negotiations take account of both employee's emotions and legal provisions. Chinese managing level can also distinguish the conflicts caused by cultural differences. For example, Brazilians don't like to be confronted or reprimanded in person. Most labor disputes are filed by employees to the court after they quitted. In terms of punishment measures, Brazilian employees are either dismissed or given a raise, leaving no space in between, so that employees have freedom to a certain extent. Brazilians do not have a strong sense of hierarchy, and will resign if not satisfied, which is different from the loyalty and dependence of Chinese employees. A major complaint from Brazilians is that the administration is bureaucratic, they have limited freedom, and everything needs to be approved. Brazil is a country with high cultural tolerance, Due to the multi-ethnic culture, there is no ethnic or cultural superiority. It advocates nature, and keeps life and work separated. Conflicts happen very often in the early stage because of the pressing management style of the Chinese enterprises. To avoid such cultural conflicts, the Chinese enterprises organized training sessions about Chinese culture. In specific, two groups of Brazilian elites were sent to China for trips, where they changed their social stereotypes. Through the introduction to corporate culture, management concept and Chinese culture within Company G, some employees were convinced to accept the management culture. Chinese managers have also realized that communication couldn't solve problems at all times. Sometimes they should meet each other halfway, and try to avoid conflicts.

In general, Company G's subsidiary in Brazil operates based on its actual situation, while its human resource management system is strictly in line with local labor laws and regulations, which leads to very desirable outcomes. This has been an important factor of supporting the sustainable development and gaining market profit of the enterprise in recent years. After the implementation of the employment law amendment in 2017, no impact was seen on the existing management system due to its relatively stable transition. According to the questionnaire survey, the management and employees also gave a relatively consistent and positive comment on the employee management system and its implementation. This is reflected in eight working hours, the level of wage (higher than the minimum wage) determined by collective bargaining, overtime wages paid in accordance with the law, various social insurance, labor contracts and on-the-job training, etc. The company has begun to pay attention to the cultural differences between employees of the two countries and their performances. By training Brazilian employees on management with Chinese characteristics, and the selection of outstanding workers, the company gradually promoted the integration of the management cultures between China and Brazil, which played a fundamental role in supporting the operation of the company and market development. Of course, there are some internal and external risks in building harmonious labor relations, which are summarized as follows.

## 2. Recognition of Multi-dimensional Risks and the Prevention & Control Measures of Chinese Enterprises

According to our analysis of Brazil's macro political and economic system and its current situation, changes in labor laws and regulations, and labor relations management of Company G, the labor relations risk index of Company G's investment projects in Brazil includes legal risk, political risk, economic risk, management risk, cultural risk, safety risk and worker's movement risk. Figure 2 shows all these risks, and highlights some important points.

According to our research, we list the risks and positions with potential risks in the human resources and labor relations management of Company G (see Table 1) from the perspective of management compliance, and propose measures and suggestions on risk prevention and control.

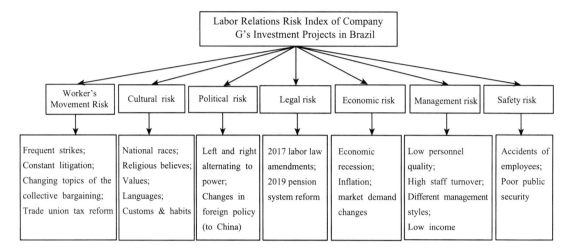

**Figure 2   Labor relations risk index of company G's investment projects in Brazil**

**Table 1       Risks of internal labor relations in the subsidiary of Company
G in Brazil and the prevention & control measures**

| No. | Positions with potential risks | Description | Prevention & control measures |
|---|---|---|---|
| 1 | Core staff | In 2018, the subsidiary of Company G in Brazil (hereinafter referred to as Company K) spent 1440.72 Reais per person on training, 15% higher than the market average, but 26% lower than the average in energy market. This indicates that the company is still relatively behind in terms of investment on staff training. | Company K has realized that by creating opportunities, selecting outstanding employees, and the internal job transfers or training, it could fully develop the potential of the best employees. It has also sent some excellent Brazilian employees to China for training, which had good outcomes – not only improved their professional skills rapidly, but also enhanced their cohesion to Chinese enterprises. Next, the company will invest in technical training to develop the necessary skills of employees based on talent assessment; invest in behavioral training to develop employees' comprehensive abilities; implement LMS and develop learning paths to improve training management; promote cultural integration programs to benefit from the cultural diversity within the enterprise. |

(continued)

| No. | Positions with potential risks | Description | Prevention & control measures |
|-----|-------------------------------|-------------|-------------------------------|
| 2 | Senior management; all staff | Generally, the payroll of Company K is relatively low across the industry. Due to the lack of competitiveness in wage and benefits, the staff turnover rate has increased significantly since 2016, both leaving willingly and passively. | Take comprehensive measures to promote equal pay for equal work, including appropriately increasing the wages of Brazilian executives, implementing an open and transparent policy of Chinese executives' wages, fine-tuning wages of all staff members to make it more reasonable. |
| 3 | Core staff | The wage standard of Company K is slightly lower than average level of the market, so there is space for further improvement. But the adjustment is relatively sluggish. | Establish a more reasonable salary and bonus system to reflect the performance of employee, timely demonstrate the improvement of employees' productivity, and improve their enthusiasm. |
| 4 | Trade union members | Trade union dues, originally compulsory, are now voluntary. This has weakened the power of trade unions and sabotaged the original balance of labor relations. | Add it as a topic in trade union's collective bargaining, and find a more stable transition approach. |
| 5 | Outsourced workers | For outsourced work, the new Labor Law stipulates that outsourced workers should enjoy the same working conditions as formal staff, such as outpatient care, food and beverage, safety, transport, training, and equipment quality. Companies implement an 18-month check to prevent it from laying off permanent workers and rehiring them as outsourced workers. Sometimes outsourced workers sue the company when their projects end, demanding equal pay for the same work as formal employees. | Follow regulation compliance in working conditions, and equal pay for outsourced workers and formal employees. |

(continued)

| No. | Positions with potential risks | Description | Prevention & control measures |
|-----|-------------------------------|-------------|-------------------------------|
| 6 | All staff | For overtime work, the main disputes are as follows: recognition of overtime work when employees work inefficiently or fail to complete the work quota during normal working hours; counting commuting time as work time because some employees' residences are far from the substation; strict clocking in/out regulation (some work is inconvenient to do so, or some work isn't completed at the work place), etc. | Scientifically review work quota of employees, and determine overtime work on this basis; Other issues about overtime can be discussed in collective bargaining. The company should draw on reasonable opinions of employees when formulating rules and regulations. |
| 7 | All staff | According to Brazilian managers of Company K, there is no need to follow the Chinese punishment measures such as warning, serious warning and demerit record, because their negative emotions will bring detrimental impact on the enterprise. The common practice is to fairly terminate the contracts with related employees who do not have any good excuses for their persistent absence from work or serious misconduct. | The issues of dismissal shall be subject to Brazilian labor law and local management practices. Communication and coordination should be rendered in the process, and the termination of contracts should be by consensus. |
| 8 | All staff | Brazilian pension system is in the process of adjustment. Many employees are concerned that pensions they will receive when retired from Company K would be significantly lower than wages of employees on active duty. To address it, most large Brazilian companies offer enterprise pension plans for their employees, but Company K does not have such plans currently. | Pay close attention to policy content and legislative process of Brazil's new Social Security Reform Act; evaluate the impact on different labor groups and the trend of labor costs, and prepare to implement the plan considering the content of social security reform policy; timely launch the enterprise pension plans in order to retain the core staff. |

(continued)

| No. | Positions with potential risks | Description | Prevention & control measures |
|---|---|---|---|
| 9 | Field workers | There are accidents of tower collapse or equipment malfunctions in recent years, causing some casualties. The regulation system of safety production is still flawed. | (1) Strengthen the rights and obligations of employees and employers. (2) Pay attention to safety production risk analysis and control. (3) Strengthen occupational safety and health training for employees. (4) Analyze accident cases regularly and take corresponding preventive measures. |
| 10 | Senior management and general staff | There are some differences and challenges in cross-cultural management among Chinese and Brazilian employees in Company K. The opinions of Brazilian executives are as follows: (1) Chinese managers are usually more resistant to different ideas. (2) Brazilian professionals (including managers and directors) have a very low degree of decision-making autonomy compared to other international or national companies in which they once worked. (3) The Chinese and Brazilian management levels have different understandings for punishment. (4) Brazilian employees are not used to being criticized by Chinese supervisors in public. (5) Brazilians are rather rigid and inflexible. They do not take on multiple roles and do additional works that are not stipulated in the contract. (6) In terms of management approach, Chinese evaluates not only the results but also the process (e.g. audit work), whereas Brazilians value results over process. (7) Brazilians | Suggestions from Brazilian executives: (1) Chinese and Brazilian managers can have a clear and shared strategic objective through clear communication on strategic direction without missing out on relevant information, i.e. the content behind decisions that are difficult for Brazilians to understand. (2) Reduce the obstacles or delay in implementing reforms. (3) Simplify decision-making process by delegating authority to those at the level that the impact would be the lowest or below strategic level. |

(continued)

| No. | Positions with potential risks | Description | Prevention & control measures |
|-----|-------------------------------|-------------|-------------------------------|
| 10 | Senior management and general staff | attach great importance to "equal pay for equal work". (8) Following the "Me Too" movement and ILO's new treaty on Eliminating Violence and Harassment in the World of Work, Brazilians emphasis more on the protection of special rights for female workers. | (4) Chinese supervisors should have more confidence in Brazilian managers, and replace those unreliable persons. |
| 11 | All staff | The most typical and risky labor dispute cases of Company K include: (1) Outsourcing workers, upon termination of their contracts, are seeking the same compensation and benefits as formal employees. (2) Complaints from former employees who claim that they were paid less than others with similar job responsibilities. (3) Complaints from former employees who claim that they did not receive overtime pay as required by law. (4) Complaints from former employees who claim that they were harrassed by supervisors (including discrimination, aggression and insult). | (1) Improve labor rules and regulations of the enterprise, making them clearer. (2) Communicate with relevant employees on risk factors of labor disputes, so that they can understand the company's management policy. (3) Organize training sessions for executives on ILO's new treaty and Brazil's national conditions, as well as enhance the awareness of the rights protection of female workers. |
| 12 | All staff | In Company L, the former distribution network construction contractor did not perform the labor legal duties to its employees, causing labor disputes. | The company first archived all the documents of major contracting companies and their employees, improving the management of employee contract documents to reduce labor disputes with these contractors and their employees. Then, the contractor of the distribution network would suspend operations in this area, and another company's service would be arranged as mitigation. |

(continued)

| No. | Positions with potential risks | Description | Prevention & control measures |
|-----|-------------------------------|-------------|-------------------------------|
| 12 | All staff | Company L was the service recipient, so that it had to bear the costs. This was one of the reasons for the numerous dispute cases. | It is suggested that Company L should strengthen the examination of labor law enforcement and the compliance of the outsourcing companies, and promote their compliance management. |

## III. Building a Harmonious Cross-cultural Labor Relations Management System Featuring Legitimacy, Cultural Advance and Manual Retreat, Talent Support

In light of this, we have established the analysis framework of the risk factors affecting the labor relations of BRI countries, analyzed labor relations of SOE in host countries according to the content structure, and clarified the status quo and potential risks. We specifically selected cases in Brazil, to study the establishment of harmonious labor relations in overseas Chinese enterprises in BRI countries in terms of legitimacy, cultural advance and manual retreat, talent support (see Figure 1).

First, risks of overseas labor relations for Chinese enterprises are caused by various factors. To prevent these risks, we need to take a multi-pronged and comprehensive approach.

Based on the current situation, labor relations risks for Chinese enterprises can be divided into three main categories. (1) Issues related to the compliance of corporate human resources and labor relation management. Take Chinese enterprises in Brazil for an example. In Brazil, the labor law was in the process of revision while the pension system was the in process of reform, which stimulated the flexible trend in labor market regulations, thus requiring numerous compliance agendas. Although this trend is advantageous to enterprises' general management, employees tend to be affected, causing short-term instability of staff management because of the huge changes. Labor relation risks mainly include low overall wage level, loose correlation between wages and performance, no annuity provision, and equal pay of outsourced employees, overtime work and compensation in dismissal, etc. These risk factors are relatively different from domestic enterprises. And the requirement for labor relations management is significantly higher than that of domestic enterprises as well. In addition, there are also problems in cross-cultural management. For example,

Brazilian managers believe that Chinese managers usually abuse power and refuse different voices, which leave Brazilian professionals little room for participating in the decision-making process; Chinese and Brazilian managers have different understandings of punishment; Brazilians are rigid and inflexible; Brazil has a lax management system that values results over process; Brazilians put more emphasis on gender equality and the protection of special rights for female workers, and so on. The above-mentioned issues of compliance, which involve local labor laws, coordination of management practices and integration of cross-cultural management, need to be quickly adjusted from the Chinese enterprises. (2) It needs to understand trade unions and their demands to safeguard rights, learn to deal with powerful trade unions, and master the related skills of collective bargaining. In 2017, Brazil's labor law modified tax policy for trade unions from compulsory to voluntary. This change seemed to be beneficial for enterprises, but it was actually a risk factor because it caused a wave of protests in Brazil. On the one hand, Chinese enterprises set a transition period to stabilize the relationship with trade unions; on the other hand, they gave full play to Brazilian managers' negotiation abilities. Meanwhile, Chinese managers learned relevant skills in participating in the negotiation, and better adapted to the requirements of collective bargaining. (3) The prevention and handling of labor disputes. Regarding labor disputes for Chinese enterprises in Brazil, the most typical and risky ones are: employees demanding equal pay for equal work, failure to pay overtime as required by the law, and allegations of sexual harassment by superiors. In general, the number of cases is rather small, while there are basically no collective dispute cases. Enterprises are required to further improve their labor rules and regulations, prevent risks of labor disputes, communicate with relevant employees, help them understand the employee relations management policies, and enhance the awareness of the rights and interest protection of female employees.

Second, promote cultural exchange, and contribute Chinese solutions and Chinese wisdom in cross-cultural management.

The report of the 19th CPC National Congress states that China will "take an active part in reforming and developing the global governance system, and keep contributing Chinese wisdom and strength to global governance". Therefore, cultural integration in transnational business does not mean the import or export of culture, but the contribution of "Chinese solutions", "Chinese wisdom" and "Chinese strength". Promote the localization of human resources, improve the quality while reduce the quantity of Chinese international talents assigned to abroad. Thus, human capital and costs are saved, talents of both sides are improved, leaving a long-term and effective mechanism of cultural exchange with great achievements in cross-cultural management. In addition, daily communication mechanism is the catalysts for cultural exchange. A good and unimpeded communication mechanism is not only the basis for building a harmonious labor relationship, but also the basis for consolidating corporate cultural order and guiding corporate values. The key point here is to strengthen communication initiated by Chinese senior executives, with approaches such as public email and hotline, open day, discussions and daily visits, communication between Chinese and Brazilian senior executives, and their participating in dismissal talk. Meanwhile, it should build an environment conducive to daily communication. Besides, the cross-border sharing of the labor relations coordination with Chinese characteristics is the guarantee of cultural exchange. We suggest that it should set up a "home of workers" to stabilize the Chinese team, establish a staff congress to further strengthen communication and participation, promote model worker culture to guarantee excellent performance, advance the building of the industrial workforce, and optimize local human resources. These are the Chinese solutions and Chinese wisdom in the field of labor relations.

Third, strengthen the talent support for international strategies of enterprises, and inherit the enterprises' cultural genes in the process of BRI.

The stable process of cross-culture management depends on two indispensable conditions: the improvement of the quality of Chinese staff and the talent localization. There are a series of specific management measures. (1) Risk prevention and control of Chinese personnel: the risk of international talent's quality and the risk of reserve of talents. In terms of prevention and control of quality risks, more attention should be paid to the clear, universal and practical implementation of the standards for the assignment of persons. Also, personnel dispatch standards for overseas projects should be formulated to improve the efficiency of global allocation of human resources. The international talent training system should be improved and systematized. Considering the actual needs of overseas work and the demands of employees, the original training system should be specifically adjusted to improve the quality of international talents. The reserve of international talent depends on the quality, dispatch willingness and talent retention. While improving the training system for international talents, we should also build a pool of high-potential talents and establish an international talent reserve system as soon as possible. At the same time, we need to ensure that the high-quality international talents in our pools are willing to be dispatched, cherish the overseas experience, and speed up the process of identification, training, development of international talents born in the 1990s. (2) Local talent strategy: attract and cultivate outstanding talents to inherit enterprises' cultural genes. First, the local talent strategy for short and medium terms: career attraction and training programs. For example, the salary of basic positions should be in line with the average level of the market. For senior executives and core employees, more attention should be paid to career vision and management besides the salary. At the same time, optimize human capital through strengthening special training. Increase investment in special training to improve labor productivity of employees, and encourage employees to participate in general training through social training institutions. Second, the local talent strategy for long terms: strengthen special training and cultural integration to pass on Chinese genes. There are some specific measures to address it. (a) Introduce "enterprises' cultural genes" through special training. Employees are trained to adapt to the culture and requirements of the enterprise in this way. And the bond formed in this process can weaken employee's intention of resignation. This process can also be interpreted as the process of inserting corporate genes. (b) Strengthen and stabilize  cross-culture management by passing on "enterprises' cultural genes". For example, recruit and training fresh graduates to become local managers, so that they can be familiar with the culture of the parent company. Through the long-term "special training" and the immersive management, which are also the process of building cultural order, the enterprises' gens has already been passed on to these local employees. We can pass on "enterprises' cultural genes"  in the long-term to build an invisible talent pool for Chinese enterprises and promote the sustainable development of enterprises.

We are now undergoing profound changes of this increasingly complex world, in which there are more and more instabilities and uncertainties. The outbreak of COVID-19 in early 2020 around the world leads to a sharp economic recession and prolonged stagnation. The economic and trade frictions between China and the US are escalating. There are all-dimensional confrontations in ideology, geopolitics, science and technology, culture and education. In term of economy, there is a trend of anti-globalization, or even "de-Sinicization". The global industrial chain has begun to re-organize. The fourth industrial revolution and the development of digital economy are promoting the further upgrading of industrial structure and economic restructuring. All of these have a significant impact on the development of compliance of overseas Chinese enterprises during the period of the "14th Five-year Plan". Therefore, we suggest that the compliance management and the establishment of harmonious labor relations of overseas Chinese enterprises should be included in the Outline for the Development of Human Resources and Social Security during the period of the "14th Five-year Plan", and improve the appropriate index system to better promote the high-quality development of Chinese enterprises in abroad.

## References

[1] Pan Yue, Chen Lusha. The Research on Chinese Companies' Labor Issue under "the

Belt and Road" Initiative: Taking Kenyan and Indonesian Cases as Examples [J]. Crossroads: Southeast Asian Studies, 2018(1): 84-90.

[2] Ma Weihua. How Do Chinese Enterprises "Go Global" under the Background of New Normal of Chinese Economy? [J]. Zhongguancun, 2014 (10): 60-61.

[3] Xiao Zhu. Foreign Labor Relations Governance of Chinese Overseas Enterprises under the Background of "the Belt and Road" [J]. Human Resource Development of China, 2018(4): 144-150.

[4] Li Xueting. Research on the Legal Risk of Overseas Mergers and Acquisitions of Chinese Enterprises [D]. Chengdu: Southwest University of Political Science and Law, 2011.

[5] Zhao Lin, Xia Yunyun. Study on Labor Legal Risk Prevention in Overseas Mergers and Acquisitions of Chinese Enterprises [J]. Guizhou Social Sciences, 2012(7):117-120.

[6] Liu Zhen. Research on the Legal Risks and Measures of Chinese Enterprises in the Promotion of the Belt and Road Initiative [J]. Journal of Hubei University (Philosophy and Social Sciences Edition), 2016 ( 6): 105-111.

[7] Zhuang Xizhen. Human Resource Development of " the Belt and Road" Relating Countries: Current Situation and Problems[J]. Research in Education Development, 2017 (17): 54-61.

[8] Shi Meixia, Zhang Zujie, Zhu Wangli. Research on Trade Union Issues from the Perspective of the Belt and Road Initiative [J]. Journal of China University of Labor Relations, 2020 (1): 12-19.

[9] Huang Yan, Wu Qianhua. Vietnam's Labor Regulation Policies and Chinese Firms' Adaptive Strategies under the Belt and Road Initiative [J]. Human Resources Development of China, 2019 (7): 121-129.

[10] Hong Yonghong, Huang Xingyong. Labor Risks Control Mechanism for Chinese Enterprises' Investment in Africa under the B&R Initiative[J]. Journal of Xiangtan University (Philosophy and Social Sciences), 2019 (3): 66-71.

[11] Chen Yuhua. Risk Factors and Prevention of Human Resource Management in Brazil[J]. Management Observer, 2016 (33).

[12] Dai Xiaochu. Strengthening Labor Risk Management, Promoting Decent Work and Achieving Sustainable Development [J]. China Employment, 2018(10)

[13] Russell Lansbury, Nick Wailes, Greg Bamber. The Global Financial Crisis and Its Impact on Employment Relations: An Internationally Comparative Approach [J]. Journal of Shanghai Normal University (Philosophy and Social Sciences Edition), 2013 (6): 41-51.

[14] International Labor Organization. Social Dialogue and Industrial Relations: Global Trends, Challenges and Opportunities. 2018.

[15] Chang Kai et al. International Comparison of Employment Relations: National Regulations and Global Changes (Sixth Edition) [M]. Beijing: China Labor and Social Security Press, 2016.

[16] Qiao Jian, Li Cheng. Study on Prevention of Labor Relations Risks of Chinese Enterprises in BRI Countries: A Case Study of Brazil [J]. Human Resources Development of China, 2018 (35):7.

[17] N Askitasklau, Janna Besamusca, Kea Tijdens. Comparing Collective Bargaining Agreements for Developing Countries [J]. International Journal of Manpower, 2015 (4).

[18] Wang Lili. Risk and Adaptive Prevention of Collective Labor Relations Adjustment under the Background of "Belt and Road" [J]. Human Resource Development of China, 2018,35 (12): 95-102.

[19] Han Xiping, Zhang Jiaxin. Classified Research on the Coordination of Labor Relations in Countries along "One Belt and One Road" [J]. Journal of Management World, 2019 (4): 70-76.

[20] Yang Weiguo, Zhou Ning. Comparative Industrial Relations Theory: Development and Challenges [J]. Teaching and Research, 2019 (7): 37-47.

[21] Zhang Hao. Stakeholders and Labor Relations Governance: A New Framework for Comparative Industrial Relations Analysis [J]. Teaching and Research,2019 (7): 59-73.

[22] Aycan, Z. The Interplay between Cultural and Institutional/Structural Contingencies in Human Resource Management Practices [J]. International Journal of Human Resource Management, 2005, 16(7) :1083-1119.

[23] Zhao Shuming, Peter J. Dowling, Denice E. Welch. Human Resource Management in Multinational Corporations [M]. Beijing: China Renmin University Press, 2001.

[24] Peng Diyun, Gan Xiaoqing. Economic Globalization and the Strategic Choice of Accelerating China's Transnational Business Operation [J]. Journal of Nanchang University (Humanities and Social Science), 2000,(1): 38-43.

[25] Chen Lingyu, Wei Liqun. Human Resource Localization Strategies in Multinational Corporations [J]. Human Resource Development of China, 2003(5): 58-60.

[26] Yao Xiaojun. The Influence of Cross-cultural Differences on Psychological Contract [J]. Enterprise Vitality, 2006 (10).

[27] Lin Xinqi. International Human Resource Management Practice [M], Liaoning: Dongbei University of Finance and Economics Press, 2012.

[28] Wang Bei, Jiang Linyao. Labor Legal Risks and Precautions against Chinese Enterprise Overseas M&A under the Background of "the Belt and Road" [J]. Journal of Shandong University of Finance and Economics, 2018 (6): 5-12.

[29] Zhang Yuan, Liu Li. Comparison and Labor Market of Countries along "the Belt and Road" and Its Implications [J]. West Forum, 2017(6): 93-110.

[30] Tian Yongpo. Human Resources of Countries along "the Belt and Road" Initiative: Current Situation, Characteristics and International Cooperation [J]. Chinese Personnel Science, 2019(8): 55-66.

# Labor Dispute Settlement

- A Root Cause Analysis on the Existence, Nature and Arbitration-Litigation Relationship of China's Labor Dispute Arbitration System

# A Root Cause Analysis on the Existence, Nature and Arbitration-Litigation Relationship of China's Labor Dispute Arbitration System[*]

*Jiang Ying, Shen Jianfeng[**]*

**Abstract:** China's existing labor dispute arbitration system is the result of historical development. Its legitimacy is supported by both international experience and domestic practices. It is built on the special characteristics of labor relations, labor laws and labor disputes, and on the theoretical basis of social governance innovation. Unlike general civil or commercial mediation and arbitration in China, the labor dispute arbitration is a mandatory quasi-judicial mechanism for settling disputes. The so-called "quasi-judicial mechanism" means that it has characteristics resembling those of a court, but its arbitration award is not final and it lacks enforceability in terms of procedures. The similarity between arbitration institutions and judicial organs in structures leads to their overlapped functions. Thus, clarifying their relationship will be the key to explain the coexistence of arbitration and litigation. Such coexistence has diverse manifestations at different development stages of the country. Since the enactment of the Labor Dispute Mediation and Arbitration Law of the People's Republic of China, the relationship between arbitration and litigation has been revealed by the facts that arbitration filters cases for litigation, while litigation, in turn, supports arbitration enforcement and supervises arbitration indirectly. At present, we should continue to ensure the smooth connection between arbitration and litigation. Going forward, we should realize the integration of arbitration and litigation by promoting the judicialization of arbitration and advancing judicial development through the participation of various parties.

**Keywords:** labor dispute arbitration; litigation; arbitration-litigation relationship; quasi-judicial

---

[*] This paper is the initial progress and outcome of the general project "Establishment of Beijing Labor Courts and improvement of Labor Trial Procedures" (Project No. 16FXB016), funded by Beijing Social Science Fund in 2016.

[**] Jiang Ying, Professor, China University of Labor Relations; Shen Jianfeng, Professor, Dean of the School of Law, China University of Labor Relations.

The relationship between labor dispute arbitration and litigation (hereinafter referred to as the arbitration-litigation relationship) has seen long-term debates. Now there are five major opinions in theory and practice. (1) The "litigation-only mode": arbitral tribunals will be established to settle labor disputes, instead of arbitration institutions. The judgement of the second instance will be the final one. (2) The "arbitration-only mode": a standing arbitration committee will be set up to completely take over the role of courts in settling labor disputes. Finality can be reached through one or two arbitrations (Wang, 2001). (3) The "one-arbitration and one-trial mode": the disputing parties must first apply to an arbitration committee for arbitration. If they refuse to accept the arbitration committee's award, they could file a lawsuit with the intermediate people's court. The decision of the intermediate court is final. (4) The "two-arbitration and one-trial mode": two tiers of arbitration committees will be established. The disputing parties must first apply to the base-level committees, then to prefectural committees, and at last to the intermediate people's courts at the prefectural level. (5) The "arbitration-or-litigation mode" (or "separated finality of arbitration and litigation mode"): the disputing parties are free to choose labor dispute arbitration or litigation. The two systems' procedures are parallel and independent of each other. The former allows two arbitrations before one final trial, while the latter allows three tiers of trial (Qin, 2010; Dong, 2008).

One important reason why there are different opinions on the relationship between labor dispute arbitration and litigation is that the analysis of various modes are based on different definitions of the labor dispute arbitration and the court. In addition, scholars failed to further explore what constitutes labor dispute arbitration and what constitutes a court in China. In particular, many of the understandings about labor arbitration are just a copy of commercial mediation and arbitration, without considering their differences in this country. This leads to a controversial relationship arbitration-litigation relationship, which even threatens the existence of the labor dispute arbitration. For a long time, in theory and practice, there have been voices of abolishing labor dispute arbitration. For example, some localities have merged the labor dispute arbitration and commercial mediation and arbitration institutions in the ongoing new round of institutional reforms. [1]

In this paper, we believe that the relationship between labor dispute arbitration and litigation is a unique issue that is rooted in China's reality, which does not have any existing answers or a universal model. It is not an issue to be solved only by logical thinking. In fact, researches should first focus on the labor dispute arbitration system with Chinese characteristics itself, and discuss the root of its existence and

---

[1] See Article 14, *Notice of the General Office of the CPC Shenyang Municipal Committee on Issuing "Optimization and Integration Programs of Shenyang Municipal Public Welfare Institutions".*

nature. Only on this basis can we discuss the relationship between labor dispute arbitration and litigation.

## I. Premise of Discussing Arbitration-Litigation Relationship: Root Causes of Labor Dispute Arbitration in China

Labor dispute arbitration has come neither from subjective assumptions nor hasty decisions. On the contrary, it is an inevitable outcome of China's social development and evolves with the constantly changing situation. Only with this in mind can we understand the root causes of existence of China's labor dispute arbitration system, and establish a basic premise for clarifying the arbitration-litigation relationship in the new era.

### 1. Root Cause Analysis from a Historical Perspective: Deficiency and Significance

China's current labor dispute arbitration system owns its birth and growth to the social progress in the country. When the Labor Dispute Mediation and Arbitration Law of the People's Republic of China (PRC) was enacted, the legislature pointed out that "the existing procedures for settling labor disputes have been accepted by the public after more than twenty years of practice, and should not be denied thoughtlessly." (Xin, 2008) In fact, if we look back, we will find that Articles 72 and 73 of the Labor Law of the Chinese Soviet Republic introduced in 1931 were the earliest provisions about settling labor disputes in the country (Huang, 2017). According to the two articles, arbitration is separated from litigation, as violations of labor laws and collective contracts are under the jurisdiction of courts, while other violations of rules related to working conditions are either arbitrated by arbitration institutions established by the Labor Bureau or heard by courts. The new Labor Law of the Chinese Soviet Republic in 1933 stipulated that "In the event of a dispute or conflict between government authorities, enterprises, agencies and their employees over labor conditions, labor authorities at all levels should, with the consent of both parties, conduct mediation and arbitration. However, in the event of a major dispute, labor department at all levels should conduct arbitration even without the parties' consent." This indicates that China's compulsory arbitration was introduced as early as in the 1930s. The practice of compulsory arbitration was not abolished during the War of Resistance against the Japanese aggression and the War of Liberation, and the idea of applying compulsory arbitration became even clearer. For example, Decisions on the Current Task of China's Workforce, adopted by the Sixth National Labor Conference in August 1948, stipulated in Chapter 3, Section 4, Item 9, Point 2 that "Labor disputes shall be handled through negotiation, mediation and arbitration, with arbitration as the last procedure. The parties may file an appeals with the court if the arbitration award is objected by one or more of the parties in dispute". After the founding of the PRC, a system of compulsory arbitration and arbitration before litigation was eventually established. Articles 5, 6, and 7 of the 1950 Provisions on Procedures for Settling Labor Disputes stipulate procedures for negotiation, mediation and arbitration, and provide that those who object the arbitration award could notify the administrative organ and file an appeal with the court within five days after the award is issued. The provisions related to the arbitration and litigation concerning labor dispute settlement after 1950, such as the 1987 Interim Provisions on Settling Labor Disputes in State-owned Enterprises, the 1993 Regulations of the PRC on Settling Labor Disputes in Enterprises, and the Labor Dispute Mediation and Arbitration Law of the PRC in 2007, are all continuation and improvement of the above-mentioned compulsory arbitration system formed in the early days of the founding of the PRC.

There is no doubt that, as far as the system is concerned, what existed in the past does not necessarily exist in the future, and what was reasonable in the past is not necessarily reasonable at the present day and in the future. It should be noted that from 1950 to now, labor relations in China have undergone profound changes, and the existing procedures for settling labor disputes may need changes as well. Although it is somewhat inadequate to argue the legitimacy of the existing labor dispute arbitration system only from the perspective of historical development, the aforementioned development course at least shows us the following things:

(1) The formation of China's labor dispute arbitration system has nothing to do with the idea of commercial mediation. It is more of a compulsory intervention, and is fundamentally different from the civil dispute settlement mechanism based on autonomy and voluntariness as in commercial mediation. Take the formation of labor dispute arbitration in China as an example, for a long period of time after the establishment of the PRC, courts in China were more understood as organs to perform the duties of the people's democratic dictatorship than dispute settlement institutions. Peng Zhen noted in his Report at the National Conference on Procuratorial Work in 1954, "Public security organs, courts, and procuratorates are all weapons against our enemies." (Peng, 1991) Therefore, disputes were considered as problems among the people and more often resolved through non-judicial means at that time. Dong Biwu also pointed out in his report at the same conference that "Acts that are wrong but not illegal, or illegal but not criminal, should not be handled via judicial means." (Dong, 2006) In other words, disputes arising from labor relations, as problems among the people, should not be settled by traditional judicial ways. It is

against such a background that labor dispute arbitration came into being. Therefore, when improving the existing labor dispute settlement system, it is important to keep in mind that labor dispute arbitration should not be mistaken for commercial mediation, and the relationship between commercial mediation and litigation cannot be applied to arbitration and litigation of labor disputes. In this sense, it is not appropriate to put forward that such disputes could be settled by "either arbitration or litigation".

(2) Attention should be paid to the objective law of institutional development itself. "The most important argument on institutional change is that most of these changes are gradual and incremental." (Douglass, 2014) Changes in form do not necessarily bring about changes in practice. For example, according to Article 17 of the Labor Dispute Mediation and Arbitration Law, labor dispute arbitration committees shall be established by provincial governments in cities and counties rather than by multiple administrative divisions. In practice, however, multiple-tier committees that are set up according to administrative divisions are found in most parts of the country, and provincial labor dispute arbitration committees are just a common thing. This reveals that rules should be set progressively, and fundamental changes in the system should not happen without a good reason, otherwise the previous rules will only continue to work as "hidden rules", which will eventually undermine the effectiveness of new rules. The clarification of arbitration-litigation relationship should also respect the unique development path of China's labor dispute arbitration system.

## 2. Root Cause Analysis from the Perspective of Effectiveness: Effects and Concerns

In recent years, as there are intensifying debates over whether China's labor dispute arbitration system should continue to exist, the competent authorities have increasingly sought to support its legitimacy through the perspective of effectiveness, that is, to prove the legitimacy of the system through its effectiveness in practice. In this regard, three reasons are often mentioned. (a) Arbitration is fast, efficient, flexible and of low cost compared to judicial means. (b) According to current statistics, almost 65% of labor disputes in China are solved through arbitration institutions. As seen from the table below, the settlement rate of arbitration in 2016 reached 47%, while the rate of arbitration awards as final results stood at 28.4%. This makes the total proportion of cases in which the parties could not file a lawsuit (by principle) as high as 62% [47% + (53% * 28.4%) = 62%]. We may take a look at the figures in some specific regions. In Zhejiang, 37,292 cases of disputes that had applied for arbitration were settled by mediation under the arbitration system in 2017 according to our survey, accounting for 74.9% of the year's total settled cases in this province. The average rate of settlement with one-time arbitration award in different parts of Zhejiang is above 40%. In total, more than 80% of labor disputes are settled without a litigation process. In Guangzhou, according to the white paper on trials of labor and personnel disputes issued by the city's intermediate court, the cases that needed a post-arbitration litigation process only accounted for 26.0% of total cases of labor disputes in 2016. (c) Labor dispute arbitration is a very effective tool, as without such a system, the courts nationwide may be overwhelmed by the tremendous number of cases[1] each year, which, in turn, may lead to backlog of cases and intensify risks of social conflicts (see Table 1).

**Table 1**　　　　**Statistics of Cases Handled by China's Labor Dispute Arbitration Institutions Since 2008**

| Year | 2008 | 2009 | 2010 | 2011 | 2012 | 2013 | 2014 | 2015 | 2016 | 2017 | 2018 | 2019 |
|---|---|---|---|---|---|---|---|---|---|---|---|---|
| Total cases settled | 69.3 | 108.78 | 126.4 | 118.7 | 126.1 | 138.8 | 136.2 | 161.0 | 163.9 | 157.5 | 171.5 | 202.3 |
| Cases settled by mediation | 45.8 | 38.78 | 52.69 | 51.64 | 53.66 | 57.05 | 56.35 | 60.30 | 60.61 | 59.8 | 67.2 | 79.5 |
| Cases settled by arbitration | 62.3 | 70.0 | 63.4 | 59.3 | 64.3 | 66.9 | 71.1 | 81.2 | 82.8 | 79.0 | 88.4 | 106.8 |
| Number of cases where arbitration awards as final results | 1.69 | 3.60 | 3.70 | 4.20 | 5.20 | 5.43 | 6.06 | 6.88 | 10.41 | 11.1 | 13.6 | 17.7 |
| Rate of arbitration awards as final results | 6.2% | 12.3% | 13.9% | 17.2% | 19.3% | 19.2% | 19.4% | 18.7% | 28.4% | 33.1% | 37.9% | 41.2% |
| Number of mediation cases under arbitration | 22.1 | 25.1 | 25.0 | 27.9 | 30.25 | 31.2 | 32.2 | 36.3 | 38.9 | 39 | 45.8 | 55.3 |

---

[1] The volume of cases handled by labor dispute arbitration institutions has reached 1.66 million, according to the 2017 Annual Statistical Bulletin on the Development of Human Resources and Social Security, issued by the Ministry of Human Resources and Social Security. See http://www.mohrss.gov.cn/SYrlzyhshbzb/zwgk/szrs/ tjgb/201805/ W020180521567611022649.pdf.

(continued)

| Year | 2008 | 2009 | 2010 | 2011 | 2012 | 2013 | 2014 | 2015 | 2016 | 2017 | 2018 | 2019 |
|---|---|---|---|---|---|---|---|---|---|---|---|---|
| Rate of mediation cases under arbitration | 35.5% | 36.6% | 39.5% | 47% | 47% | 46.6% | 45.2% | 44.7% | 47.0% | 49.4% | 51.8% | 51.8% |

The number of cases in the table is calculated in ten thousands (wan).

Sources: China Labor Statistics Yearbook, China Statistics Press, 2009–2019 edition, and annual Statistical Bulletins on the Development of Human Resources and Social Security, published on the website of the Ministry of Human Resources and Social Security.

Although the above three reasons well support the arbitration system, there remain several challenges. First, civil procedure system can also be employed to resolve disputes quickly after introducing procedure of small claims cases and summary procedure. For example, according to the revised Civil Procedure Law of the PRC in 2012, summary proceedings should be concluded within three months. In fact, our survey shows that most of the cases handled by the court of summary jurisdiction or the small claims courts in many places are cases of labor disputes. Second, as for "flexibility", on the one hand, summary proceedings in civil procedure can be flexible too. On the other hand, arbitration procedure is getting less flexible as they enter into the stage of normalization and standardization. Third, nearly 65% of cases were settled through arbitration ways, but will the courts have the same capacity if human and financial resources in arbitration are channeled to them? So far, no data could prove that the effectiveness of the arbitration system is necessarily higher than the courts. Fourth, a dedicated arbitral tribunal can be established if there are concerns about case backlog caused by the shortage of court staff. Fifth, while nearly 65% of the cases mentioned above can be resolved within a relatively short time, is it reasonable that the settlement of the remaining over 30% cases may take one year or more? Thus, from the perspective of effectiveness, we can only prove that the existing labor dispute arbitration system can play an important role, but it remains a question whether this system is the best choice and has enough legitimacy. To answer this question, further research is needed.

## 3. Factual Support for the Existence of an Independent Arbitration System

The fundamental reason for the existence of a labor dispute arbitration system lies in the unique characteristics of labor relations, labor laws and labor disputes (Linsenmaier, 2004). Labor relations, as a product of organized production, is a kind of legal relation concerning management with a strong sense of trust and sympathy.

As there are many legal systems to deal with labor relations (Shen, 2015), the settlement of disputes arising from labor relations involves not only legal knowledge, but also social security, collective contracts, regulations of employers and the autonomy of employers in production and operation. These issues go beyond the legal scope and extend to the field of human resources and even the balance of interests and rights of different walks of life. Therefore, the relevant institutions need to settle labor disputes from multiple positions and perspectives and with rich knowledge, which, however, are usually unavailable to the traditional judicial institutions that take legal knowledge as the basic standard for the selection of judges. That is why some scholars point out that "Though the judicial workers in the courts have received legal professional education and training, but most of them are not taught or trained to handle labor relations. When dealing with labor dispute litigation cases, they mainly resort to the written laws that often could not reflect the reality of labor world. Consequently, their judgments may fail to touch the essence of labor relations" (Huang, 2011). One way to solve this issue is to ask those who have knowledge about labor relations and can represent the stakeholders to participate in the trial process, so that the labor dispute adjudication institutions are equipped with members from diversified backgrounds and inclusive mechanisms, which is the most fundamental reason for the existence of independent labor dispute adjudication system in a market economy. In some countries, this is the main reason for the existence of the labor court under an independent and general court. Scholars in Germany usually believe that "workers or employers become members of labor courts as representatives of different classes. In this way, for neutral judges, every right dispute becomes a case of extensive class struggle. The representatives of workers and employers eliminate the differences in such cases through mutual agreement. Through this recall of the social impact of a single decision, the judge can make a more reasonable judgment than without jurors." (Gustav, 1959) This is what makes labor arbitration systems truly irreplaceable. Other features, such as speed and flexibility, are meaningful but not fundamental to the independent existence of a labor dispute settlement system outside of the general courts.

## 4. New Characteristics in the New Era Encouraging an Independent Arbitration System

China's labor dispute arbitration system is also built on social governance and dispute settlement systems with Chinese characteristics. As stated in the Decision of the Central Committee of the Communist Party of China on Some Major Issues Concerning Comprehensively Deepening the Reform, which was adopted at the Third Plenary Session of the Eighteenth Central Committee of the Communist

Party of China (CPC), "We will persist in implementing systematic governance, strengthen leadership by the Party committee, give full play to the leading role of the government and encourage and support the participation of all sectors of the society, so as to achieve positive interaction between the government management on the one hand and social self-management and residents' self-management on the other."[1] These statements show that all sectors of society are encouraged to participate in dispute settlement. The CPC Central Committee Recommendations for the 13th Five-year Plan for Economic and Social Development also emphasizes that "We will continue the Peaceful China initiative, improve the social governance system to help see that Party committees play a leadership role, government plays a guiding role, social organizations play a cooperative role, the general public participates, and the rule of law acts as a guarantee. We will work to make social governance more refined and see that everyone contributes to and benefits from social governance ."[2] The report of the 19th Party Congress once again took social governance innovation to a new high. The above idea of social governance is of profound significance, which highlights the participation of the public in social governance, as well as their contribution and wellbeing (Dou, 2014). In this sense, the settlement of disputes also welcomes the participation of people from different sectors. As far as labor dispute arbitration is concerned, such an idea will support its innovation in organization mode, personnel structure, and tribunal form, and will provide legal means for social governance in the field of labor dispute settlement. At the same time, a social governance perspective also helps us avoid looking solely at labor dispute settlement itself, but understand it in the context of overall social governance. Labor dispute arbitration is a manifestation of ideas for innovation in social governance, and its system should continue to improve under the guidance of these ideas.

## 5. International Experience Justifying an Independent Arbitration System

From a perspective of comparative law, different countries have different labor dispute settlement systems, and there is neither a uniform pattern nor unified institution for labor dispute settlement (Dong, 2008). However, this comparison does reveal some common points.

(1) Labor disputes are seldom settled in traditional civil courts. In both Germany and the United States, labor disputes are resolved through procedures different than that of traditional civil courts. The reasons include lengthy and complex procedures,

---

[1] Decision of the CCCPC on Some Major Issues Concerning Comprehensively Deepening the Reform, adopted at the Third Plenary Session of the 18th Central Committee of the Communist Party of China.

[2] Recommendations for the 13th Five-year Plan for Economic and Social Development (adopted at the Fifth Plenary Session of the 18th Central Committee of the Communist Party of China on October 29, 2015).

high costs and a lack of judges with relevant knowledge in traditional courts.

(2) Labor dispute settlement institutions often have persons from non-legal backgrounds take part in the arbitration process. In Germany, there are honor judges recommended by trade unions and employers' federations, and in the United States, not all members of labor dispute arbitration institutions are legal professionals. In Japan, some labor disputes are resolved through civil courts by professional judges, but scholars often criticize that those judges do not have necessary knowledge in labor law or labor relations, and suggest that professionals in relevant fields should be included as judges (Satoshi, 2003).

(3) According to the studies of Chinese scholars, the jurisdiction of these institutions over labor disputes is mandatory. (Dong, 2008) Despite differences in form, China's independent labor dispute arbitration system is in line with the general practices of its international counterparts mentioned above.

### 6. Why Commercial Mediation is not Applicable to Labor Dispute Arbitration

It is common in China to take arbitration in labor dispute settlement as mediation in commercial affairs. The widely accepted viewpoint of taking an "arbitration or trial" mode or a mode in which "arbitration and litigation are separated and their respective results are final" (Qin, 2010; Lin, 2016) is a typical example. However, it is not feasible to simply apply commercial mediation to labor dispute settlement for two reasons.

(1) Commercial mediation is based on the parties' full autonomy. The parties can choose the institution, procedure, and mediator under mutual consent, which guarantees the legitimacy of mediation decisions. However, this kind of willingness and autonomy is difficult to achieve in labor relations and disputes. As employees are the weaker party in practice, allowing them to freely reach an agreement with employers on dispute issues means their right of enjoying relief would be deprived, not to mention that the parties are highly unlikely to reach an agreement by themselves – they are in dispute after all. Here we see a contradiction in the mainstream belief: it advocates to reduce or even cancel the autonomy of workers and employers in substantive law, yet when it comes to procedural law, it turns to an autonomous commercial mediation model (Shen, 2016).

(2) The civil and professional nature of commercial mediation is based on mediators' professionality.[1] In labor arbitration, however, there are simply not enough

---

[1] Arbitration Law of the People's Republic of China stipulate the following qualifications of arbitrators: "Arbitrators shall meet one of the following conditions: (a) having obtained legal professional qualification through the national unified legal professional qualification examination, and has engaged in arbitration work for eight years; (b) having worked as a lawyer for eight years; (c) having worked as a judge for eight years; (d) engaged in legal research or teaching, and have a senior title in these fields; (e) have legal knowledge, engaged in economic and trade or other professional work, and have a senior title or the same professional level."

arbitrators with expertise relative to the large number of cases. Even if there are enough expert arbitrators, low arbitration fees could not support their participation in the long run. Is it appropriate to charge high fees? Can employees afford them? Due to these concerns, the German Employment Law provides that arbitration in the sense of commercial arbitration can only be arranged through group agreement in very exceptional cases (Waltmann, 2014).

In summary, China's labor dispute arbitration system is a result of the nation's development and supported by international experience, with its legitimacy assured by its effectiveness in practice. Against the current social and economic background, this system stems from the unique characteristics of labor relations, labor laws, labor disputes, and the theoretical foundation of social governance innovation in China. It is a compulsory dispute settlement mechanism with the participation of multiple parties. Different from traditional civil and commercial mediation, its application, structure, procedures and awards are all based on the mandate from the state. The above root causes of the existence of labor dispute arbitration system lead to its similarities and differences with the traditional litigation mechanism. This phenomenon is not only the starting point of understanding the arbitration-litigation relationship, but also the reason for the complexity of this relationship.

## II. Focus of the Debates on the Arbitration-litigation Relationship: Nature and Positioning of Labor Dispute Arbitration

Based on the above understanding of the root causes of China's labor dispute arbitration, it is necessary to further consider what is the nature of arbitration and how it is positioned in order to clarify their relationship. At present, theories (Wang, 2017) and political documents[1] mostly define arbitration institutions as quasi-judicial ones, but what is the meaning of "quasi-judicial"? Does it mean that arbitration is similar to the judiciary? According to the existing theories and practices, both "judicial" and "quasi-judicial" have already become legal jargons, but this analogy will have no theoretical or practical value without specific connotation. Therefore, to correctly understand the arbitration-litigation relationship, we must first discuss what "quasi-judicial" truly is.

### 1. Existing Views on "Quasi-Judicial"

There is no systematic theory or research in China on the concept of

---

[1] See Ministry of Human Resources and Social Security, Supreme People's Court, Ministry of Justice, etc., Opinions on Further Strengthening Multiple Methods for Settling Labor Personnel Disputes (issued by Ministry of Human Resources and Social Security).

"quasi-judicial". This term was first used in administrative laws: when defining administrative adjudication, scholars proposed that "a quasi-judicial procedure falls between general administrative procedures and judicial procedures. It pays more attention to procedural fairness than general administrative procedures, but is simpler and faster than judicial procedures" (Hu and Jiang, 2012). In studies on competition laws, scholars suggested the adjudication power of anti-monopoly institutions to be quasi-judicial as well (Zhu and Wang, 2012; Shi, 2008). They believe that "being quasi-judicial means that the administration organs hold hearings on and conduct investigations into certain disputes to perform their governance duties, while in term of form, quasi-judicial procedures should have an adjudication step similarly to those in courts" (Shi, 2008). The term is generally believed to be originated from the UK and the United States: according to the definition by scholars in these countries, "quasi-judicial" describes a function that resembles the judicial function in that it involves deciding a dispute and ascertaining the facts and any relevant law, but differs in that it depends ultimately on the exercise of an executive discretion rather than the application of law (Elizabeth, 2003). At present, the term "quasi-judicial" is still associated with the adjudication of administrative organs under a strict procedure within limits of discretion, no matter in China, the UK or the US.

However, this understanding of quasi-judicial function is not in line with the actual provisions and practices of labor dispute arbitration. First, according to the current law, arbitration institutions are not administrative organs, and it is agreed by both theory and current regulations that filing an administrative lawsuit could not lead to a review of the awards of labor arbitration. However, as an administrative adjudication falls into the category of a specific administrative act, the above-mentioned quasi-judicial administrative adjudications are subject to reviews and lawsuits (Hu and Jiang, 2012). Secondly, one of the main features of "quasi-judicial" function mentioned above is to make an award within the scope of discretion, but the basic feature of labor dispute arbitration is to make an award according to law. Therefore, the existing views about the term "quasi-judicial" cannot cover labor dispute arbitration.

## 2. Premise of Discussing Labor Dispute Arbitration's Quasi-Judicial Nature: What is the Administration of Justice?

As mentioned above, it is necessary to redefine the "quasi-judicial nature" of the labor dispute arbitration. This definition should start from what "administration of justice" is, and then discuss the common places between an arbitration mode and a judicial mode to deal with labor disputes, and whether these commonalities lead to the quasi-judicial nature of labor dispute arbitration. Although the term "justice" is common, there is no definition of justice in current legislation. In theory, however, "there are three main schools for interpreting the administration of justice in China. The first school equates administration of justice with trial, the second regards it as an act or procedure of the administrations that handle cases through litigation, and the third takes it as an act of settling disputes in a broad sense" (Chen and Cui, 2008). According to the third school, the administration of justice for resolving disputes in the broad sense "refers to a legal activity with dispute settlement as its basic function, including arbitration, mediation, administrative judgment, judicial review, international trial and other dispute resolution mechanisms, which has the same basic functions as the courts have. It takes the court as its core, the agreement of the parties as its base, and the state's coercive power as its final guarantee" (Yang and Yu, 1997). Labor dispute arbitration institutions would be judicial organs if we take this definition, but in fact the mainstream views believe that such a definition is too broad to be useful, because the administration of justice is a functional activity of the state, and judicial activities reflect the will of the state and are backed by the coercive power of the state (Chen and Cui, 2008). As for the other opinions, one believes the administration of justice is similar to trial, and judicial activities are considered as the trial activities of the courts, while another holds that the administration of justice refers to litigation activities, that is, judicial activities include the activities of the procuratorial organs in addition to the trial activities of the courts. The fundamental difference between the two lies in whether the procuratorial organs are a part of the judicial organs and whether the procuratorial organs' participation in litigation is a judicial activity. But this is not the focus of this paper. The issue discussed in this paper is how to define the administration of justice from the perspective of trial.

How the administration of justice is defined from the perspective of trial depends on our understanding of its characteristics, or the criteria (elements) for defining it. Whether labor dispute arbitration is quasi-judicial also depends on evaluations on its existing powers and practices based on these criteria. According to the limited studies in China, the administration of justice has eight elements:

a. Disputes over rights or interests;

b. Two or more specific parties are involved in those disputes;

c. One of the parties files the dispute case to an institution, organization or individual (judge or adjudicator) that has judicial power;

d. The judge or adjudicator, as a third party independent of the disputing parties, participates in and presides over the settlement of the dispute;

e. A hearing is then held with the participation of all disputing parties in a bid to influence the judge's or adjudicator's decisions by oral argument;

f. If the dispute involves fact finding, the disputing parties are required to submit evidence to the adjudicator and the court shall subpoena witnesses; if the dispute is over a point or points of law, then the disputing parties are required to present related evidence accordingly;

g. The adjudicator or judge makes and announces a decision to resolve the parties' dispute; and

h. On the basis of taking into account the claims, evidence and opinions of the disputing parties, the adjudicator or judge shall determine the facts of the dispute and apply the relevant principles and rules established by the substantive law to the facts. If it is only a legal dispute, the decision shall be made in accordance with legal principles, rules, precedents or jurisprudence (Chen, 2000).

To sum up, the core point of the above elements is that the administration of justice is an activity that the dispute is finally and compulsorily adjudicated by a neutral third party through procedures such as presenting evidence, cross-examination, etc, according to law, with the participation of all the disputing parties.

Scholars have different opinions on the features of the administration of justice. Some of them believe that judicial power has 10 features: a) passivity, b) neutrality, c) emphasis on procedure, d) stability, e) exclusivity, f) legal nature of legal professions, g) finality, h) negotiating nature of operation, i) different responsibilities of courts at different levels, and j) fairness priority (Sun, 1998). Some others believe that judicial activities have five features, with "trial as its center, fairness as its soul, strict legal procedures as its form, judgment as its basic requirement, and authority as its important symbol" (Chen and Cui, 2008). There is also a four-feature opinion: a) independence of judicial power, b) passivity of judicial power, c) finality of judicial decisions (authority), and d) the negotiating nature of judicial operations (Liu, 2003). Despite differences, these opinions all view justice as a function of the state, a kind of adjudication, and has features of neutrality, passivity, negotiating nature of its operations, and finality, etc. The above characteristics and elements could serve as a yardstick for us to determine whether an institution is judicial, whether a power is judicial power, and whether a labor dispute arbitration is quasi-judicial.

## 3. What's the Meaning of "Quasi" in "Quasi-Judicial"?

### 3.1 The fundamental element of "Quasi": non-finality of arbitration awards

From the perspectives of system and practice, labor dispute arbitration is also an activity that disputes are compulsorily adjudicated by a neutral third party designated by the state, with the participation of disputing parties through procedures such as presenting evidence, cross-examination, etc. Arbitration institutions also resemble courts: adjudicators are neutral, the principle of "no action, no jurisdiction" indicates passiveness, and the arbitration process is negotiation in essence, as disputing parties express their views through means of providing evidence and conducting cross-examinations and debates.

However, labor dispute arbitration lacks finality in China, which means the arbitration award is not considered as a final result. According to the current law, the parties can file an appeal if they are not satisfied with the arbitration award. This makes the arbitration different from a traditional judicial activity and thus have the "quasi-judicial" function. It should be noted, however, that arbitration has gained a sense of finality in the current law: arbitration awards were to be "final and binding" except for certain circumstances, which leads to a large amount of cases being settled at the stage of arbitration. From the perspective of finality, this can be considered a step towards the judicialization of labor dispute arbitration.

### 3.2 The second element of "quasi": relatively weak enforceability of arbitration awards

As we can see from the discussions above on the features and elements of the administration of justice, an important element of judicial power would be compulsory enforcement of adjudication through the state power. Labor dispute arbitration is also compulsory in its initial phase, as disputing parties cannot choose its initiation, legal basis or procedure. But unlike civil procedures, it has no enforceability in procedures, such as the power to detain, preserve and implement, as well as to investigate and punish financial institutions with wrongdoings. In fact, further enforcement is still largely based on the parties' willingness to cooperate, which is different from the enforceability of a traditional judicial activity that is underpinned by the state power.

### 3.3 Quasi-judicial is not quasi-court

Some hold the opinion that although labor dispute arbitration institutions are engaged in adjudication, they are just quasi-judicial bodies, not courts. This view equates courts with judicial organs, and regards a quasi-judicial nature as a quasi-court nature. But judicial organs are not just courts, and courts are a part of judicial system. Moreover, what is a court? Is it merely an institution named "court"? The definition of court goes back to the definitions of judicial power and trial power, while the discussion of "quasi-judicial" should also return to the above-mentioned criteria for the administration of justice instead of dwelling on the names of relevant institutions.

### 3.4 The "quasi" nature of arbitration is not because arbitrators are not judges

Some think the persons presiding over court proceedings in the judicial system must be judges who have gained qualification through judicial examination. Since arbitrators are not required to pass the judicial examination, they are not judges, and arbitration is therefore quasi-judicial. However, judges of arbitral tribunals in other countries can also be honorary judges who have not passed judicial examinations.

This is also true in the general judiciary: "The participation of the general public, as laymen, in the exercise of the power of adjudication by becoming jurors through a certain selection process, has always been regarded as an important feature of the judicial power in terms of organization" (Chen, 2000). From a logic perspective, it is the power to adjudicate that determines requirements of the adjudicator or judge, not the opposite. Whether one is an adjudicator or judge is the result, not the cause. Of course, it must be admitted that many factors lead to the non-finality nature of labor dispute arbitration in China, including the lack of strict qualification requirements for adjudicators, which makes legislators doubts about the quality of awards. From this point of view, there is indeed a correlation between arbitration's quasi-judicial nature and adjudicators' competence.

To sum up, labor dispute arbitration conforms to the basic characteristics of the administration of justice. The differences between a labor dispute arbitration institution and a traditional judicial organ is that the arbitration award is not the final result, and its ruling process is not fully mandatory, which is the essence of the quasi-judicial nature of the labor dispute arbitration. Given the provisions of the current laws, it can be considered that a labor dispute arbitration committee is a dispute adjudication body established by the provincial people's government with the participation of the government, trade unions and enterprises. It has the basic features of a judicial body, but the adjudication process is not completely mandatory and the adjudication awards are not completely final. As a result of the similarity between labor dispute arbitration institutions and judicial organs in structure, their functions overlap to some extents, thereby leading to overlaps and poor connection between labor dispute arbitration and litigation in China.

## III. Arbitration-Litigation Relation: History, Current Improvement and Development Outlook

The analysis on the arbitration-litigation relationship should be based on the quasi-judicial nature of arbitration. In other words, discussions on this relationship should begin from the particularities that "labor dispute arbitration has the basic characteristics of a judicial activity, but its award is not the final result, and its ruling process is not fully mandatory". At the same time, this analysis should not be limited to discussions on formalities or focus on the things on the surface, such as the binary decision: choose an arbitration or a litigation mode. What it should do is to find out the source of the quasi-judicial nature and analyze the essence of arbitration-litigation relationship. On this basis, we will further discuss how to improve this relationship at present and in the future.

## 1. Arbitration-Litigation Relationship in History

As mentioned above, labor dispute arbitration has always featured in non-finality and relatively weak enforceability throughout its development in China. However, these features come from different ideas at different stages of its development, which leads to substantial differences in the relationship between labor dispute arbitration and administration of justice despite their resemblance in form. On the one hand, understanding these differences can help us more deeply understand the mechanism behind the arbitration-litigation relationship in China, and on the other hand, they can also provide us some clues for the development direction of this relationship.

### 1.1 Stage one: two types of contradictions and arbitration's role of filtering

At the early stage of arbitration in China, its non-finality was mainly due to understandings on different dispute settlement institutions at that time. As mentioned in the beginning of this paper, for a long time after the founding of the PRC, courts were more understood as organs "upholding the people's democratic dictatorship" than resolving disputes. Labor disputes were not taken as severe conflicts as they were internal problems among the people, thus being resolved through arbitration. This is also a continuation of the Soviet tradition, "Labor disputes in the USSR do not create irreconcilable conflicts between the parties, so such disputes can always be resolved on the basis of coordinating interests between individual workers and the socialist society" (Aleksandrov, 1955). However, since the labor dispute arbitration conducted by the administrative organs does not solve severe conflicts, if the dispute between the parties has not been settled after an arbitration, the nature of the disputes may have changed into a conflict. Then the parties will turn to the court. Following this idea, we can see arbitration serves as a natural filter for litigation in this stage. What arbitration can solve is non-confrontational contradictions and vice versa, and there is no need to establish a special system to handle the arbitration-litigation relationship. This relationship worked well as it met the social, political and economic conditions at that time.

### 1.2 Stage two: arbitration's administrative nature and judiciary's supervision over arbitration

After China launched reform and opening up, a consensus was gradually reached among scholars, legislative bodies and the public, i.e. the administration of justice is for the people and disputes could be settled by judicial means. There was no longer any theoretical or conceptual obstacle to the court in handling problems among the people and non-confrontational conflicts. Nevertheless, after being restored in 1987, the labor dispute arbitration system continued the arbitration-before-trial pattern due to various reasons. In this stage, the existence of labor dispute arbitration, its non-finality and its weak enforceability were shaped by its own administrative nature, not by the nature of judicial organs.

Since its birth, China's labor dispute arbitration has had close relations to the administration bodies. Article 3 of the 1950 Provisions on Procedures for Settling Labor Disputes stipulated that "labor administrative organs of the people's governments at all levels shall be designated as organs for resolving labor disputes." This remained mostly the case after the restoration of labor dispute arbitration in 1987. Article 13 of the Regulations on China's Settlement of Labor Disputes in Enterprises stipulated that "the labor dispute settlement institution of an administrative department of labor is the office of the arbitration committee", and a later Responses to Questions towards Regulations on China's Settlement of Labor Disputes in Enterprises further explained that "the labor dispute settlement institution of the administrative department of labor" is "an institution with functions of labor dispute mediation and arbitration, which is established by the administrative department of labor, and shall work with the arbitration committee at the same level as one office." In practice, however, arbitration was solely conducted by administrative organs. Although the Supreme People's Court made it clear through the Reply on the Issue of Litigants in Hearing Labor Dispute Cases that administrative lawsuit does not apply to a labor dispute arbitration body, the Reply itself reflects that in terms of both theory and practice, arbitration was considered almost equal to a government function. In this context, a need for supervision over arbitration emerged, and the non-finality of labor arbitration result had its legitimacy. The judicial organs began to play the role of supervising and became the supervisor, while the arbitration institutions became the supervised party. At the second stage, all labor disputes may go through litigation procedures after arbitration.

*1.3 Stage three: complex relationship due to traditions, reality and logic*

This stage takes place after the enactment of Labor Dispute Mediation and Arbitration Law of the PRC in 2007. The Law aimed at minimizing administrative interference and increasing social participation, but in institutional design, it kept the quasi-judicial function of labor dispute arbitration as mentioned above. There are mainly five reasons for this.

(1) Respecting tradition. As legislators of Labor Dispute Mediation and Arbitration Law of the PRC noted, "the existing procedures for settling labor disputes have been accepted by the public after more than twenty years of practice, and should not be denied thoughtlessly" (Xin, 2008).

(2) Concerns on the quality of arbitration. One drawback of the original system, as raised in the draft of Labor Dispute Mediation and Arbitration Law of the PRC, is that "the weakness of non-professional labor arbitration institutions and

personnel becomes increasingly obvious" (Xin, 2008). However, the final Law did not specify quality management for arbitration personnel, and the requirements for arbitrators were easily met and rather flexible. In the absence of a guarantee for the personnel, assets and belongings of arbitration institutions, coupled with the fact that qualification requirements for arbitrators are unlikely to be stricter, it would be unwise to improve the legal effect of arbitration awards.

(3) Inadequate support. Although a labor dispute arbitration institution is an adjudication body that requires compulsory enforcement, it is not provided with enough power to ensure such enforcement. Arbitration institutions do not have the power to subpoena witness, preserve evidence, investigate financial institutions or punish disruptions of hearings. As a result, the initialization of labor dispute arbitration is mandatory, but its procedures are not mandatory. Due to this lack of enforceability, arbitration proceedings may be unable to ascertain facts or move forward because of institutional reasons, thus weakening the effectiveness of arbitration awards.

(4) Debates on whether to divert cases. With the increasing number of labor disputes, concerns raise on whether it is possible for one institution to handle all the cases. Some people hope to have arbitration institutions to divert cases, but others are worried about their handling capacity. The existing arbitration system is a compromise between the two opinions.

(5) The logic of the dispute settlement process itself. In theory, "In order to ensure the objectivity and correctness of judgment, and also to allow the parties to recognize its legitimacy, a mandatory system like trial often has to adopt extremely cautious procedures... On the other hand, dispute settlement institutions outside the trial system have more freedom in procedures, as they gain legitimacy through the parties' consent – after all, their decisions are not binding" (Takao, 2004). The legitimacy of a compulsory adjudication system is based on strict procedural guarantees, while a non-compulsory adjudication system relies on the parties' full consent. Currently in China, however, labor dispute arbitration is a compulsory dispute resolution mechanism without a consensual basis. On the other hand, its procedure design is not strict and has space for improvement. Therefore, neither the procedure nor the consensual basis can provide sufficient legitimacy for the arbitration results, and thus the finality of its award could not be recognized.

The above quasi-judicial nature determined by tradition and logic leads to the current complex relationship between arbitration and litigation.

(1) Labor arbitration filters and diverts cases for the judiciary. In fact, the essential purpose of labor dispute arbitration is neither letting cases enter into the litigation stage after arbitration nor causing three trials before finality by filing

an appeal, but to settle as many disputes as possible outside the courts. This was mentioned in Notes on the Draft of Labor Dispute Mediation and Arbitration Law: "After analyzing arbitration cases in recent years, we find that most labor disputes can be resolved through arbitration in accordance with the above provisions of the draft" (Xin, 2008). Other provisions such as "arbitration awards shall be final and binding" and "mediation priority" also reflect this purpose.

(2) The court helps the enforcement of arbitration procedures. Due to their quasi-judicial nature, labor institutions are not provided with enough powers, such as the compulsory enforcement of their awards. Therefore, for matters such as implementing protective measures and enforcing awards, labor dispute arbitration institutions rely on the judiciary's authority to ensure the effectiveness of their decisions. Article 44 of Labor Dispute Mediation and Arbitration Law stipulates rules for making an award on advance enforcement and transferring it to the people's court for enforcement. Article 51 stipulates rules on applying to the court for award enforcement. In addition, some regions see practices that arbitration institutions entrust courts to examine evidence, preserve property, etc.

(3) Labor dispute arbitration is supervised indirectly by the judiciary. As judicial organs and labor dispute arbitration institutions are independent of each other, they are not a leader-led relation and the former is not the appellate body of the latter. The arbitration institution is not an administrative organ, so in a strict sense, the relationship between arbitration and litigation is not a supervisor-supervised one. For general arbitration awards, Article 50 of Labor Dispute Mediation and Arbitration Law stipulates that, where a party has objection to the arbitral award of a labor dispute case, it may initiate a litigation to a people's court within 15 days from the date it receives the award. This parallel structure is also reflected in practice: if a party refuses to accept the arbitral award and turns to the court, the judicial organ does not review the legitimacy of the arbitral award, but hears the case as a completely new case. Under this litigation-after-arbitration pattern, the court may correct an illegal or wrong arbitration award, which leads to de facto supervision. In other words, after the Law's enactment, arbitration filters cases for litigation, while litigation, in turn, supports arbitration enforcement and supervises arbitration indirectly.

## 2. Suggestions for Current Improvement in Arbitration-Litigation Relationship

By "current improvement", this article means to improve arbitration-litigation relationship without making fundamental changes in the arbitration system or altering its quasi-judicial nature. The starting point would be to understand its current trends. At present, the most important trends of labor dispute arbitration in China is the establishment of arbitration entities, the standardization of arbitration process and the increasing judicial elements in arbitration. In 2012, the Ministry of Human Resources and Social Security and relevant ministries issued the Guidelines on Strengthening the Effectiveness of Labor Dispute Settlement. On this basis, the substantive and standardized construction of the arbitration courts has been strengthened. As of December 2016, a total of 3,189 labor dispute arbitration courts had been established nationwide, which means that 98.4% of administrative divisions above the county level have established labor dispute arbitration courts. As of April 30, 2017, there had been 26,500 full-time and part-time arbitrators in China, including 15,800 full-time arbitrators. At the same time, the training of arbitrators carried out by human resources and social security departments at all levels was in full swing, and the proportion of arbitrators who passed the judicial examination in some regions was on the rise. The construction of various systems of labor dispute arbitration and the standardization of arbitration procedures have been continuously strengthened, and the ability of arbitration institutions to solve disputes have also been greatly improved. The above-mentioned establishment of arbitration courts, the specialization of arbitrators and the standardization of arbitration procedures lead to the phenomenon known as the judicialization of arbitration. Affected by the above factors, arbitration and litigation have become increasingly similar in both procedures and functions. We can even expect them to overlap more with the further standardization of arbitration procedures and the improvement of arbitration institutions' ability in handling cases. Therefore, the current core approach of improving arbitration-litigation relationship would be to reduce overlapping functions.

As mentioned above, labor arbitration filters and diverts cases for the judiciary, while the judiciary supervises arbitration indirectly. Bearing this relation in mind, we propose to connect arbitration and litigation in a sound way and minimize their overlapped functions through the following ways.

(1) Unify the acceptance scope of cases, standards of adjudication and rules of providing evidence. The differences between labor dispute arbitration and litigation should not lie in these aspects, but in the composition and expertise of adjudicators, as well as the combination of legal means and legal effects. Only by unifying the criteria above can we truly realize labor arbitration's role of filtering cases for the court and uphold the authority of arbitration. Those differences will only lead the parties to continue to resort to the court after arbitration, causing high litigation costs and lengthy procedures.

(2) Gradually strengthen the enforceability of arbitration institutions in proceedings. As mentioned above, labor dispute arbitration is a kind of compulsory arbitration, and its compulsory initiation means the parties' involuntary participation.

From this perspective, with improved expertise of arbitrators and further standardization of arbitration institutions, compulsory enforcement in the process of handling cases by labor dispute arbitration institutions should be strengthened, including the power to summon witnesses and the power to obtain evidence from relevant institutions. We should ensure that compulsory initiation is followed by compulsory enforcement, and prevent procedures from being formalities.

(3) Gradually increase the application of arbitration awards as final results. This is an effective way to prevent overlapping procedures. The legitimacy of the finality of adjudication awards lies in the judicial aspect of labor dispute arbitration and the efficiency principle of dispute resolution. If we examine the provisions of China's civil procedure law or the practice of labor courts in other countries, we can find that it is not rare that the award of the first instance is the final award and a further appeal is not allowed (Dong, 2008; Shen, 2015).

(4) Enhance the capability of the judiciary in supporting arbitration procedures in those areas where labor dispute arbitration institutions do not have relevant power. According to the current law, this mainly involves the preservation of evidence and property and award enforcement. Labor dispute arbitration procedures should have the same status as those of the first instance. In particular, property preservation in arbitration should be treated equally as in litigation.

## 3. Outlook for Future Arbitration-Litigation Relationship

If the ability and authority of arbitration cannot be improved after years of development, and the arbitration and litigation continue to converge, the finality of arbitration awards will be widely accepted in the long run and then arbitration and litigation will get homogeneous. Arbitration will no longer be a quasi-judicial institution and complete the final transformation to a judicial institution. If so, the time has come for us to make a choice between arbitration and litigation or to merge them into one. It is not a future to be feared of, but a natural result of our system. Should arbitration be abolished when it resembles litigation in every aspect? From the essence of labor disputes and labor relations, arbitration should be judicialized, but if the judiciary gets ready to replace arbitration, it should also include some elements of arbitration, such as introducing judges from different backgrounds in order to competently settle labor disputes. This constitutes the premise for future development of China's independent arbitration-litigation system: the future of labor dispute resolution in China will be the integration of arbitration and judicial functions. This convergence can be achieved through the following ways.

(1) Set up independent labor dispute adjudication bodies at district (county),

city (prefecture), and provincial levels. They can be jointly established by existing arbitration institutions and departments of the judiciary engaged in labor dispute settlement. At the central level, a coordinating body in physical form can be jointly set up by the courts, human resources & social security departments, trade unions, business federations, etc. Such an organ should be responsible for developing rules for handling cases as well as coordinating and managing disputes, but should not involve in specific procedures.

(2) Provide institutional guarantee for diversified personnel composition of the adjudicative body. The judges of the labor dispute adjudication institutions shall include the personnel with judicial qualification and the representatives who are from trade unions and enterprises and have professional knowledge on social security, human resources and labor and social security laws. The institutions responsible for handling cases are arbitral tribunals that are equipped with the above professionals. A three-person panel or a single-person system may be adopted to carry out arbitrations.

(3) Apply the mode of the second instance as final instance plus a retrial. Given the particularity of labor disputes, clear rules should be set to limit appeal and retrial. To well manage the relationship between the first instance and the second instance, the current model of "finality of the first adjudication + withdrawal of award" could be adopted.

## IV. Conclusion

Ten years after the enactment of Labor Dispute Mediation and Arbitration Law, it is time for us to reflect on the relationship between labor dispute arbitration and litigation. Rather than simply permuting or merging procedures, we should analyze the root causes of the labor dispute arbitration system's existence as well its nature, and consider its future direction. Labor dispute arbitration should be recognized as a quasi-judicial dispute settlement mechanism which is based on the special characteristics of labor relations and labor disputes and guided by the innovation thoughts of social governance. The similarity between arbitration and judicial activities provides a basis for clarifying their relationship, while their differences pave the way for their coexistence. At present, we should continue to promote the judicialization of labor dispute arbitration and make arbitration and litigation well connected. Going forward, we should realize the integration of arbitration and litigation by promoting the judicialization of arbitration and advancing judicial development through the participation of various parties.

## References

[1] Wang Zhenqi. Legislative Suggestions for China's Labor Dispute Settlement System [J]. China Labor, 2001(2): 9-10.

[2] Qin Guorong. The Choice of Legal Mechanism for China's Labor Dispute Settlement [J]. Jianghai Academic Journal, 2010(3): 142-148.

[3] Dong Baohua, ed. Research on Labor Dispute Settlement System [M]. Beijing: China Labor and Social Security Publishing House, 2008.

[4] Xin Chunying. Explanation on the Labor Dispute Mediation and Arbitration Law of the PRC (Draft), Bulletin of the Standing Committee of the National People's Congress, Issue 1, 2008:28-31.

[5] Huang Xudong. On the Evolution and Trends of Labor Dispute Arbitration-Litigation Relationship in China//Lin Jia, ed, Social Law Review [M], Beijing: China Renmin University Press, 2017.

[6] Peng Zhen. Report at the National Conference on Procuratorial Work//Peng Zhen. Selected Writings of Peng Zhen[M]. Beijing: People's Publishing House, 1991.

[7] Dong Biwu biography team eds. Dong Biwu (1886-1975) [M] Beijing: Central Literature Publishing House, 2006.

[8] Douglass C. North. Translated by Hang Xing. Institutions, Institutional change, and Economic Performance[M] Shanghai: Gezhi Press, Shanghai Sanlian Bookstore and Shanghai People's Publishing House, 2014.

[9] China Labor Statistics Yearbook[M], Beijing: China Statistics Press, 2009-2019.

[10] Linsenmaier, Von Lyon nach Erfurt - Zur Geschichte der deutschen Arbeitsgerichtsbarkeit,in:NZA 2004, S402.

[11] Shen Jianfeng. Interactions of Individual Autonomy, State Coercion and Collective Autonomy in Coordinating Labor Relations[J]. China Human Resources Development, 2015(9): 90-96.

[12] Huang Chengguan. Current Situation and Concerns of Labor Litigation in China, Labor, Society and Law[M]. Taipei: Yuanzhao Publishing Company, 2011.

[13] Gustav Radbruch. Vorschule der Rechtsphilosophie, Verlag Scherer, S.100, 1959.

[14] Dou Yupei. From Social Management to Social Governance: A Major Innovation in Theory and Practice[J]. Administrative Reform, 2014(4): 20-25.

[15] Satoshi Nishitani. Vergleichende Einführung in das japanische Arbeitsrecht, Carl Heymanns Verlag KG2003, S. 357.

[16] Waltmann. Translated by Shen Jianfeng. Employment Law of Germany[M]. Beijing: Law Press, 2014.

[17] Wang Quanxing. Labor Law[M].Beijing: Law Press, 2017.

[18] Hu Jianmiao and Jiang Lihong. Administrative Law[M]. Beijing: China Renmin

University Press, 2012.

[19] Zhu Hongwen and Wang Jian. From Integrating Two Powers to Integrating Three Powers: Theory, Method and Content of Introducing Quasi-Judicial Powers into China's Antitrust Enforcement Agencies[J]. Law Review, 2012(5): 105-112.

[20] Shi Jianzhong. Building a Quasi-Judicial System in Antitrust Law[J]. Oriental Law, 2008(3): 53-62.

[21] Elizabeth A.Martin. A Dictionary of Law[M]. Oxford: Oxford Unversity Press, 2003.

[22] Chen Guangzhong and Cui Jie. A Chinese Interpretation of Judicial and the Judiciary[J]. Chinese Jurisprudence, 2008(2): 76-84.

[23] Yang Yiping and Yu Jingyao. A Modern Interpretation of the Concept of Judicial[J]. Journal of the Graduate School of the Chinese Academy of Social Sciences, 1997(2): 62-70.

[24] Chen Ruihua. The Nature of Judicial Power[J]. Jurisprudence Research, 2000(5): 30-58.

[25] Sun Xiaoxia. Essence of Judicial Power Lies in the Right to Judge[J]. Jurisprudence, 1998(8): 3.

[26] Liu Rui' an. Characteristics of Judicial Power[J]. Modern Jurisprudence, 2003(3): 87-93.

[27] Aleksandrov. Translated by Li Guangmo and Kang Baotian. A Course on Soviet Labor Law[M]. Beijing: China Renmin University Press, 1955.

[28] Takao Tanase.Translated by Wang Yaxin. Dispute Resolution and the Trial System[M]. Beijing: China University of Political Science and Law Press, 2004.